Translating the Bible

from William Tyndale to King James

by Gerald Bray

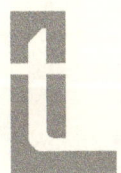

The Latimer Trust

Translating the Bible: From William Tyndale to King James

© Gerald Bray 2010

ISBN 978-0-946307-75-3

Published by The Latimer Trust, July 2010

Cover photograph: © JMB – Fotolia.com

The Latimer Trust (formerly Latimer House, Oxford) is a conservative Evangelical research organisation within the Church of England, whose main aim is to promote the history and theology of Anglicanism as understood by those in the Reformed tradition. Interested readers are welcome to consult its website for further details of its many activities.

The Latimer Trust
PO Box 26685, London N14 4XQ UK
Registered Charity: 1084337
Company Number: 4104465
Web: www.latimertrust.org
E-mail: administrator@latimertrust.org

Views expressed in works published by The Latimer Trust are those of the authors and do not necessarily represent the official position of The Latimer Trust.

Contents

Translating the Bible 1
In the beginning 1
William Tyndale 5
The Great Bible 9
The Geneva Bible 12
The Bishops' Bible 15
The Douai-Reims (Roman Catholic) Bible 17
The Authorised (King James) Bible 22
How to read this book 26

1. Tyndale's Preface to the New Testament, 1526 28
2. Tyndale's Preface to the Pentateuch, 1530 48
3. Coverdale's Dedication and Preface to the Bible, 1535 60
4. Cranmer's Preface to the Great Bible, 1540 79
5. A Fruitful Exhortation to the Reading and Knowledge of Holy Scripture, 1547 92
6. Preface to the Geneva New Testament, 1557 100
7. Preface to the Geneva Bible, 1560 103
8. Preface to the Bishops' Bible, 1568 113
9. Preface to the Revised Geneva New Testament, 1576 131
10. Preface to the Reims New Testament, 1582 143
11. Preface to the Douai Old Testament, 1609 187
12. Preface to the Authorised (King James) Version, 1611 201

For further reading: 236

Translating the Bible

In the beginning

Five hundred years ago you could have gone into a bookshop in England and bought a range of books on different subjects that catered to the interests and tastes of a growing reading public. Printing was a new technology in those days, and as its techniques improved prices were coming down, making books more affordable than they had been when everything had to be copied out by hand. But there was one potential best seller that you could not have bought anywhere – a Bible. The most important book of all was simply not available, except perhaps in a very expensive and rare Latin edition which few people had the money to purchase and only a minority could understand. People knew about the Bible, of course, because they heard extracts from it read in church, and although the reading itself was in Latin, there was often an explanation in English for the benefit of those who could not follow it. There were also plays based on Bible stories, and stained-glass windows that portrayed characters from both the Old and New Testaments. The festivals of the church year highlighted the key events in the life of Jesus, and the apostles too were commemorated at different times. But although there was a general familiarity with these great Biblical themes, few people knew what the Bible really said and almost nobody could have questioned the official teaching of the church by comparing it with the source material from which it was supposed to be drawn.

It is hard for us to think ourselves back into that situation or to understand how it had come about. Mostly it had happened by accident in an age when books were expensive and few people could read, but there were also forces in both church and state that did not want people to know too much. Just as today there are civil servants who would rather conduct their business in private without being accountable to the public they are meant to serve, so in earlier times there were churchmen, the civil servants of their day, who found it more convenient not to expose themselves or their methods to popular scrutiny. By operating in Latin they distanced themselves from the general population, but at the same time they could link up with others of their type all across Europe. Latin was a class barrier at home but a useful means of international communication abroad, and those who really wanted to know what the Bible said could always enter a monastery or university, become priests, monks or nuns, and indulge their passion to their heart's content. If they wanted to, they could then go and tell everyone else what the Bible said, and that was felt to be enough. Ordinary people who lacked special training were no more expected to understand the Bible for themselves than most of us would be expected to understand a legal or medical textbook today.

It had not always been like that. In the early days of Christianity, the Bible was freely available in Greek, the language in which most public preaching and worship was conducted. Even before the coming of Christ, the Jews of Alexandria had translated the Hebrew Scriptures for the benefit of those who could no longer read them in the original, and that version was generally used by the first Christian communities. It was called the Septuagint, from the Latin word for 'seventy,' because legend had it that seventy (or perhaps seventy-two) scholars had translated it during the reign of Ptolemy II Philadelphus (285–246 BC), the founder of the great library at Alexandria. The Septuagint (often abbreviated as LXX, the Roman numeral for 'seventy') had its faults, and contained a number of books that were not in the Hebrew original, and by the second century AD other translations were starting to appear. These were the work of particular individuals like Aquila, Symmachus and Theodotion, each of whom tried to improve on the LXX, with varying degrees of success. Theodotion's translation of Daniel, in particular, was so good that it virtually superseded the LXX version, but that was exceptional. On the whole, the LXX was firmly entrenched both in the synagogue and in the church, and these newer translations never really caught on. The New Testament was originally written in Greek, but parts of it can legitimately be called a translation, because Jesus and his disciples spoke Aramaic, a language closely related to Biblical Hebrew. A few Aramaic words were incorporated into the Greek New Testament to remind us of this (like *abba, talitha cumi* and *marana tha*) but on the whole the language of Jesus was not widely used in the early church, at least not outside the communities where it was generally spoken.

When Christianity became a legal religion in the Roman Empire, translations of the Bible into languages other than Greek became common. In the east, versions appeared in Coptic (Egyptian), Syriac (a form of Aramaic), Ge'ez (the ancient language of Ethiopia) and Armenian. In the west, there were many attempts to produce a Latin translation, but this soon led to confusion as different translators produced different versions, and around the year 375 Pope Damasus asked Jerome, the leading scholar of his time, to prepare an authoritative text for the use of the Latin-speaking world. Jerome took the trouble to learn Hebrew, and insisted that it should form the basis of all translations of the Old Testament, which involved rejecting the extra books that had crept into the LXX. Those books, which we now call the Apocrypha, are not quoted in the New Testament but they had been used from time to time in the church and there was opposition to letting them go, particularly from Augustine, the greatest theologian of the time. Augustine and Jerome corresponded with each other on the subject without reaching agreement, and the argument did not go away. In the middle ages, the church compromised by using Jerome's translation with the Apocrypha included, but at the time of the Reformation the Protestant churches sided with Jerome, which is why the Apocrypha is not normally included in English Bibles now.

Jerome produced an excellent translation, based on the best manuscripts available to him and it soon superseded all other Latin versions to become the 'popular' one – the *Vulgata*, or Vulgate, as we call it. As Christianity spread northwards, beyond the bounds of the Roman Empire, the Latin language and the Vulgate went with it. The languages of the north, whether Celtic or German, were not written at that time, and although Christians introduced a script and started recording them, there were only limited attempts made to produce translations of the Bible. The great scholar Bede, for example, wrote commentaries on the Latin text that were widely used, but he did not spend much time on translation. It is recorded that he produced an English version of John's Gospel, but that was all. By the time of the Norman conquest in 1066, when the English language was suppressed as a medium of government and administration, the Gospels and parts of the Old Testament had appeared in Old English (Anglo-Saxon) but they were never widely circulated. Very different was the situation in eastern Europe, where the conversion of the Slavs led not only to the development of a Slavonic literary language but to a complete translation of the Scriptures, which is still in use today. The reason for this was that the Slavs were evangelised by the eastern church, which had preserved the translation principle, and not by the western church, based on Rome, which preferred to keep everything in Latin. Some westerners even claimed that because Pontius Pilate had written the words 'Jesus of Nazareth, king of the Jews' on the cross in Hebrew, Greek and Latin, the Bible could only be read in one of those three sacred languages. But as Hebrew was the language of the Jews who had rejected Christ, and Greek was the language of the eastern church which had broken away from Rome, Latin was the only one that could be relied on to convey the truth!

The notion that translating the Bible into other languages would lead to distortion of its meaning was reinforced by the fact that those who dissented from the Roman church often wanted vernacular translations to be made. The first one was done by (or at the request of) Peter Waldo, the leader of the Waldensians, a proto-Protestant movement that appeared in southern France in the twelfth century. Interestingly enough, Waldo's activities spurred others to produce translations of their own, not to support him but to counteract his teachings by issuing an approved version of the Bible in the language of the people. In other words, translation was disapproved of, but when it occurred anyway, it was matched by opponents on the principle that 'if you can't beat 'em, join 'em.'

The most important translation of this dissenting type was the one sponsored by John Wycliffe (1328–84) in England. Wycliffe believed that the church of his day was corrupt and teaching false doctrines that were not in agreement with the Bible. He thought that people were being hoodwinked by the church authorities, who kept the Scriptures to themselves and manipulated them for their own purposes. Making the Bible available in English was a way of challenging this monopoly, and two different versions made their appearance. The first was done during Wycliffe's lifetime and he may have taken part in it, though this is uncertain. It was too stiff and literalistic though, using Latin turns of phrase that sound odd in English, and around 1388 a second attempt was made, this time in a language that was much more accessible and natural. The first translation was condemned by the authorities however, and in 1407 Thomas Arundel, the archbishop of Canterbury, convened a synod of his province in Oxford which made Bible translation illegal. From that time onwards Wycliffite Bibles were destroyed and their owners were punished, but the fact that over 250 copies still survive shows what a mammoth task that was. Wycliffe's followers, known as Lollards (from the old *lollen*, a word that meant 'mumble'), went underground and in parts of England they remained influential right up to the time of the Reformation, when they resurfaced and became leading supporters of change in the established church.

The Wycliffite translations were circulated in manuscript, because printing was not invented until nearly a century later, but even when printed books became available, it was illegal to publish them and no edition was produced until 1850! Meanwhile the English language had been changing fast. By 1500 people could no longer read the

Wycliffite version with ease, and it was becoming clear that if an English Bible was ever to be issued for general use it would have to be in a new translation. This is where William Tyndale comes into the picture.

William Tyndale

Born about 1494, William Tyndale belonged to a new generation whose intellectual horizons were vastly expanded by the unexpected discovery of new worlds by Spanish and Portuguese explorers, by the spread of knowledge through printing and by the interest being shown in a 'return to the sources' of traditional western civilisation which was part of the revival of learning that we now call the Renaissance. The most important figure of this movement was Desiderius Erasmus (1466–1536), who was known all over Europe for his insistence on the highest standards of critical scholarship and for his ferocious attacks on the corruption of the Roman church, which had been made even worse by the vast influx of new wealth coming from the Americas. Spain was using its money to take over as much of Europe as it could, and dominating the papacy was one of its prime goals. The Spanish Pope Alexander VI (1492–1503) was one of the most corrupt in history, even allowing the government of Rome to fall into the hands of his son (by a marriage he had contracted when still a layman). Cesare Borgia, as this son was known, and his equally famous sister Lucrezia, became a byword for wickedness in high places, and once the papacy had been sucked into that, getting out was virtually impossible. Every reasonable observer recognised that root and branch reform of the institution was necessary, but who would do it and how was unclear. In the meantime, at a lower level, the church went on performing its customary tasks and imposing as much conformity to its wishes as it could.

The explosion, when it finally came, took place in an unexpected quarter. In 1503 a young German law student called Martin Luther (1483–1546) fell from his horse in a thunderstorm and was very nearly killed. Believing that his life had been spared for a purpose, Luther entered a monastery and dedicated himself to finding peace with God. Like most people at the time, he thought that if he performed the right devotional exercises he could atone for his sins and be spared the punishment that he would otherwise deserve for them. But unlike other people, Luther had no idea when to stop. He fasted more than anybody else and prayed longer and harder than they did. So fanatical did he become that his superiors in the monastery feared for his health, and when in 1512 he was invited to become the first professor of Biblical studies at the newly-funded university of Wittenberg, it was with some relief that they encouraged him to take up the post. Luther threw himself into his new task with the same determination that he showed in everything else he did, and it was during the next few years that he came to understand what the true secret of spiritual peace was. The New Testament teaches that we are not saved by our own efforts, however praiseworthy they may be, but by trust in the Son of God who has paid the price for our sins by his death on the cross. What I cannot do for myself he has done for me, and it is by clinging to him that I can know that I am saved from my sins. Jesus died for me quite apart from anything I might have done to deserve that, and I can do no more than bow to his wisdom and receive him as the Lord and Saviour of my life.

At first Luther kept this discovery to himself, because it never occurred to him that most people had no idea what the Bible really taught. He thought that the problem was his own misunderstanding, and was embarrassed that he had not realised this earlier. But as he began to teach and preach the Gospel, he came to see that there were many others who also needed to hear it because they did not understand it either. In 1517 a fund-raising campaign to raise money for the pope was launched in Germany, promising people that for a small sum of money they could have their time in purgatory reduced. Luther was incensed by this perversion of the truth, and wrote ninety-five theses arguing against it. He published them on the church door at Wittenberg, hoping to stimulate an academic debate, but before long they were circulating all over Europe. This was the match that lit the fire, and within a few years the papacy found itself confronting not only Luther, but many others who were caught up in the ferment, including a substantial proportion of Erasmus' disciples (though not Erasmus himself). The pope appealed to the rulers of Europe for support, but most of them knew that the church needed reform and were unwilling to offer him any help. The one exception was Henry VIII of England, who wrote a book attacking Luther's teaching and was somewhat grudgingly rewarded for his pains with the title 'defender of the faith,' which his successors still bear today.

It was in the midst of this turmoil that William Tyndale saw a chance to reverse the prohibition of 1407 and produce an English Bible. He needed a sponsor if the project was ever to get off the ground, but his own diocese of Worcester, then in the hands of Italian appointees of the papacy, was not willing to help. However, in 1522 Cuthbert Tunstall, a man noted for his scholarly interests and open-mindedness, was appointed bishop of London, and Tyndale decided to make an appeal to him. Whatever Tunstall may have thought about it personally, he knew that translating the Bible was illegal and warned Tyndale of the danger he was putting himself in. Tyndale took the hint and left England, never to return. His first stop abroad was Wittenberg, where he enrolled in the university and thus became probably the first Englishman to meet Martin Luther personally. Tyndale's arrival there coincided with the publication of Luther's German New Testament, which he had come to see as vital if ordinary people were ever going to come face to face with the Word of God. Tyndale needed no further encouragement, and in no time at all he had produced an English equivalent, complete with Luther's prefaces to the individual books, which he had translated (and slightly modified in the process).

In 1526 Tyndale managed to get his New Testament printed in Germany, from where it was smuggled back into England. We have no idea how many copies were seized and destroyed, but probably not many. Only three now survive, one of which is in Stuttgart and was discovered as recently as 1996. But enough people were able to obtain it to make it clear that a translation was both possible and sorely needed, and after 1526 there could be no going back. A revised version appeared in 1534, by which time the first books of the Old Testament had also appeared. Tyndale was working on the Old Testament prophets when he was arrested and his work was brought to a halt, but it was carried on by others. A complete English Bible was finally published by Miles Coverdale in 1535, shortly before the Spanish authorities in Antwerp, which was then subject to the king of Spain, had Tyndale tried and executed for heresy.

Tyndale's New Testament is a Lutheran document, as the preface and the prologues to the various books clearly indicate. Tyndale went beyond Luther, however, in his understanding of the Bible as covenant – a view which would later give rise to the most characteristic type of Puritan theology. In the preface to the New Testament he gives us a very clear explanation of what this means. Later, in the response to George Joye appended to the preface in the 1534 revision, he developed his belief in *sola Scriptura*, a Lutheran formula which he nevertheless understood in his own way. Tyndale not only wished to affirm what Scripture affirms; he also wanted to deny what Scripture does not clearly affirm. It was this second aspect of his thinking that was later to become a major bone of contention between conformists and non-conformists in England, which would end in civil war and the permanent division of what had previously been a single Protestant church.

Tyndale's preface to the Old Testament contains an account of his attempts to secure the bishop of London's support for his translation work, and also hints at the reasons why he felt obliged to leave England. It was reprinted in the 1534 edition, though the prologue received a substantial addition, which deals specifically with what we would now call 'covenant theology.'

Tyndale's overriding concern was to point out that the Bible was given for the 'learning and comfort' of believers, and that this is the main reason why everyone needs a translation in his or her own language. He demonstrated his point by several quotations from the New Testament (which refer to the use of the Old), and also by rehearsing the main events of patriarchal history. Particularly noteworthy are his assertions that even the most obnoxious stories from the Old Testament are full of consolation for the Christian, and also that believers today are subjected to exactly the same kinds of suffering and persecution as the figures whose stories are told in the Old Testament. The unity of the covenants was therefore not merely theoretical or historical, but had practical significance for the lives of individual Christians.

Tyndale's reputation as a translator has endured because he had a gift for finding the right phrase and an ability to cast the original text in an English which was just right for it – not too Latinate but not too popular, dignified but not archaic. He was also able to make use of rare English words (like *atonement*), and even coin some (like *passover*), which were so successful that they have entered the common vocabulary and are still used as much today as they were in the sixteenth-century. Because he was an outlaw and his activities were strictly illegal, his name could never be mentioned officially, even after the Reformation, but it has been estimated that up to ninety percent of the Authorised Version of 1611 goes back to him. In a very real sense therefore, Tyndale was to the English Bible what Luther was to the German, even though it would be King James I (1603–25) who would be given the credit in later times!

Miles Coverdale (1488–1569) took up where Tyndale left off, but his preface indicates just how much things had changed in the space of only a few years. In 1534, submitting to Henry VIII's somewhat questionable desire to annul his marriage to Katharine of Aragón, the Church of England had formally renounced papal jurisdiction, a decision which was subsequently ratified by parliament. Henry was not intending to reform the church in any significant way, but the break with Rome gave the would-be reformers hope that further change might be possible. This is why Coverdale starts with a preface intended for the king, before proceeding to explain to lesser mortals how and why they should read the Bible. In addressing Henry VIII, Coverdale pointed out various instances in the history of Israel where God had used kings to clean up corruptions that had crept into public worship, and he made it very clear where he thought Henry's duty lay in this regard. He then went on to tell people that reading the Bible was essential for their Christian growth. Only in the Bible was it possible to learn what God's will is, how he has accomplished our salvation and what we must do in response to that.

Today Coverdale's translation is remembered mainly for its psalter, which was incorporated into the Book of Common Prayer in 1549 and retained in later editions, even after a new translation had been made. By then, the words had become familiar and much loved, and they can still be heard, especially in the chanting of cathedral and collegiate church choirs, where the ancient traditions have been maintained.

The Great Bible

Within months of the final break with Rome in 1534, the convocation of the province of Canterbury had petitioned the king to order 'that the Holy Scripture should be translated into the vulgar English tongue by certain good and learned men, to be nominated by his Majesty, and should be delivered to the people for their instruction.' Coverdale produced his Bible even before the king could respond to this request, and two years later John Rogers, using the pseudonym of Thomas Matthew, came out with another version, which was essentially a combination of Tyndale and Coverdale. It was this translation which Thomas Cromwell sought the king's permission to publish, with the encouragement of Thomas Cranmer, the newly-appointed archbishop of Canterbury, who was himself quickly moving down the road to reform. The king gave his consent, and his advisers thought it best to authorise Coverdale to make a further revision of the so-called 'Matthew's Bible.' In 1538 the king directed that a copy of the Bible in English (which would in effect be this revision) should be placed in every parish church by Easter [6 April] 1539.

The work itself was soon ready, and was sent to Paris late in 1538 for typesetting and printing. Unfortunately, it fell foul of the inquisition there, just as the printing was nearly complete, and the whole operation had to be started over, this time on English soil. The result was that the Great Bible, as it came to be called, was not ready until April 1539, too late to meet the requirement of the king's injunction. A new order was therefore issued, extending the publication date to All Saints' Day [01 November] 1539. Once again there were difficulties, though this time it was because demand for the edition was such that supplies were soon exhausted!

A second edition was quickly prepared, and was issued in April 1540. For this edition, Archbishop Cranmer provided a preface, which soon became its hallmark. The Great Bible, or 'Cranmer's Bible' as it now came to be called, went through a total of seven editions before publication was suspended at the end of 1541. An eighth edition came out in 1549, and a ninth appeared in 1553, though as a result of Mary I's accession, most of it remained unsold. It was reprinted in 1562 and at least seven more times over the next few years, but it was cumbersome to use and had already been displaced in many quarters by a new translation, made by the exiles in Geneva. Even the bishops of the Church of England recognised that the Great Bible had no future, and set about replacing it with a translation of their own, which appeared in 1568. Not until 1611 was there to be another version of the Scriptures appointed and authorised to be read in churches.

Cranmer's preface to the Great Bible rapidly became a classic statement of the Reformation principle of *sola Scriptura*, as this applied to the English situation. He drew on the patristic tradition, and in particular the work of the great exegete John Chrysostom (d. 407), and the great theologian Gregory of Nazianzus (d. 390), to explain to his readers how the Bible should be read for spiritual profit, as well as for intellectual stimulation. This combination of patristic theology and Reformation concerns became typical of the Anglican tradition, and in many ways served to distinguish it from other types of Protestantism which were less clearly rooted in the early church. Cranmer was also concerned to uphold royal authority, and the rights of the king over the church were clearly stated in his preface. He knew better than anyone that the success or failure of the Reformation would depend on the king's good will, which was not to be taken for granted. This aspect of the matter does not much appeal to us today, but we have to remember that a social change as deep as that of the Reformation was likely to cause civil unrest, and indeed did so in parts of England, not to mention other European countries. The last thing that the Reformers needed was to be caught up in a popular revolt which would use their concerns as an excuse to overturn the established order and do untold damage to the church, as well as to the state, in the process. Cranmer wanted change, but he wanted it in an orderly and peaceful way, and this was always one of the main concerns of the English Reformers. On matters of theological principle they were usually in agreement with their continental colleagues, and in particular they had great admiration for Calvin and his associates in Geneva, but in terms of practical politics they found themselves resisting the demands of impatient enthusiasts and looking for what to them were harmless compromises with the traditional order so as to ease the pain of transition.

Shortly after writing the preface, Cranmer got involved in another, related project, which aimed to provide ready-made sermons for uneducated clergy to read to their flocks. The first of these was the sermon or 'homily' on Scripture, which was composed about 1542 (but not published until 1547), in which Cranmer outlined his teaching more clearly. Unlike the preface, the homily was actually read out to congregations, which is why it is so important. It was the first, and for many people the only, instruction that they ever received on how they should read the Bible. In it, Cranmer clearly expounded the divine inspiration and authority of the text, and explained how and why ordinary Christians should read it for their own spiritual growth. To this day the *Homilies* are considered to be part of the Church of England's official teaching, and although they are seldom read now, they still remain the most authoritative guide that the church has to the reading of the Bible.

In the homily on Scripture nothing is said about royal authority. Instead, Cranmer concentrates on the spiritual profit that is to be gained from reading the sacred text. The Bible contains everything we need to know for our salvation, and Christians must read and study it in order to learn how they can fulfil God's will more perfectly. The words of Scripture are the words of everlasting life, and instead of listening to the vain arguments of other people, true believers should spend their time praying and meditating on it, so as to understand how to apply it to their own lives. Not to know the Bible well is dangerous, because then it is easy to fall into error. Cranmer knew that some parts of the text are harder to understand than others, but he insisted that anyone whose heart was in the right place would be given the grace needed to make sense of it. In his words: 'Although many things in the Scripture be spoken in obscure mysteries, yet there is nothing spoken under dark mysteries in one place but the selfsame thing, in other places is spoken more familiarly and plainly, to the capacity of both learned and unlearned.'

The Geneva Bible

Soon after the accession of Mary I a number of prominent English Protestants found it advisable to leave the country. Some of them eventually made their way to Geneva, where they were welcomed by John Calvin and his followers. One of these exiles, William Whittingham, later took the initiative in Bible translation, and became dean of Durham from 1562 until his death in 1579.

Working under the direction of the greatest Greek and Hebrew scholars of the day, in particular Théodore de Bèze (1518–1605), or Beza as he is usually known in English, Whittingham and his associates, who included Miles Coverdale and John Knox, proceeded to revise the work of their predecessors. First came a New Testament, ready as early as 1557 and modelled on Beza's Latin version which had appeared the year before. Then in 1559 appeared the Psalter, followed shortly thereafter by the rest of the Old Testament. Based for the first time on a critical edition of the original Hebrew and Greek texts, and benefitting from the enormous strides in scholarship that had been made on the continent, the Geneva Bible was a version which for quality far outstripped its rivals in the field. Among its many novel features was a division into verses, which had first appeared in Robert l'Estienne's great edition of the Greek New Testament in 1550. (Chapters had been in use since about 1200.) Another feature was the addition of copious marginal notes, helping readers to understand the meaning of difficulties in the text and guiding them to other Scriptural passages which dealt with the same subject. Most useful of all, the Geneva Bible was printed in a handy quarto format that could be packed into a saddle-bag, instead of the cumbersome folio editions that had been the norm with the Great Bible. Another innovation that was to become standard was the introduction of words in *italic* script, to indicate additions to the original text that the translators felt were necessary for the flow of the English. A frequent example of this is the simple phrase 'I the LORD' which becomes 'I *am* the LORD' when that is needed to make the text read more naturally. The words 'Lord' and 'God' were also printed in capital letters when they represented the Hebrew YHWH ('Yahweh'), the sacred name of God which was never pronounced and which is rendered in the New Testament as *Kyrios* ('Lord'). Unlike the use of italic script, this habit has persisted to the present day and can be found in modern translations like the English Standard Version.

The Geneva Bible appeared in 1560, at a propitious moment in British history. The translators hoped that it would replace the Great

Bible, but their desire was thwarted by the outspoken Calvinism of the marginal notes which accompanied the text. There was no official prohibition on the printing of the Geneva Bible in England, and royal permission for it was obtained as early as 1561, but the fact is that no such edition was forthcoming. The Geneva translation was printed in England for the first time in 1575, and great emphasis was laid on the fact that it was done on royal authority. This was important, because it signalled the establishment's determination to tie the Genevan strand of Protestantism to its own purposes. The 1560 edition had appeared before the rise of Puritanism and so it could not be tarred with that particular brush, and in fact most of the ritual issues that exercised the Puritans were not mentioned in the notes to the Geneva Bible at all. This made it possible for defenders of the state church to use it for their own purposes, and they gladly did so. Even John Whitgift, archbishop of Canterbury from 1583 to 1604 and a stickler for authority, used it in his theological writings far more often than any other translation.

In 1566 Théodore Beza revised his edition of the New Testament, on which the original Geneva translation had been passed, and overhauled the notes, which made it desirable for the English translation to be updated. This work was undertaken by Laurence Tomson (1533–1608), who added his own preface, which is a stirring call to spiritual revival through the reading of God's word. Tomson's revision became standard and was incorporated into all subsequent printings of the Geneva Bible. The years 1575–83 were a breathing space for English Calvinism, and it was during this time that the classical editions of the Geneva Bible appeared, often accompanied by theological tracts supporting a distinctively Reformed position. In particular, from 1579 most of them included a treatise on predestination which maintained a strict Calvinist line and led most people to believe that it was the Church of England's official teaching. In Scotland, the Geneva Bible received official sanction, and did much to spread the use of standard English as the spoken language in that country. It was also the Bible that the pilgrim fathers took to America on board the *Mayflower* in 1620, though by then its days were numbered. The last edition came out in 1640, by which time the Authorized (King James) Version had replaced both it and the Bishops' Bible. Throughout this period, the Geneva Bible was printed with the full authority of the crown and the church, and its immense popularity guaranteed that the teaching of Geneva became the religion of the English people. What had previously been understood as a national enterprise was now tied to an international network of churches, and in turn, the theology that bound those churches together was domesticated in England.

The Geneva Bible was famous, or notorious, for its Calvinist theology, but this was mostly contained in the marginal notes, which directed the reader to consider the application of various texts to particular points of theological dispute. In the text itself, the version's Calvinism can mostly be seen in its preference for words like *congregation* and *elder* instead of *church* and *priest*. However it was the accompanying notes and the treatises printed alongside the Bible itself that ensured the spread of Reformed orthodoxy. Church politics made it seem like the Bible of Puritanism, but this is a misunderstanding. It was much more widely used than that, and the Puritans had no particular investment in it as a translation. By the time they were in control of the government the Geneva Bible was on the way out, and it did not resurface as the Bible of Protestant Dissent after the Restoration. It was always just a means to an end, never the end in itself, and when a better translation appeared it was gradually laid aside as the last generation to be brought up on it quietly passed away.

The historical importance of the Geneva Bible for the history of English Bible translation is that it moved the discussion to a new level. Earlier translators had been content to put the best available Hebrew and Greek editions into good English, assuming that if that was done, the text would speak for itself. The Geneva translators understood that things are not as simple as that. The Bible could indeed be read and understood, but the true meaning of individual passages had to be gathered from the overall context of the entire work. People who lifted verses out of context could easily misapply them, and even learned scholars might not grasp the full dimensions of their teaching without a theological framework to guide them. This framework was not imposed on the text from outside, as the critics claimed, but emerged from within as the ramifications of God's covenant with man became clearer. Those who looked back to Tyndale and Cranmer might find that hard to take and continue to press for a plain, unadorned reading of the text, but the rise of theological controversy made their position look increasingly naive. As the Roman Catholic counter-offensive against Protestantism became stronger, so the Geneva Bible became more popular because whatever its faults might be, it sought to provide answers to the sorts of objections the Roman side was raising and to defend the Protestant cause with greater sophistication than had previously been the case.

The Bishops' Bible

When Queen Elizabeth I came to the throne on 17 November 1558 there were great hopes among the Reformers both at home and abroad that she would lead England back to the Protestantism the country had known before 1553. As soon as they heard the news, the exiles began streaming home, bringing with them the Geneva New Testament and Psalter, and after 1560 the complete Bible. The Psalter and the Bible were both dedicated to the queen, but their tone is markedly less deferential than the one used towards Henry VIII by Miles Coverdale in 1535. The Geneva reformers did not deny that the queen had the responsibility to govern the church according to the law of God, but neither did they doubt that it was their responsibility to tell her how to go about it. They were convinced that Calvin's Geneva was the model Christian state and thought that it should be replicated as closely as possible in England, despite the fact that Geneva was a republican city-state and that episcopal church government had been overthrown even before Calvin got there in 1536. Neither of these features commended themselves to Elizabeth or her advisers and so, despite the fact that the Bible was dedicated to her, she was lukewarm towards it. Her bishops soon realised that another solution to the problem of providing an English Bible for general use would have to be found.

Unfortunately, the appearance of the Geneva Bible was a reminder that the Great Bible had been a product of its time and was no longer in step with the most recent scholarship. It did not take into account the advances that had taken place since 1540, which were considerable. There were also problems with the English in some places, where the earlier translators had either struck the wrong note or produced a version which seemed to many to be too crude or colloquial for church use. Some form of revision was clearly required, and the task was entrusted to Archbishop Matthew Parker and his episcopal colleagues. They worked on it for a few years, borrowing many things from the Geneva Bible in the process, and finally issued their version in 1568. One of the most important differences between it and the Geneva Bible was the nature of the explanatory notes in the margin. Parker would probably have liked to dispense with them altogether, but even he realised that that was no longer possible. Instead, he toned down the theological content and concentrated more on linguistic and historical questions that could be regarded as more objective. Of particular concern to him was the need to make sure that the translation and its notes were in harmony with the official teaching of the Church of

England. Though on the whole it was a Protestant reading that he preferred, he was also sensitive to Catholic tradition and wherever possible tried to accommodate it. The Geneva translators had offered a solidly Reformed (Calvinist) theological interpretation of the text which was designed to clarify difficulties in what to them was the right way. Of course, not all of their explanations commanded general assent. For example, when they translated the Greek word *ekklêsia* as 'congregation' instead of 'church' or *presbyteros* as 'elder' rather than as 'priest,' they were making a statement about the nature and government of the institutional church. It had always been the policy of the English state to leave the medieval church organisation intact as much as possible, in order to minimise the dislocation which the Reformation otherwise caused, but the Genevans were challenging this by claiming that the Scriptural grounds for that form of church government were decidedly weak. What appeared to be simple translation thus became a polemic for a more radical reformation of the church, and the accompanying notes clarified this still further.

To counter this tendency, the bishops refrained from using words that might undermine the church's official government and doctrine, even if they could be justified on purely academic grounds. They were also determined to claim the inheritance of the Great Bible, to which end they reprinted Cranmer's preface to it. Archbishop Matthew Parker (1559–75) nevertheless added another preface of his own, in which he emphasised the need for individuals to 'search the Scriptures' in order to test the rival claims of the different churches and spiritual movements which were competing for the allegiance of the population.

The Bishops' Bible stands out for the way in which it reinserts the Apocryphal books into the main body of the Old Testament, thereby obscuring their status as sub- or deutero-canonical and provoking the ire of those used to the Genevan tradition. The original New Testament was sufficiently faulty to need a number of revisions, which were made to the 1572 edition, and popular attachment to the Coverdale Psalter brought about its reinstatement as the official text in 1582. This was a clear case in which the guardians of the Bishops' Bible were prepared to fly in the face of scholarly opinion, which had moved on from Coverdale, and it severely compromised the text in the eyes of those whose first concern was for accuracy in translation. The growing popularity of the Geneva Bible about this time, and the emergence of a Roman Catholic translation that challenged a number of the assumptions underlying both Protestant versions, produced a situation of general discontent with the *status quo* that would not be resolved until 1611. The Bishops' Bible enjoyed an extended lease of life, perhaps more accurately viewed as a stay of execution, thanks to the policies of Archbishop John Whitgift, who after 1583 tried to insist that it should be brought back into the everyday use of the church. New editions soon appeared to meet this somewhat artificial demand for them, but the Geneva Bible was not suppressed and there is little sign that it lost its popularity with the general public. Long before the decision to prepare a fresh translation was taken in 1604, even the staunchest supporters of the Bishops' Bible had come to recognise that it had failed in its purpose of uniting the church behind a common translation and that its faults were such that only a substantially new version could correct them.

In his preface, Matthew Parker concentrated on the Cranmerian theme of 'search the Scriptures,' seeing that as the best way to grow in the Christian life and forestall theological disagreements. He also attacked the canons of the Oxford council held in 1407, calling them the prime example of how the Roman church tried to keep the Bible out of the hands of the people. As an antiquarian, Parker was particularly interested in old translations of the Bible into English, and he even claimed that they were widespread before the prohibition was issued, though we now know that that was not true. The only translations that circulated at all widely were the Wycliffite ones, which Parker did not mention, perhaps because of their initially subversive character!

The Douai-Reims (Roman Catholic) Bible

The rapid progress of Protestantism, due in no small measure to the widespread circulation of the vernacular Scriptures, finally persuaded the Roman Catholic Church that it too, needed Bibles in the language of the people. Needless to say, the existing Protestant translations were all held to be full of heresy and error, but the reason given for this was somewhat odd. Ignoring the progress made by humanistic scholars, many of them loyal sons of the Roman church, in finding and translating Hebrew and Greek manuscripts of the Bible, they insisted that only Jerome's Latin translation, the famous Vulgate, had ultimate authority. Jerome, they maintained, had used texts of greater authenticity than any that were available in the sixteenth century, which was a defensible position since no manuscripts in the original languages of that antiquity were then available. Because of that, in the places where he differed from what appeared to be the original reading, it was he, and not the surviving Hebrew and Greek texts, who was right. Today we have a higher opinion of Jerome than the humanist scholars of the sixteenth century did, and in some cases, like the omission of the doxology at the end of the Lord's Prayer in Matthew 6:13, we now agree that he was right and the Greek manuscripts used by Erasmus and l'Estienne were wrong. But we only think this because we now have access to better Greek manuscripts. Nobody today would defend the Latin (or any) translation as the supremely authoritative text, which is what the Council of Trent decided to do in 1546.

The attachment to Jerome was buttressed by a desire to maintain the unity of the church and to stave off heresy. It was taken almost for granted that vernacular translations of the Bible would be heretical, either because they were done by heretics in the first place (the position taken by Sir Thomas More in his attack on William Tyndale) or because the inherent differences between languages was bound to produce variant readings and thus open the door to heresy. It is important to notice here that this argument was the exact opposite of the one advanced by Thomas Cranmer and Matthew Parker. They believed that it was because the Bible had *not* been translated into the vernacular that heresy had been given a chance to spread, because it profited from the ignorance of gullible people who did not know what the truth was.

Alongside this determination to maintain the authority of Jerome, there was another Catholic view that was more moderate and eventually came to supplant it in scholarly circles. This was that the Hebrew and Greek originals must be respected for what they were, but that for the sake of unity, the church had the right to authorise a Latin text which would then be preferred to any vernacular version. Translations into modern languages could be allowed for pastoral purposes but not for the establishing of doctrine. Gradually Rome got around to putting this principle into practice, and in 1590 a new Latin Bible appeared, which was essentially the Vulgate touched up by modern scholarship. Unfortunately it was so defective that it was withdrawn almost as soon as it was published, and reissued two years later in a substantially corrected revision. That revision, known as the Clementine Vulgate because it was issued by Pope Clement VIII, remained the standard Catholic text until the mid-twentieth century.

It is therefore easy to understand why, when the Catholic exiles at Reims undertook to produce their own translation of the Bible into English, they based it on the Latin Vulgate. More controversially, they also did their best to make the English language sound as much like Latin as possible. They knew that English had already absorbed many Latin and Greek words, especially in its religious terminology, and wanted it to accept more. Why, they argued, was it all right to use a word like Pentecost, the original meaning of which was not generally understood, but not Pasch (for Easter)? What made the Protestants invent a word like 'foreskin' when the Latinate 'prepuce' could be employed instead? These are not theological questions but linguistic ones, and there is no simple answer to them. The Catholics were traditionalists, and traditionalists always have trouble with change, whatever it is. Were they alive today, they would be mortified to discover that modern English has allowed *thou, thee* and *ye* to fall into disuse in favour of the now universal *you.* This obscures what is sometimes a convenient distinction between the singular and the plural, and we can understand why some people would be upset at losing that. But can we really go back and restore *thou* to its traditional place in the language? Logic might suggest that it would be a good idea to do so, but the 'feel' of the language is against it and it would never catch on. This was the basic problem the Catholic translators faced with their proposals for a revamped English vocabulary. However justifiable their arguments might have been, they were swimming against the tide and so were doomed to failure from the start.

The sad result of all this is that the Reims New Testament was often unintelligible, even to contemporaries. Catholic apologists have spared no effort to defend the translators, and it is true that in some ways – notably in their use of the definite article – they were more accurate than their Protestant counterparts. But technical excellence of this kind could not outweigh the enormous defects of their translation, and the Reims New Testament never became the household version that the Geneva Bible did. Considering that it could not be freely sold in England, that the church actively discouraged the private reading of the Scriptures and that most of those who might want to read it knew Latin anyway, it is surprising that any copies were distributed at all. Certainly it never became familiar to any large body of people and it is now more of a curiosity than anything else.

Having said that however, the preface is of great interest as a statement of Catholic opposition to the Reformers' pretensions, and it gives us a flavour of the continuing opposition which the Protestants had to face. Bible translation has always been a theological enterprise, but seldom more so than in the Catholic response to the Reformers. At stake was nothing less than the source of Christian truth, and the right of the church to interpret it according to tradition. The Catholics of the sixteenth century were committed, not merely to a defence of the patristic heritage (something which they shared in large measure with

Anglicans) but also – and at that time more important – to the tradition represented by the Vulgate. The main target of their attacks was therefore Théodore Beza, whom they rightly regarded as their most formidable adversary. Ironically, the attacks they made on him only served to increase his reputation as a scholar who could rise above the prejudices of his age. For Beza did not rely on his theological position in order to justify his choice of textual variants, but on the sense of the text itself and the weight of manuscript evidence, to which he then made his theological position conform. In this respect he was a humanist scholar in the tradition of Erasmus and even Sir Thomas More, who would probably have agreed with him over against the Reims translators.

This does not mean that the men of Reims could not win on points. An example of this can be found in Mark 7:3, which talks about the Jewish ceremonial washings which the Pharisees practised. The problem was to know whether this was something they did 'often' (as the Vulgate said, reading the Greek as *pykne*) or 'up to the elbow' which is what the extant Greek manuscripts apparently say (*pygme*). Here a good case can be made for accepting the superiority of the Vulgate reading, even if there is no original Greek text to base it on, and Beza recognised this, even though in the end he felt bound to go with the Greek. A modern scholar might concur, on the ground that the Greek is more difficult to understand, which is why the Reims translators rejected it. The principle is that of the so-called *lectio difficilior*, which says that a harder reading is more likely to have been 'simplified' into something comprehensible than the other way round, and that may be what Jerome or his immediate Greek source did. It is interesting to note here that the King James Version followed the Latin whereas most modern English translations simply leave the word out on the ground that its meaning is unclear! But if the Reims translation occasionally scores on points like this, it loses the overall argument because its intention is to justify the superiority of the Latin over the Greek, which is nonsensical, even if in one or two cases like this one it appears to be justified.

In one important respect, the Reims translators implicitly acknowledged the superiority of Beza's methods. Rather than prepare a simple translation which would find its way into the hands of ordinary English Catholics, who might then interpret it in ways far removed from the official teaching of the church, they decided to add notes of their own to guide potential readers. Naturally the content of these notes was very different from anything Beza wrote, but the underlying principle was the same. A Catholic Bible that circulated in England could not be effectively controlled by a hierarchy which did not exist, and so the stipulations for Catholic vernacular Bibles that had been laid down by the Council of Trent were ignored in the English case. Instead, it was to be the techniques of the most determined Protestants that would become the Catholic norm, and it was on that basis that the translation proceeded.

Shortly after the completion of the Reims New Testament, the English College was transferred to Douai, where it had originally been founded in 1568, but difficulties of organization delayed the production of the Old Testament for many years. During that time, the definitive edition of the Latin Vulgate was produced, which made a revision of the original New Testament possible and encouraged the translators to press on with the Old. In general however, it is fair to say that the advantages and defects of the Reims New Testament reappear in the Old Testament produced at Douai, in spite of the lapse of time.

The Douai-Reims translation, taken together, is now usually known as the Douai Bible, and was officially imposed on English-speaking Catholics as the only vernacular translation permitted for use. However, its defects soon made themselves felt, and many revisions were attempted. The most successful of these were the ones made by Bishop Richard Challoner (1691–1781), who was a convert from Protestantism, and therefore familiar with the Authorised (King James) Version. His revisions, which were made between 1749 and 1772, removed most of the unintelligible Latinisms and replaced them by phraseology taken from the Authorised Version. It is in this form that the Douai Bible has survived until the present day, although, like the Authorised Version, its use has declined in recent years, particularly since the appearance of *The Jerusalem Bible* in 1966. Thus, in a curious and quite unintended way, the Authorised Version became in effect the Catholic as well as the Protestant Bible, thereby demonstrating its innate superiority to any of its contemporary rivals.

The anti-Protestant polemic characteristic of the Reims New Testament is continued in the Old Testament preface. Perhaps the only difference to note is that between 1582 and 1609 the fortunes of English Catholicism had declined dramatically, thanks to the failure of the Spanish Armada (1588) and the Gunpowder Plot (1605). In the seventeenth century, the foreign character of Catholicism became much more marked, and religious dissension in England, though still very lively, became largely a matter of disputes within the Protestant camp, rather than arguments with Rome, as had been the case during most of the sixteenth century. There is no doubt that the preface to the Old

Testament, and especially its concluding sections, reflects an atmosphere of persecution, with little hope of immediate deliverance. The emphasis is very much on patient endurance, and there is open recognition that few are heeding the call to sacrifice themselves, if necessary, for the sake of the cause.

The Authorised (King James) Bible

The appearance of a Catholic vernacular New Testament, however defective, changed the nature of Bible translation in England. Until 1582 it had been almost taken for granted that the English Bible was a Protestant enterprise, the only difference of opinion being as to how detailed its Protestantism was. Nobody seriously doubted that the Scriptures taught Protestant doctrine and that Catholic teachings were accretions made by popes, church councils and canon lawyers. The defence of Roman Catholicism on the basis of Scripture therefore came as a surprise to many, and the detailed accusations made in the preface to the New Testament could not be allowed to go unanswered. One of the strongest Catholic arguments was the perceived disunity of Protestantism. How could it be that people who read the same Bible came to such different conclusions about it? Why were they constantly changing even the text itself? It was not simply that there were two main versions, the Geneva and the Bishops' Bible, which competed for attention, but that every new edition of each of these Bibles was subtly different. They were not fixed texts, protected by some kind of copyright, but ongoing projects in which printers and politicians could play a rôle almost as important as that of the actual translators. Gradually people came to see that something had to be done about this if the credibility of Protestantism as the truth contained in God's Word was to be maintained.

Nothing much could be done as long as Queen Elizabeth I was alive, because she resisted even the smallest changes to her religious settlement, and the Bishops' Bible had been part of that. With the accession of James VI of Scotland (1567–1625) to the throne of England in 1603 however, the pressures for further reform of the church which had been gathering steam in the 1590s came to a head. A conference was held at Hampton Court in January 1604, which attempted to resolve these, but it met with little success. In spite (or more probably because) of the king's presbyterian upbringing, he was not prepared to see the Church of England move towards a type of Reformation similar to that of Scotland. One exception to this rule however, was his decision to accept a proposal, put forward by Dr John Reynolds of Corpus Christi

College, Oxford, a leading Puritan, that a new translation of the Bible should be prepared for general use. The uneasy co-existence between the Bishops' Bible, read in church but generally unloved, and the Geneva Bible, with its many marginal notes proclaiming a strident Calvinism, had to be resolved, and the only way to do this fairly was to start again. James agreed to this proposal, but stipulated that the Bishops' Bible should form the basis of any new translation and that it must appear without any notes to 'guide' the reader into adopting a particular theological position. If that was not clear from the text itself, then it should be left to the reader's judgement, a sentiment which would have warmed the heart of Thomas Cranmer but which was quite daring in the climate of 1604, when even the Catholics were preparing extensive notes to their translation.

The king took a personal interest in the work, which eventually involved 47 different translators. His stipulation that the Bishops' Bible must be used as the basis of the new translation barely limited the freedom of the translators, who worked from the best Hebrew and Greek manuscripts then available and were free to consult any translation they chose. They were even happy to borrow from the Reims New Testament, as the example of Mark 7:3 given above shows. But the real clue as to where their heart lay can be found in the translators' preface, which was composed by Miles Smith (1554–1624) who became bishop of Gloucester in 1612. Smith made an able, elegant and reasonably concise defence of the new translation, but when it came to quoting the text of the Bible, he did not use it. Instead, his Biblical citations all come from the Geneva version! That was the one people knew and more often than not it was also the one that was closest to the original meaning.

In the case of the Old Testament, the Hebrew text available in 1611 was not substantially different from that we use today, but things were very different in the case of the Greek New Testament. King James' men used the edition of Robert l'Estienne, which in 1633 would come out in Holland as the *Textus Receptus* ('Received Text'), a title which it has borne ever since. However, subsequent manuscript discovery has revealed that this Received Text is quite different in many places from the best Greek sources, and this has now made the Authorised Version out of date scientifically, as well as linguistically. As far as the language was concerned, it was archaic even before it was printed, a fact not often appreciated by modern readers. The translators were not trying to be modern or colloquial, but the very opposite. They were searching for a vanished past, in theory for the world of William

Tyndale and Thomas Cranmer, but in reality (as is almost always the case in such situations) for something that had never existed. Looking back on William Tyndale, they did not find him old-fashioned but the very opposite – he was too racy for their tastes! Anyone who doubts this need only compare the two versions, as in Genesis 30:16, for example, where the Authorised Version says of Jacob and Leah: 'And he lay with her that night' whereas Tyndale wrote: 'And he slept with her that night,' the expression we still use today. We could even say that had the translators stuck with Tyndale instead of trying to clean him up, the AV might not seem as outdated now as it does!

In other respects, the AV tried to accommodate the sensitivities of the established church when choosing potentially controversial religious terminology, though often the result was a compromise, with 'congregation' for example being used in the Old Testament and 'church' in the New to designate much the same thing. But we must be careful not to say that 'congregation' was the preferred Puritan word, since most Puritans were quite happy to speak of Israel as the Old Testament church! There are also inconsistencies due to the practices of different translating committees, of which the most noticeable is the tendency to use Hellenised forms of Hebrew names in the New Testament but pseudo-Hebraic ones in the Old. Hence the distinction between Elijah and Elias, Noah and Noe, though the pattern is not carried through. Following this logic consistently, Joshua ought to become Jesus in the New Testament, but he does not, although the identity of the name of our Saviour with the successor of Moses is duly obscured, which was not true in either the Greek or the Latin Bibles (which used 'Jesus' for both). On the other hand, Solomon, a more-or-less Greek form,[1] stays the same in both testaments and does not become Shlomo, as it would if the Hebrew were being strictly followed in the Old Testament.

The translators of the AV knew that they were under attack, and that they would be criticised for their efforts however hard they tried. They also knew that if their version was to have any hope of success, the support of the king was essential, which helps to explain their somewhat fawning attitude to him. But these considerations were preliminary and ultimately peripheral to their work. Their main purpose was to exalt the Scriptures as the Word of God, to let them speak to an entire nation, from the most learned to the most humble and to provide

---

[1] The Greek is *Salomon*.

as accurate and reliable a text as they could. They knew that there were some passages that could be translated in different ways, and they reserved the right to put variants in the margin, despite the king's injunction against notes. They also understood that it would be impossible to produce an exactly literal translation without doing violence to the English, and although they knew they would be attacked by the Catholics for taking liberties with the originals, they resisted the temptation to produce a wooden and unreadable text as their predecessors at Reims and Douai had done.

The Authorised Version was a compromise and it betrays its origins, but although it would eventually win the day, it did not immediately establish itself as the classic English text of the Bible. That took another generation, and it was not until the civil war period that its position was finally secure. It is one of the great ironies of English history that just as the Church of England broke up into competing denominations, the overall unity of its Protestantism was sealed by the acceptance of a common Bible. Whatever else Baptists, Presbyterians and Methodists may have done, they have never tried to produce their own Bibles, an activity which is today associated with sects like the Jehovah's Witnesses. Even in an age of multiple translations, denominationalism plays virtually no part and the modern study of the Bible remains an ecumenical enterprise, as it has always been in the English-speaking world.

Few people now realise it, but the text of the AV was not finalised for 150 years after it was first issued. As with the Bishops' and Geneva Bibles before it, the AV underwent subtle but progressive updatings with each new edition, a process which did not end until 1761. There was no serious attempt to revise or replace it until 1881, when the so-called Revised Version appeared. That failed to catch on, largely because of its wooden and pedantic rendering of the original texts, and it was not until the 1960s that the Authorised Version faced serious competition from modern translations. It is now falling into disuse, though its status as a literary classic remains unchallenged, and on this score at least, none of the modern versions can hope to rival it. For better or for worse, it has entered into the substance of the language itself and will always sound like the 'real' Bible to those whose mother tongue is English.

Perhaps the last word should be given to the translators themselves. As Miles Smith came to the end of his explanation of the translation and the motives that lay behind it, he reached out to his readers with the following exhortation, which remains as challenging to us today as when it was first uttered:

> *It is a fearful thing to fall into the hands of the living God,*[2] *but a blessed thing it is, and will bring us to everlasting blessedness in the end, when God speaketh unto us, to hearken; when he setteth his Word before us, to read it; when he stretcheth out his hand and calleth, to answer: 'Here am I; here we are to do thy will, O God.' The Lord work a care and conscience in us to know him and serve him, that we may be acknowledged of him at the appearing of our Lord Jesus Christ, to whom with the Holy Ghost, be all praise and thanksgiving. Amen.*

How to read this book

The present edition of the prefaces to the main translations of the Bible into English between 1525 and 1611 has been prepared to coincide with the four-hundredth anniversary of the first edition of the Authorised or King James Version. The texts have been taken from the Bibles and Testaments themselves, apart from the Homily on Scripture, which comes from the *Book of Homilies*, which was last edited in 1859.

In many cases the spelling has been modernised and the punctuation has been rearranged to correspond with current practice, so as to make the texts easier to read. On the other hand, obsolete words have been retained and a modern equivalent has been provided in the footnotes.

Each of the texts has been provided with notes indicating the sources of the various quotations and allusions, something which has never been done before. In many cases the original Bibles contain useful information of this kind in their margins, but the references are often out of date and some are simply wrong. As an aid to scholars seeking to locate patristic citations, references are given to J. P. Migne's *Patrologia Graeca* (PG) and *Patrologia Latina* (PL). In many cases newer editions are now available along with translations, but Migne remains a standard reference, covering the entire field in a way that no other series as yet does. Biblical texts are cited according to the standard English system, even if the original text did not do this (as the Roman Catholic texts, for example, did not). Similarly, Biblical names have been standardised for ease of reference, on the principle that

---

[2] Hebrews 10:31.

comprehensibility is more important in a work intended for the general public than strict (but confusing) accuracy.

1. Tyndale's Preface to the New Testament, 1526

01. Here thou hast (most dear reader) the New Testament or covenant made with us of God in Christ's blood. Which I have looked over again (now at the last) with all diligence, and compared it unto the Greek, and have weeded out of it many faults, which lack of help at the beginning, and oversight, did sow therein. If aught seem changed, or not altogether agreeing with the Greek, let the finder of the fault consider the Hebrew phrase or manner of speech left in the Greek words. Whose preterperfect tense and present tense is oft both one, and the future tense is the optative mode also, and the future tense is oft the imperative mode in the active voice, and in the passive ever. Likewise person for person, number for number, and an interrogation for a conditional, and such like as with the Hebrews is a common usage.[1]

02. I have also in many places set light in the margin to understand the text by. If any man find faults either with the translation or with aught beside (which is easier for many to do, than so well to have translated it themselves of their own pregnant wits, at the beginning without fore-example) to the same it shall be lawful to translate it themselves and to put what they lust thereto. If I shall perceive either by myself or by the information of other, that aught be escaped me, or might be more plainly translated, I will shortly after cause it to be mended. Howbeit in many places, me thinketh it better to put a declaration in the margin, than to run too far from the text. And in many places, where the text seemeth at the first chop hard to be understood, yet the circumstances before and after, and often reading together, maketh it plain enough etc.

03. Moreover, because the kingdom of heaven, which is the Scripture and Word of God, may be so locked up, that he which readeth or heareth it cannot understand it; as Christ testifieth how that the

---

[1] Tyndale means that the verb structure of Hebrew is less developed than that of Greek, with the result that the true meaning of the Greek does not always correspond to the verbal tense or mood actually used.

scribes and Pharisees had so shut it up[2] and had taken away the key of knowledge[3] that the Jews which thought themselves within, were yet so locked out, and are to this day that they can understand no sentence of the Scripture unto their salvation, though they can rehearse the texts everywhere and dispute thereof as subtly as the popish doctors of dunces' dark learning, which with their sophistry, served us, as the Pharisees did the Jews. Therefore (that I might be found faithful to my Father and Lord in distributing unto my brethren and fellows of one faith, their due and necessary food: so dressing it and seasoning it, that the weak stomachs may receive it also, and be the better for it) I thought it my duty (most dear reader) to warn thee before, and to show thee the right way in, and to give thee the true key to open it withal, and to arm thee against false prophets and malicious hypocrites, whose perpetual study is to leaven the Scripture with glosses, and there to lock it up where it should save thy soul, and to make us shoot at a wrong mark, to put our trust in those things that profit their bellies only and slay our souls.

04. The right way; yea, and the only way to understand the Scripture unto our salvation, is that we earnestly, and above all things, search for the profession of our baptism, or covenants made between God and us. As for an example: Christ saith: *Happy are the merciful, for they shall obtain mercy.*[4] Lo, here God hath made a covenant with us, to be merciful unto us, if we will be merciful one to another, so that the man which sheweth mercy unto his neighbour may be bold to trust in God for mercy at all needs. And contrariwise, judgement without mercy shall be to him that showeth not mercy.[5] So now, if he that showeth no mercy trust in God for mercy, his faith is carnal and worldly, and but vain presumption. For God hath promised mercy only to the merciful. And therefore the merciless have no God's word that they shall have mercy; but contrariwise, that they shall have judgement without mercy. And: *If ye shall forgive men their faults, your heavenly Father shall forgive you, but if ye shall not forgive men their faults, no more shall your Father forgive you your faults.*[6]

---

[2] Matthew 23:1-4.
[3] Luke 11:52.
[4] Matthew 5:7.
[5] James 2:13.
[6] Matthew 6:14-15.

Here also, by the virtue and strength of this covenant wherewith God of his mercy hath bound himself to us unworthy, may he that forgiveth his neighbour be bold when he returneth and amendeth to believe and trust in God for remission of whatsoever he hath done amiss. And contrariwise, he that will not forgive cannot but despair of forgiveness in the end, and fear judgement without mercy.

05. The general covenant wherein all other are comprehended and included is this. If we meek ourselves to God, to keep all his laws after the example of Christ: then God hath bound himself to us to keep and make good all the mercies promised in Christ throughout all the Scripture.

06. All the whole law which was given to utter our corrupt nature, is comprehended in the ten commandments. And the ten commandments are comprehended in these two: love God and thy neighbour. And he that loveth his neighbour in God and Christ fulfilleth these two, and consequently the ten, and finally all the other. Now if we love our neighbours in God and Christ: that is to wit, if we be loving, kind and merciful to them, because God hath created them unto his likeness, and Christ hath redeemed them and bought them with his blood, then may we be bold to trust in God through Christ and his deserving, for all mercy. For God hath promised and bound himself to us, to show us all mercy and to be a Father Almighty to us, so that we shall not need to fear the power of all our adversaries.

07. Now if any man that submitteth not himself to keep the commandments do think that he hath any faith in God, the same man's faith is vain, worldly, damnable, devilish and plain presumption, as it is above said, and is no faith that can justify or be accepted before God. And that is it that James meaneth in his Epistle.[7] *For how can a man believe,* saith Paul, *without a preacher?*[8] Now read all the Scripture and see where God sent any to preach mercy to any, save unto them only that repent and turn to God with all their hearts, to keep his commandments. Unto the disobedient that will not turn is threatened wrath, vengeance and damnation, according to all the terrible curses and fearful

---

[7] See James 2:14-26.
[8] Romans 10:14.

examples of the Bible.

08. Faith now in God the Father through our Lord Jesus Christ, according to the covenants and appointment made between God and us, is our salvation. Wherefore I have ever noted the covenants in the margins, and also the promises. Moreover, where thou findest a promise and no covenant expressed therewith, there must thou understand a covenant. For all the promises of the mercy and grace that Christ hath purchased for us are made upon the condition that we keep the law. As for an example, when the Scripture saith: *Ask and it shall be given you, seek and ye shall find, knock and it shall be opened unto you.*[9] It is to be understood, if that when thy neighbour asketh, seeketh or knocketh to thee, thou then show him the same mercy which thou desirest of God, then hath God bound himself to help thee again, and else not.

09. Also ye see that two things are required to begin a Christian man. The first is a steadfast faith and trust in Almighty God, to obtain all the mercy that he hath promised us, through the deserving and merits of Christ's blood only, without all respect to our own works. And the other is that we forsake evil and turn to God, to keep his laws and to fight against ourselves and our corrupt nature perpetually, that we may do the will of God every day better and better.

10. This have I said (most dear reader) to warn thee, lest thou shouldest be deceived and shouldest not only read the Scriptures in vain and to no profit, but also unto thy greater damnation. For the nature of God's Word is that whosoever read it or hear it reasoned and disputed before him, it will begin immediately to make him every day better and better, till he be grown into a perfect man in the knowledge of Christ and love of the law of God; or else make him worse and worse, till he be hardened that he openly resist the Spirit of God, and then blaspheme after the example of Pharaoh, Korah, Abiram, Balaam, Judas, Simon Magus and such other.

11. This to be even so, the words of Christ do well confirm. *This is condemnation,* saith he, *the light is come into the world but the*

---

[9] Matthew 7:7.

men loved darkness more than light, for their deeds were evil.[10] Behold, when the light of God's word cometh to a man, whether he read it or hear it preached and testified, and he yet have no love thereto, to fashion his life thereafter, but consenteth still unto his old deeds of ignorance; then beginneth his just damnation immediately, and he is henceforth without excuse, in that he refused mercy offered him. For God offereth him mercy upon the condition that he will mend his living, but he will not come under the covenant. And from that hour forward he waxeth worse and worse, God taking his Spirit of mercy and grace from him for his unthankfulness' sake.

12. And Paul writeth that the heathen, because when they knew God they had no lust to honour him with Godly living, therefore God poured his wrath upon them and took his Spirit from them, and gave them up unto their hearts' lusts to serve sin from iniquity to iniquity, till they were thoroughly hardened and past repentance.[11]

13. And Pharaoh, because when the word of God was in his country and God's people scattered throughout all his land, and yet neither loved them or it; therefore God gave him up, and in taking his Spirit of grace from him, so hardened his heart with covetousness that afterward no miracle could convert him.[12]

14. Hereto pertaineth the parable of the talents. The Lord commandeth the talent to be taken away from the evil and slothful servant, and to bind him hand and foot and to cast him into utter darkness, and to give the talent unto him that had ten, saying: *to all that have, more shall be given. But from him that hath not, that he hath shall be taken from him.*[13] That is to say, he that hath a good heart toward the Word of God and a set purpose to fashion his deeds thereafter and to garnish it with godly living and to testify it to other, the same shall increase more and more daily in the grace of Christ. But he that loveth it not, to live thereafter and to edify other, the same shall lose the grace of true knowledge and be blinded again and every day wax worse and worse and blinder and blinder, till he be an utter enemy of the Word of God, and his heart so hardened, that it shall be

---

[10] John 3:19.
[11] Romans 1:19-23 (paraphrased).
[12] See Exodus 7-11.
[13] Matthew 25:29.

impossible to convert him.

15. And: *The servant that knoweth his master's will and prepareth not himself shall be beaten with many stripes; that is, shall have greater damnation.*[14] And: *all that hear the Word of God and do not, thereafter build on sand,*[15] that is, as the foundation laid on sand cannot resist violence of water, but is undermined and overthrown, even so the faith of them that have no lust nor love to the law of God, built upon the sand of their own imaginations, and not on the rock of God's Word according to his covenants, turneth to desperation in time of tribulation and when God cometh to judge[16].

16. And the vineyard planted and hired out to the husbandmen that would not render to the Lord of the fruit in due time, and therefore was taken from them and hired out to other, doth confirm the same.[17] For Christ saith to the Jews, *the Kingdom of Heaven shall be taken from you and given to a nation that will bring forth the fruits thereof,*[18] as it is come to pass. For the Jews have lost the spiritual knowledge of God and of his commandments and also of all the Scripture, so that they can understand nothing godly. And the door is so locked up that all their knocking is in vain, though many of them take great pain for God's sake. And the fig tree that beareth no fruit is commanded to be plucked up.[19]

17. And finally, hereto pertaineth with infinite other, the terrible parable of the unclean spirit which, after he is cast out, when he cometh and findeth his house swept and garnished, taketh to him seven worse than himself, and cometh and entereth in and dwelleth there, and so is the end of the man worse than the beginning.[20] The Jews, they had cleansed themselves with God's Word, from all outward idolatry and worshipping of idols. But their hearts remained still faithless to Godward and toward his mercy and truth, and therefore without love also and lust to his

---

[14] Luke 12:47.
[15] Matthew 7:26.
[16] Tyndale means that a faith built on sand will crumble as soon as it is put to the test.
[17] Matthew 21:33-43.
[18] Matthew 21:43
[19] Luke 13:6-9.
[20] Luke 11:24-26.

law, and to their neighbours for his sake, and through false trust in their own works (to which heresy, the child of perdition, the wicked Bishop of Rome with his lawyers hath brought us Christians), were more abominable idolaters than before, and become ten times worse in the end than at the beginning. For the first idolatry was soon spied and easy to be rebuked of the prophets by the Scripture. But the later is more subtle to beguile withal, and an hundred times of more difficulty to be weeded out of men's hearts.

18. This also is a conclusion, nothing more certain, or more proved by the testimony and examples of the Scripture, that if any that favoureth the Word of God be so weak that he cannot chasten his flesh, him will the Lord chastise and scourge every day sharper and sharper, with tribulation and misfortune, that nothing shall prosper with him but that all shall go against him, whatsoever he taketh in hand, and shall visit him with poverty, with sickness and diseases, and shall plague him with plague upon plague, each more loathsome, terrible and fearful than other, till he be at utter defiance with his flesh.

19. Let us therefore that have now at this time our eyes opened again through the tender mercy of God, keep a mean[21]. Let us so put our trust in the mercy of God through Christ, that we know it our duty to keep the law of God and to love our neighbours for their Father's sake which created them, and for their Lord's sake, which redeemed them, and bought them so dearly with his blood. Let us walk in the fear of God and have our eyes open unto both parts of God's covenants, certified that none shall be partaker of the mercy save he that will fight against the flesh, to keep the law. And let us arm ourselves with this remembrance, that as Christ's works justify from sin and set us in the favour of God, so our own deeds through working of the Spirit of God help us to continue in the favour and the grace into which Christ hath brought us; and that we can no longer continue in favour and grace than our hearts are to keep the law.

20. Furthermore, concerning the law of God, this is a general conclusion, that the whole law, whether they be ceremonies, sacrifices, yea or sacraments either, or precepts of equity between

---

[21] 'Balance'

man and man throughout all degrees of the world, all were given for our profit and necessity only, and not for any need that God hath of our keeping them, or that his joy is increased thereby or that the deed, for the deed itself, doth please him. That is, all that God requireth of us when we be at one with him and do put our trust in him and love him, is that we love every man his neighbour to pity him and to have compassion on him in all his needs and to be merciful unto him. This to be even so, Christ testifieth saying: *This is the law and the prophets.*[22] That is, to do as thou wouldst be done to (according, I mean, to the doctrine of the Scripture) and not to do that which thou wouldest not have done to thee, is all that the law requireth and the prophets. And Paul affirmeth also that *love is the fulfilling of the law, and that he which loveth doth of his own accord all that the law requireth.*[23] And Paul saith that *the love of a pure heart and good conscience and faith unfeigned is the end and fulfilling of the law.*[24] For faith unfeigned in Christ's blood causeth to love for Christ's sake. Which love is the pure love only and the only cause of a good conscience. For then is the conscience pure, when the eye looketh to Christ in all her deeds, to do them for his sake and not for her own singular advantage, or any other wicked purpose. And John both in his gospel and also epistles, speaketh never of any other law than to love one another purely, affirming that we have God himself dwelling in us and all that God desireth, if we love one the other.

21. Seeing then that faith to God and love and mercifulness to our neighbours, is all that the law requireth, therefore of necessity the law must be understood and interpreted by them. So that all inferior laws are to be kept and observed as long as they be servants to faith and love, and then to be broken immediately, if through any occasion they hurt, either the faith which we should have to Godward in the confidence of Christ's blood, or the love which we owe to our neighbours for Christ's sake.

22. And therefore, when the blind Pharisees murmured and grudged at him and his disciples, that they broke the sabbath day and traditions of the elders, and that he himself did eat with publicans

---

[22] Matthew 7:12.
[23] Romans 13:10.
[24] 1 Timothy 1:5.

and sinners, he answereth alleging Isaiah the prophet: *go rather, and learn what this meaneth – I require mercy and not sacrifice.*[25] And: *Oh that ye wist what this meaneth, I require mercy and not sacrifice.*[26] For only love and mercifulness understandeth the law, and else nothing. And he that hath not that written in his heart, shall never understand the law, no: though all the angels of heaven went about to teach him. And he that hath that graven in his heart shall not only understand the law, but shall also do of his own inclination all that is required of the law, though never law had been given: as all mothers do of themselves without law unto their children, all that can be required by any law, love overcoming all pain, grief, tediousness or loathsomeness; and even so, no doubt, if we had continued in our first state of innocency, we should ever have fulfilled the law, without compulsion of the law.

23. And because the law (which is a doctrine through teaching every man his duty, doth utter our corrupt nature) is sufficiently described by Moses, therefore is little mention made thereof in the New Testament, save of love only, wherein all the law is included, as seldom mention is made of the New Testament in the old law, save here and there are promises made unto them, that Christ should come and bless them and deliver them, and that the Gospel and New Testament should be preached and published unto all nations.

24. The gospel is glad tidings of mercy and grace and that our corrupt nature shall be healed again for Christ's sake and for the merits of his deservings only; yet on condition that we will turn to God, to learn to keep his laws spiritually, that is to say, of love for his sake, and will also suffer the curing of our infirmities.

25. The New Testament is as much to say as a new covenant. The Old Testament is an old temporal covenant made between God and the carnal children of Abraham, Isaac and Jacob, otherwise called Israel, upon the deeds and observing of a temporal law. When the reward of the keeping is temporal life and prosperity in the land of Canaan, and the breaking is rewarded with temporal death and punishment. But the New Testament is an everlasting covenant

---

[25] Matthew 9:13, citing Hosea 6:6, not Isaiah.
[26] Matthew 12:7.

made unto the children of God through faith in Christ, upon the deservings of Christ. Where eternal life is promised to all that believe, and death to all that are unbelieving. My deeds, if I keep the law, are rewarded with the temporal promises of this life. But if I believe in Christ, Christ's deeds have purchased for me the eternal promise of the everlasting life. If I commit nothing worthy of death, I deserve to my reward that no man kill me; if I hurt no man, I am worthy that no man hurt me. If I help my neighbour, I am worthy that he help me again, etc. So that with outward deeds with which I serve other men, I deserve that other men do like to me in this world, and they extend no further. But Christ's deeds extend to life everlasting unto all that believe, etc. This be sufficient in this place concerning the law and the gospel, New Testament and Old; so that as there is but one God, one Christ, one faith and one baptism, even so thou understand that there is but one gospel, though many write it and many preach it. For all preach the same Christ and bring the same glad tidings. And thereto Paul's epistles, with the gospel of John and his first epistle, and the first epistle of Saint Peter, are most pure gospel and most plainly and richly described the glory of the grace of Christ. If ye require more of the law, seek in the prologue to the Romans and in other places where it is sufficiently treated[27] of.

26. Repentance. Concerning this word repentance, or (as they used) penance, the Hebrew hath in the Old Testament generally *sob* [*shub*] – turn, or be converted. For which the translation that we take for Saint Jerome's hath most part *converti* – to turn, or be converted, and sometime yet, *agere paenitentiam*. And the Greek in the New Testament hath perpetually *metanoeo* – to turn in the heart and mind, and to come to the right knowledge, and to a man's right wit again. For which *metanoeo* St. Jerome's translation hath sometime *ago paenitentiam* – I do repent, sometime *paeniteo* – I repent, sometime *paeniteor* – I am repentant, sometime *habeo paenitentiam* – I have repentance, sometime *paenitet me* – it repenteth me. And Erasmus useth much this word *resipisco* – I come to myself, or to my right mind again. And the very sense and signification both of the Hebrew and also of the Greek word is – to be converted and to turn to God with all the heart, to know his will and to live according to his

---

[27] Original text says 'intreated'.

laws, and to be cured of our corrupt nature with the oil of his Spirit and wine of obedience to his doctrine. Which conversion or turning, if it be unfeigned, these four do accompany it and are included therein: Confession, not in the priest's ear, for that is but man's invention, but to God in the heart and before all the congregation of God, how that we be sinners and sinful, and that our whole nature is corrupt and inclined to sin and all unrighteousness, and therefore evil, wicked and damnable, and his law holy and just, by which our sinful nature is rebuked; and also to our neighbours, if we have offended any person particularly. Then, Contrition – sorrowfulness that we be such damnable sinners, and not only have sinned but are wholly inclined to sin still. Thirdly: Faith (of which our old doctors have made no mention at all in the description of their penance), yet God for Christ's sake doth forgive and receive us to mercy, and is at one with us and will heal our corrupt nature. And fourthly: Satisfaction, or amends-making, not to God with holy works, but to my neighbour whom I have hurt, and the congregation of God whom I have offended, (if any open crime be found in me), and submitting of a man's self unto the congregation or church of Christ, and to the officers of the same, to have his life corrected and governed henceforth of them, according to the true doctrine of the church of Christ. And note this: that as satisfaction or amends-making is counted righteousness before the world and a purging of the sin, so that the world when I have made a full amends, hath no further to complain. Even so, faith in Christ's blood is counted righteousness, and a purging of all sin before God.

27. Moreover, he that sinneth against his brother sinneth also against his Father, Almighty God. And as the sin committed against his brother is purged before the world with making amends and asking forgiveness, even so is the sin committed against God purged through faith in Christ's blood only. For Christ saith: *Except ye believe that I am he, ye shall die in your sins.*[28] That is to say, if ye think that there is any other sacrifice or satisfaction to Godward than me, ye remain ever in sin before God, howsoever righteous ye appear before the world. Wherefore now, whether ye call this *metanoia*, repentance, conversion or turning again to

---

[28] John 8:24.

God, either amending and etc. or whether ye say repent, be converted, turn to God, amend your living or what ye lust, I am content so ye understand what is meant thereby, as I have now declared.

28. Elders. In the Old Testament the temporal heads and rulers of the Jews which had the governance over the lay or common people are called elders, as ye may see in the four Evangelists. Out of which custom, Paul in his epistles and also Peter, call the prelates and spiritual governors which are bishops and priests, elders. Now whether ye call them elders or priests, it is to me all one: so that ye understand that they be officers and servants of the Word of God, unto the which all men both high and low that will not rebel against Christ, must obey as long as they preach and rule truly and no longer.

29. A prologue into the four Evangelists, showing what they were and their authority. And first of St Matthew. As touching the Evangelists, ye see in the New Testament clearly what they were. First Matthew (as ye read Matthew 9[:9], Mark 2[:14], Lk 5[:27]) was one of Christ's apostles, and was with Christ all the time of his preaching, and saw and heard his own self almost all that he wrote.

30. Of Mark read how Peter (after he was loosed out of prison by the angel) came to Mark's mother's house, where many of the disciples were praying for his deliverance.[29] And Paul and Barnabas took him with them from Jerusalem and brought him to Antioch.[30] And Paul and Barnabas took Mark with them when they were sent out to preach; from whom he also departed, as it appeareth in the said chapter, and returned to Jerusalem again.[31] And Paul and Barnabas were at variance about him, Paul not willing to take him with them, because he forsook them in their first journey.[32] Notwithstanding yet, when Paul wrote the epistle to the Colossians, Mark was with him, as he saith in the fourth chapter; of whom Paul also testifieth, both that he was Barnabas'

---

[29] Acts 12:12.
[30] Acts 12:25.
[31] Acts 13:13.
[32] Acts 15:37-39.

sister's son and also his fellow worker in the Kingdom of God.[33]

31. And Paul commandeth Timothy to bring Mark with him, affirming that he was needful to him, to minister to him.[34] Finally, he was also with Peter when he wrote his first epistle, and so familiar that Peter calleth him his son.[35] Whereof ye see, of whom he learned his gospel, even of the very apostles, with whom he had his continual conversation, and also of what authority his writing is, and how worthy of credence.

32. Luke was Paul's companion, at the least way from the sixteenth chapter of Acts forth and with him in all his tribulation. And he went with Paul at his last going up to Jerusalem. And from thence he followed Paul to Caesarea, where he lay two years in prison. And from Caesarea he went with Paul to Rome, where he lay two other years in prison. And he was with Paul when he wrote to the Colossians, as he testifieth in the fourth chapter, saying: *The beloved Luke the physician saluteth you.*[36] And he was with Paul when he wrote the second epistle to Timothy, as he saith in the fourth chapter, saying: *Only Luke is with me.*[37] Whereby ye see the authority of the man, and of what credence and reverence his writing is worthy of, and thereto of whom he learned the story of his gospel, as he himself saith, how that he learned it and searched it out with all diligence of them that saw it and were also partakers at the doing. And as for the Acts of the Apostles, he himself was at the doing of them (at the least) of the most part, and had his part therein, and therefore wrote of his own experience.

33. John, what he was, is manifest by the first three Evangelists. First, Christ's apostle, and that one of the chief. Then Christ's nigh kinsman, and for his singular innocency and softness, singularly beloved and of singular familiarity with Christ, and ever one of the three witnesses of most secret things. The cause of his writing was certain heresies that arose in his time, and namely two, of which one denied Christ to be very man and to be come in the very flesh and nature of man. Against which two heresies he

---

[33] Colossians 4:10.
[34] 2 Timothy 4:11.
[35] 1 Peter 5:13.
[36] Colossians 4:14.
[37] 2 Timothy 4:11.

wrote both his gospel and also his first epistle, and in the beginning of his gospel saith that the word or thing was at the beginning, and was with God, and was also very God, and that all things was created and made by it, and that it was also made flesh; that is to say, became very man. *And he dwelt among us* (saith he) *and we saw his glory.*[38]

34. And in the beginning of his epistle he saith: *We show you of the thing that was from the beginning, which also we heard, saw with our eyes and our hands handled.*[39] And again: *We show you everlasting life, that was with the Father and appeared to us, and we heard and saw, and etc.*[40]

35. In that he saith that it was from the beginning, and that it was eternal life, and that it was with God, he affirmeth him to be very God. And that he saith, we heard, saw and felt, he witnesseth that he was very man also. John also wrote last, and therefore touched not the story that the other had compiled. But writeth most of faith and promises, and of the sermons of Christ.

36. This be sufficient concerning the four Evangelists and their authority and worthiness to be believed.

37. A warning to the reader if aught be escaped through negligence of the printer, as this text is that followeth, which if thou find any more such: compare the English to the other books that are already printed, and so shalt thou perceive the truth of the English.

38. In the twenty-third chapter of Matthew and in the thirty-third leaf on the second side and last line, read the sentence thus: *Thou blind Pharisee, cleanse first the inside of the cup and platter, that the outside of them may be clean also.*[41]

William Tyndale, yet once more to the Christian Reader [1534]:

39. Thou shalt understand most, dear reader, when I had taken in hand to look over the New Testament again, and to compare it with the Greek, and to mend whatsoever I could find amiss, and

---

[38] John 1:14.
[39] 1 John 1:1.
[40] 1 John 1:2.
[41] Matthew 23:26.

had almost finished the labour; George Joye[42] secretly took in hand to correct it also, by what occasion his conscience knoweth; and prevented me, insomuch that his correction was printed in great number, ere mine began. When it was spied and word brought me, though it seemed to divers other that George Joye had not used the office of an honest man, seeing that he knew that I was in correcting it myself; neither did walk after the rules of the love and softness which Christ and his disciples teach us, how that we should do nothing of strife to move debate, or of vainglory, or of covetousness; yet I took the thing in worth as I have done divers other in time past, as one that have more experience of the nature and disposition of the man's complexion, and supposed that a little spice of covetousness and vainglory (two blind guides) had been the only cause that moved him so to do, about which things I strive with no man: and so followed after and corrected forth and caused this to be printed, without surmise or looking on his correction.

40. But when the printing of mine was almost finished, one brought me a copy and showed me so many places, in such wise altered that I was astonished[43] and wondered not a little what fury had driven him to make such change, and to call it a diligent correction. For throughout Matthew, Mark and Luke perpetually: and oft in the Acts, and sometime in John and also in the Hebrews, where he findeth this word *resurrection*, he changeth it into 'the life after this life,' or 'very life' and such like, as one that abhorred the name of the resurrection.

41. If that change, to turn resurrection into life after this life, be a diligent correction, then must my translation be faulty in those places, and St Jerome's,[44] and all the translators that ever I heard of, in what tongue soever it be, from the apostles unto this; his

---

[42] (1495-1553). A Cambridge graduate, he fled to the continent to escape persecution at the hands of Cardinal Wolsey and engaged in Bible translation. Noticing that Tyndale's New Testament had been published without having been proof-read by a native English speaker, he undertook the work for the second edition, but went further and tampered with the word *resurrection*, which he believed often referred to the intermediate state between death and the resurrection of the dead as we would understand it. Tyndale therefore attacked him in this addition to his original preface, although Joye apologised to him in February 1535.

[43] Original text says 'astonied'.

[44] Jerome (340-420) translated the Bible into Latin.

diligent correction (as he calleth it) which whether it be so or no, I permit it to other men's judgements.

42. But of this I challenged George Joye, that he did not put his own name thereto and call it rather his own translation; and that he played boo peep, and in some of his books putteth in his name and title, and in some keepeth it out. It lawful for who will to translate and show his mind, though a thousand had translated before him. But it is not lawful (thinketh me) nor yet expedient for the edifying of the unity of the faith of Christ, that whosoever will, shall by his own authority, take another man's translation and put out and in and change at pleasure, and call it a correction.

43. Moreover, ye shall understand that George Joye hath had of a long time marvellous imaginations about this word resurrection, that it should be taken for the state of the souls after their departing from their bodies, and hath also (though he hath been reasoned with thereof and desired to cease) yet sown his doctrine by secret letters on that side of the sea, and caused great division among the brethren. Insomuch that John Frith, being in prison in the Tower of London, a little before his death, wrote that we should warn him and desire him to cease, and would have then written against him, had I not withstood him.[45] Thereto I have been since informed that no small number, through his curiosity, utterly deny the resurrection of the flesh and body, affirming that the soul, when she is departed, is the spiritual body of the resurrection, and other resurrection shall there none be. And I have talked with some of them myself, so doted in that folly, that it were as good persuade a post, as to pluck that madness out of their brains. And of this all is George Joye's unquiet curiosity the whole occasion, whether he be of the said faction also or not – to that, let him answer himself.

44. If George Joye will say (as I wot well he will) that his change is the sense and meaning of those Scriptures, I answer that it is sooner said than proved; howbeit let other men judge. But though it were the very meaning of the Scripture, yet if it were lawful after his example to every man to play boo peep with the translations that are before him, and to put out the words of the text at his

---

[45] (1503-33). He was imprisoned in the Tower of London from October 1532 until shortly before he was martyred for his faith on 4 July 1533.

pleasure, and to put in everywhere his meaning or what he thought the meaning were; that were the next way to stablish all heresies and to destroy the ground wherewith we should improve them. As for an example, when Christ saith: *The time shall come in the which all that are in the graves shall hear his voice and shall come forth; they that have done good unto resurrection of life (or with the resurrection of life), and they that have done evil, unto the resurrection (or with the resurrection) of damnation.*[46] George Joye's correction is: *They that have done good shall come forth into the very life, and they that have done evil into the life of damnation*, thrusting clean out this word resurrection. Now by the same authority, and with as good reason, shall another come and say of the rest of the text: They that are in the sepulchres shall hear his voice, and so put in his diligent correction and mock out the text, that it shall not make for the resurrection of the flesh, which thing also George Joye's correction doth manifestly affirm. If the text be left uncorrupt it will purge herself of all manner false glosses, how subtle soever they be feigned, as a seething pot casteth up her scum. But if the false gloss be made the text, diligently overseen and correct, wherewith then shall we correct false doctrine and defend Christ's flock from false opinions and from the wicked heresies of ravening of wolves? In my mind therefore, a little unfeigned love after the rules of Christ, is worth much high learning, and single and slight understanding that edifieth in unity, is much better than subtle curiosity, and meekness better than bold arrogance and standing overmuch in a man's own conceit.

45. Wherefore, concerning the resurrection, I protest before God and our Saviour Jesus Christ, and before the universal congregation that believeth in him, that I believe according to the open and manifest Scriptures and Catholic Faith, that Christ is risen again in the flesh which he received of his mother, the Blessed Virgin Mary, and body wherein he died. And that we shall all, both good and bad, rise both flesh and body, and appear together before the judgement seat of Christ, to receive every man according to his deeds. And that the bodies of all that believe and continue in the true faith of Christ shall be endued with like immortality and glory as is the body of Christ.

---

[46] John 5:28-29.

46. And I protest before God that our Saviour Christ, and all that believe in him, that I hold of the souls that are departed as much as may be proved by manifest and open Scripture, and think the souls departed in the faith of Christ and love of the law of God, to be in no worse case than the soul of Christ was from the time that he delivered his spirit into the hands of his Father, until the resurrection of his body in glory and immortality. Nevertheless, I confess openly, that I am not persuaded that they be already in the full glory that Christ is in, or the elect angels of God are in. Neither is it any article of my faith, for if it so were, I see not but then the preaching of the resurrection of the flesh were a thing in vain. Notwithstanding, yet I am ready to believe it, if it may be proved with open Scripture. And I have desired George Joye to take open texts that seem to make for that purpose, as this is: *Today thou shalt be with me in Paradise*,[47] to make thereof what he could, and to make his dreams about this word resurrection go. For I receive not in the Scripture the private interpretation of any man's brain, without open testimony of any Scriptures agreeing thereto.

47. Moreover, I take God (which alone seeth the heart) to record to my conscience, beseeching him that my part be not in the blood of Christ, if I wrote of all that I have written throughout all my book, aught of an evil purpose, of envy or malice to any man, or to stir up any false doctrine or opinion in the church of Christ, or to be author of any sect, or to draw disciples after me, or that I would be esteemed or had in price above the least child that is born, save only of pity and compassion I had and yet have on the blindness of my brethren, and to bring them unto the knowledge of Christ, and to make every one of them if it were possible, as perfect as an angel of heaven, and to weed out all that is not planted of our Heavenly Father, and to bring down all that lifteth up itself against the knowledge of the salvation that is in the blood of Christ. Also, my part be not in Christ, if my heart be not to follow and live according as I teach, and also if mine heart weep not night and day for mine own sin and other men's indifferently, beseeching God to convert us all and to take his wrath from us, and to be merciful as well to all other men, as to mine own soul, caring for the wealth of the realm I was born in, for the king and

---

[47] Luke 23:43.

all that are thereof, as a tender-hearted mother would do for her only son.

48. As concerning all I have translated or otherwise written, I beseech all men to read it for that purpose I wrote it – even to bring them to the knowledge of the Scripture. And as far as the Scripture approveth it, so far to allow it, and if in any place the Word of God disallow it, there to refuse it, as I do before our Saviour Christ and his congregation. And where they find faults, let them show it me if they be nigh, or write to me if they be far off; or write openly against it and improve it, and I promise them, if I shall perceive that their reasons conclude, I will confess mine ignorance openly.

49. Wherefore I beseech George Joye, yea and all other too, for to translate the Scripture for themselves, whether out of Greek, Latin or Hebrew. Or (if they will needs) as the fox when he hath pissed in the gray's[48] hole challengeth it for his own, so let them take my translations and labours, and change and alter, and correct and corrupt at their pleasures, and call it their own translations, and put to their own names, and not to play boo peep after George Joye's manner. Which whether he have done faithfully and truly, with such reverence and fear as becometh the Word of God, and with such love and meekness and affection to unite, and circumspection that the ungodly have none occasion to rail on the verity, as becometh the servants of Christ, I refer it to the judgements of them that know and love the truth. For this I protest, that I provoke not Joye, nor any other man (but am provoked, and that after the spitefullest manner of provoking), to do sore against my will and with sorrow of heart that I now do. But I neither can nor will suffer of any man that he shall go, take my translation, and correct it without name, and make such changing as I myself durst not do, as I hope to have my part in Christ, though the whole world should be given me for my labour.

50. Finally, that New Testament thus diligently corrected, beside this so oft putting out this word resurrection, and I wot not what other change, for I have not yet read it over, hath in the end, before the Table of the Epistles and Gospels, this title: *Here endeth the New Testament diligently overseen and correct and printed now again at Antwerp, by me widow of Christopher [van Rurmund] of*

---

[48] 'Badger'.

Eindhoven. In the year of our Lord 1534 in August. Which title (reader), I have here put in, because by this thou shalt know the book the better. *Vale.*

2. Tyndale's Preface to the Pentateuch, 1530

01. When I had translated the New Testament I added an epistle unto the latter end, in which I desired them that were learned to amend if aught were found amiss. But our malicious and wily hypocrites, which are so stubborn and hard-hearted in their wicked abominations that it is not possible for them to amend anything at all (as we see by daily experience, when both their livings and doings are rebuked with the truth) say, some of them that it is impossible to translate the Scripture into English, some that it is not lawful for the laypeople to have it in their mother tongue, some, that it would make them all heretics, as it would no doubt from many things which they of long time have falsely taught, and that is the whole cause wherefore they forbid it, though they other cloaks pretend. And some or rather every one, say that it would make them rise against the king, whom they themselves (unto their damnation) never yet obeyed. And lest the temporal rulers should see their falsehood, if the Scripture came to light, causeth them so to lie. And as for my translation, in which they affirm unto the laypeople (as I have heard say) to be I wot not how many thousand heresies, so that it cannot be mended or correct, they have yet taken so great pain to examine it, and to compare it unto that they would fain have it and to their own imaginations and juggling terms, and to have somewhat to rail at, and under that cloak to blaspheme the truth, that they might with as little labour (as I suppose) have translated the most part of the Bible. For they which in times past were wont to look on no more Scripture than they found in their Duns,[1] or such like devilish doctrine, have yet now so narrowly looked on my translation that there is not so much as one i therein, if it lack a tittle over his head, but they have noted it, and number it unto the ignorant people for a heresy. Finally, in this they be all agreed, to drive you from the knowledge of the Scripture, and that ye shall not have the text thereof in the mother tongue, and to keep the world still in darkness, to the intent they might sit in the

---

[1] John Duns Scotus (1265-1308), a famous medieval theologian whose writings were often learned by rote, without understanding. For that reason, those who parroted him came to be called 'dunces.'

consciences of the people, through vain superstition and false doctrine, to satisfy their filthy lusts, their proud ambition, and unsatiable covetousness, and to exalt their own honour above king and emperor, yea and above God himself.

02. A thousand books had they lever² to be put forth against their abominable doings and doctrine, than that the Scripture should come to light. For as long as they may keep that down, they will so darken the right way with the mist of their sophistry, and so tangle them that either rebuke or despise their abominations with arguments of philosophy and with worldly similitudes and apparent reasons of natural wisdom. And with wresting the Scripture unto their own purpose clean contrary unto the process, order and meaning of the text, and so delude them in descanting upon it with allegories, and amaze them expounding it in many senses before the unlearned laypeople (when it hath but one simple literal sense whose light the owls cannot abide) that though thou feel in thine heart and art sure how that all is false that they say, yet couldst thou not solve their subtle riddles.

03. Which thing only moved me to translate the New Testament. Because I had perceived by experience how that it was impossible to establish the laypeople in any truth, except the Scripture were plainly laid before their eyes in their mother tongue, that they might see the process, order and meaning of the text; for else, whatsoever truth is taught them, these enemies of all truth quench it again, partly with the smoke of their bottomless pit whereof thou readest;³ that is, with apparent reasons of sophistry and traditions of their own making, founded without ground of Scripture, and partly in juggling with the text, expounding it in such a sense as is impossible to gather of the text, if thou see the process, order and meaning thereof.

04. And even in the Bishop of London's house I intended to have done it.⁴ For when I was so turmoiled in the country where I was that I could no longer there dwell (the process thereof were too long here to rehearse) I this wise thought in myself – this I suffer

---

² 'Rather'
³ Revelation 9:1.
⁴ Cuthbert Tunstall (1474-1559) was bishop of London from 19 October 1522 to 21 February 1530, when he was translated to Durham. Tyndale must have gone to see him shortly after his consecration.

because the priests of the country be unlearned, as God it knoweth, there are a full ignorant sort which have seen no more Latin than that they read in their portesses and missals, which yet many of them can scarcely read, (except it be Albertus *De secretis mulierum*,⁵ in which yet, though they be never so sorrily learned, they pore day and night, and make notes therein, and all to teach the midwives, as they say, and Lyndwood, *A Book of Constitutions*,⁶ to gather tithes, mortuaries, offerings, customs and other pillage, which they call not theirs, but God's part and the duty of Holy Church, to discharge their consciences withal; for they are bound that they shall not diminish, but increase all things to the uttermost of their powers) and therefore (because they are thus unlearned, thought I) when they come together to the alehouse, which is their preaching place, they affirm that my sayings are heresy. And besides that, they add to of their own heads which I never spake, as the manner is to prolong the tale to short the time withal, and accused me secretly to the Chancellor and other the Bishop's officers. And indeed, when I came before the Chancellor,⁷ he threatened me grievously and reviled me, and rated me as though I had been a dog, and laid to my charge whereof there could be none accuser brought forth, (as their manner is not to bring forth the accuser) and yet all the priests of the country were the same day there. As I this thought, the Bishop of London came to my remembrance, whom Erasmus (whose tongue maketh of little gnats great elephants, and lifteth up above the stars whosoever giveth him a little exhibition), praiseth exceedingly among other in his *Annotations on the New*

---

⁵ Albert the Great of Cologne (1193/1206-1280). He was a prominent medieval scientist and wrote on a number of topics, including 'the secrets of women' which Tyndale quotes here.
⁶ William Lyndwood's compendium of the canon law of the province of Canterbury, usually known today as his *Provinciale*. Lyndwood (1375-1446) was the greatest English canonist of his day. He wrote his compendium in 1430 and published it three years later. It was printed for the first time in 1505.
⁷ John Bell (d. 1556), bishop of Worcester from 17 August 1539 until his resignation on 17 November 1543. The see of Worcester was effectively vacant following the death of Bishop Silvestro de' Gigli on 16 April 1521. Giulio de' Medici was provided on 7 June 1521 and resigned on 26 September 1522, but he never occupied the see.

Testament, for his great learning.[8] Then thought I, if I might come to this man's service, I were happy. And so I gat me to London, and through the acquaintance of my master[9] came to Sir Harry Guildford, the King's Grace's Controller,[10] and brought him an oration of Isocrates[11] which I had translated out of Greek into English, and desired him to speak unto my Lord of London for me, which he also did as he showed me, and willed me to write an epistle to my Lord, and to go to him myself, which I also did, and delivered my epistle to a servant of his own, one William Hebblethwaite, a man of mine old acquaintance.[12] But God, which knoweth what is within hypocrites, saw that I was beguiled, and that that counsel was not the next way unto my purpose. And therefore he gat me no favour in my Lord's sight.

05. Whereupon my Lord answered me, his house was full, he had more than he could well find, and advised me to seek in London, where he said I could not lack a service. And so in London I abode almost a year, and marked the course of the world, and heard our praters, I would say our preachers, how they boasted themselves and their high authority, and beheld the pomp of our prelates, and how busied they were as they yet are, to set peace and unity in the world (though it be not possible for them that walk in darkness to continue long in peace, for they cannot but either stumble or dash themselves at one thing or another that shall clean unquiet altogether) and saw things whereof I defer to speak at this time, and understood at the last, not only that there was no room in my Lord of London's palace to translate the New Testament, but also that there was no place to do it in all England, as experience doth now openly declare.

06. Under what manner therefore should I now submit this book to

---

[8] Desiderius Erasmus (1466-1536) was a friend of Tunstall's and did praise him, but not in this work. Tyndale was probably referring to Erasmus' first *Apology against Lee*, written in March 1520, where he refers to Tunstall as '*unum exemplar sat emendatum.*' (One model of a well-educated man). See D. Daniell, *William Tyndale. A biography* (New Haven, CT: Yale UP, 1994), p. 83 and corresponding endnote.
[9] Sir John Walsh, who was born about 1490 and was then resident at Little Sodbury Manor, Gloucestershire, where Tyndale became tutor to his children. Walsh died in June 1547.
[10] Sir Henry Guildford (1489-1532) was controller of the king's household from 1515 to 1523.
[11] 436-338 BC.
[12] Not otherwise known.

be corrected and amended of them which can suffer nothing to be well? Or what protestation should I make in such a manner unto our prelates, those stubborn Nimrods which so mightily fight against God, and resist his Holy Spirit, enforcing with all craft and subtlety to quench the light of the everlasting testament, promises and appointment made between God and us; and heaping the fierce wrath of God upon all princes and rulers, mocking them with false feigned names of hypocrisy, and serving their lusts at all points, and dispensing with them even of the very laws of God, of which Christ himself testifieth, that not so much as one tittle thereof may perish, or be broken.[13] And of which the prophet saith: *Thou hast commanded thy laws to be kept* "me'od", that is in Hebrew *exceedingly*,[14] with all diligence, might and power, and have made them so mad with their juggling charms and crafty persuasions that they think it a full satisfaction for all their wicked lying, to torment such as tell them truth, and to burn the word of their souls' health, and slay whoever believe thereon.

07. Notwithstanding, yet I submit this book and all other that I have either made or translated, or shall in time to come, (if it be God's will that I shall further labour in his harvest) unto all them that submit themselves unto the Word of God, to be corrected of them, yea and moreover to be disallowed and also burnt, if it seem worthy when they have examined it with the Hebrew, so that they first put forth of their own translating another that is more correct.

A prologue showing the use of the Scripture

08. Though a man had a precious jewel and a rich, yet if he wist not the value thereof nor wherefore it served, he were neither the better nor richer by a straw. Even so, though we read the Scripture and babble of it never so much, yet if we know not the use of it and wherefore it was given, and what is therein to be sought, it profiteth us nothing at all. It is not enough therefore to read and talk of it only, but we must also desire God day and night instantly to open our eyes, and to make us understand and feel wherefore the Scripture was given, that we may apply the medicine of the

---

[13] Matthew 5:18.
[14] Psalm 119:4.

Scripture, every man to his own sores, unless that we pretend to be idle disputers and brawlers about vain words, ever gnawing upon the bitter bark without and never attaining unto the sweet pith within, and persecuting one another for defending of lewd imaginations and fantasies of our own invention.

09. Paul, in the third of the second epistle to Timothy saith, that the Scripture is good to teach (for that ought men to teach, and not dreams of their own making, as the Pope doth) and also to improve, for the Scripture is the touchstone that trieth all doctrines, and by that we know the false from the true.[15] And in the sixth to the Ephesians he calleth it the sword of the Spirit, because it killeth hypocrites and uttereth and improveth their false inventions.[16] And in the fifteenth to the Romans he saith all that are written are written for our learning, that we through patience and comfort of the Scripture might have hope.[17] That is, the examples that are in the Scripture comfort us in all our tribulations, and make us to put our trust in God, and patiently to abide his leisure. And in the tenth of the first to the Corinthians, he bringeth in examples of the Scripture to fear us and to bridle the flesh, that we cast not the yoke of the law of God from off our necks, and fall to lusting and doing of evil.[18]

10. So now the Scripture is a light and showeth us the true way, both what to do and what to hope. And a defence from all error, and a comfort in adversity that we despair not, and feareth us in prosperity that we sin not. Seek therefore in the Scripture as thou readest it

1530 edition:

first the law, what God commandeth us to do. And secondarily the promises, which God promiseth us again, namely in Christ Jesu our Lord. Then seek examples, first of comfort, how God purgeth all them that submit themselves to walk in his ways, in the purgatory of tribulation, delivering them yet at the latter end, and never suffering any of them to perish that cleave fast to his promises. And finally, note the examples which are written to fear

---

[15] 2 Timothy 3:16.
[16] Ephesians 6:17.
[17] Romans 15:4.
[18] 1 Corinthians 10:6-11.

the flesh that we sin not. That is, how God suffereth the ungodly and wicked sinners that resist God and refuse to follow him, to continue in their wickedness, ever waxing worse and worse until their sin be so sore increased and so abominable, that if they should longer endure they would corrupt the very elect. But for the elect's sake God sendeth them preachers. Nevertheless, they harden their hearts against the truth and God destroyeth them utterly, and beginneth the world anew.

1534 edition:

chiefly and above all, the covenants made between God and us. That is to say, the law and commandments which God commandeth us to do. And then the mercy promised unto all them that submit themselves unto the law. For all the promises throughout the whole Scripture do include a covenant. That is, God bindeth himself to fulfil that mercy unto thee only, if thou wilt endeavour thyself to keep his laws, so that no man hath his part in the mercy of God, save he only that loveth his law and consenteth that it is righteous and good, and fain would do it, and ever mourneth because he now and then breaketh it through infirmity, or doth it not so perfectly as his heart would.

(11). And let love interpret the law; that thou understand this to be the final end of the law, and the whole cause why the law was given – even to bring thee to the knowledge of God, how that he hath done all things for thee, that thou mightest love him again with all thine heart and thy neighbour for his sake as thyself, and as Christ loved thee. Because thy neighbour is the son of God also, and created unto his likeness as thou art, and bought with as dear blood as art thou. Whosoever feeleth in his heart that every man ought to love his neighbour as Christ loved him, and consenteth thereto, and enforceth to come thereto; the same only understandeth the law aright and can interpret it. And he that submitteth not himself in the degree he is in, to seek his neighbour's profit as Christ did his, can never understand the law, though it be interpreted to him. For that love is the light of the law, to understand it by.

(12.) And behold how righteous, how honest and how due a thing it is by nature, that every man love his neighbour unfeignedly even as himself, for his Father's sake. For it is the Father's great shame and his high displeasure, if one brother hurt another. If one brother be hurt of another, he may not avenge himself, but must complain to his Father or to them that have authority of his Father to rule in his absence. Even so, if any of God's children be hurt by any of his brethren, he may not avenge himself with hand or heart. God must avenge. And the governors and ministers of the law that God hath ordained to rule us by, concerning our outward conversation of one with another – they must avenge. If they will not avenge, but rather maintain wrong and be oppressors themselves, then we must tarry patiently till God come, which is ever ready to reap tyrants off the face of the earth as soon as their sins are ripe.

(13.) Consider also what wrath, vengeance and plagues God threateneth to them that are rebellious and disobedient.

(14.) Then go to and read the stories of the Bible for thy learning and comfort, and see everything practised before thine eyes, for according to those examples shall it go with thee and all men until the world's end. So that into whatsoever case or state a man may be brought, according to whatsoever example of the Bible it be, his end shall be according as he there seeth and readeth. As God there warneth ere he smite, and suffereth long ere he take extreme vengeance, so shall he do with us. As they that turn are there received to mercy, and they that maliciously resist perish utterly, so shall it be with us. As they that resist the counsel of God perish through their own counsel, so shall it be with us until the world's end. As it went with their kings and rulers, so shall it go with ours. As it was with their common people, so shall it be with ours. As it was with their spiritual officers, so shall it be with ours. As it was with their true prophets, so shall it be with ours until the world's end. As they had ever among them false prophets and true, and as their false persecuted the true and moved the princes to slay them, so shall it be with us until the end of the world. As there was among them but a few true-hearted to God, so shall it be among us; and as their idolatry was, so shall ours be until the end of the world. All mercy that is showed there is a promise unto thee if thou turn to God. And all vengeance and wrath showed there is threatened to thee, if thou be stubborn and resist.

(15). And this learning and...

Both editions:

16. (This) comfort shalt thou evermore find in the plain text and literal sense. Neither is there any story so homely, so rude, yea or

so vile (as it seemeth outward) wherein is not exceeding great comfort. And when some which seem to themselves great clerks say they wot[19] not what more profit is in many gests[20] of the Scripture if they be read without an allegory than in a tale of Robin Hood, say thou: that they be written for our consolation and comfort, that we despair not if suchlike happen to us. We be not holier than Noah, though he were once drunk.[21] Neither better beloved than Jacob, though his own son defiled his bed.[22] We be not holier than Lot, though his daughters through ignorance deceived him, nor peradventure holier than those daughters.[23] Neither are we holier than David, though he brake wedlock, and upon the same committed abominable murder.[24] All those men have witness of the Scripture that they pleased God and were good men, both before that those things chanced them, and also after. Nevertheless, such things happened them for our example – not that we should counterfeit their evil, but if while we fight with ourselves enforcing to walk in the law of God (as they did) we yet fail likewise, that we despair not, but come again to the laws of God and take better hold.

17. We read, since the time of Christ's death, of virgins that have been brought unto the common stews[25] and there defiled, and of martyrs that have been bound and whores have abused their bodies. Why? The judgements of God are bottomless. Such things chanced partly for examples, partly God through sin healeth sin. Pride can neither be healed nor yet appear but through such horrible deeds. Peradventure they were of the Pope's sect and rejoiced fleshly, thinking that heaven came by deeds and not by Christ, and that the outward deed justified them and made them holy and not the inward spirit received by faith and the consent of the heart unto the law of God.

18. As thou readest therefore, think that every syllable pertaineth to thine own self, and suck out the pith of the Scripture, and arm thyself against all assaults. First, note with strong faith the power

---

[19] 'Know'.
[20] 'Tales'.
[21] Genesis 9:21.
[22] Genesis 35:22.
[23] Genesis 19:30-38.
[24] 2 Samuel 11:14-27.
[25] 'Rubbish tips'.

of God in creating all of naught. Then mark the grievous fall of Adam and of us all in him, through the light regarding the commandment of God. In the fourth chapter God turneth him unto Abel and then to his offering, but not to Cain and his offering.[26] Where thou seest that the deeds of the evil appear outwardly as glorious as the deeds of the good, yet in the sight of God, which looketh on the heart, the deed is good because of the man and not the man good because of his deed. In the sixth, God sendeth Noah to preach to the wicked and giveth them space to repent; they wax hard-hearted, God bringeth them to naught, and yet saveth Noah, even by the same water by which he destroyed them.[27] Mark also what followed the pride of the building of the tower of Babel.[28] Consider how God sendeth forth Abraham out of his own country into a strange land full of wicked people, and gave him but a bare promise with him that he would bless him and defend him.[29] Abraham believed and that word saved and delivered him in all perils, so that we see how that man's life is not maintained by bread only (as Christ saith) but much rather by believing the promises of God.[30] Behold how soberly and how circumspectly both Abraham and also Isaac behave themselves among the infidels. Abraham buyeth that which might have been given him for naught[31], to cut off occasions.[32] Isaac, when his wells which he had digged were taken from him, giveth room and resisteth not.[33] Moreover, they earn and sow and feed their cattle, and make confederations, and take perpetual truce, and do all outward things, even as they do which have no faith, for God hath not made us to be idle in this world. Every man must work godly and truly to the uttermost of the power that God hath given him, and yet not trust therein, but in God's word or promise, and God will work with us and bring that we do to good effect. And then when our power will extend no further, God's promises will work all alone.

---

[26] Genesis 4:1-16.
[27] Genesis 6:9-22.
[28] Genesis 11:1-9.
[29] Genesis 12:1-3.
[30] Matthew 4:4, citing Deuteronomy 8:3.
[31] Genesis 14:21-24.
[32] 'Avoid dispute or contention'.
[33] Genesis 26:15-22.

19. How many things also resisted the promises of God to Jacob? And yet Jacob conjureth God with his own promises, saying: O God of my father Abraham, and God of my father Isaac, O Lord, which saidst unto me: return unto thine own country, and unto the place where thou wast born and I will do thee good. I am not worthy of the least of those mercies, nor of that truth which thou hast done to thy servant. I went out but with a staff, and come home with two droves, deliver me out of the hands of my brother Esau, for I fear him greatly, etc.[34] And God delivered him, and will likewise all that call unto his promises with a repenting heart, were they never so great sinners. Mark also the weak infirmities of the man. he loveth one wife more than another, one son more than another. And see how God purgeth him. Esau threatened him; Laban beguileth him. The beloved wife is long barren; his daughter is ravished, his wife is defiled, and that of his own son. Rachel dieth, Joseph is taken away, yea and as he supposed, rent of wild beasts. And yet how glorious was his end? Note the weakness of his children, yea and the sin of them, and how God through their own wickedness saved them. These examples teach us that a man is not at once perfect the first day he beginneth to live well. They that be strong therefore must suffer with the weak, and help to keep them in unity and peace one with another, until they be stronger.

20. Note what the brethren said when they were tached[35] in Egypt: We have verily sinned (said they) against our brother in that we saw the anguish of his soul when he besought us, and would not hear him, and therefore is this tribulation come upon us.[36] By which example thou seest, how that conscience of evil doings findeth men out at the last. But namely in tribulation and adversity; there temptation and also desperation, yea and the very pains of hell find us out. There the soul feeleth the fierce wrath of God, and wisheth mountains to fall on her, and to hide her (if it were possible) from the angry face of God.

21. Mark also, how great evils follow of how little an occasion. Dinah goeth but forth alone to see the daughters of the country, and how

---

[34] Genesis 32:9-11.
[35] 'Accused'
[36] Genesis 42:21.

great mischief and trouble followed?[37] Jacob loved but one son more than another, and how grievous murder followed in their hearts?[38] These are examples for our learning, to teach us to walk warily and circumspectly in the world of weak people, that we give no man occasions of evil.

22. Finally, see what God promised Joseph in his dreams.[39] Those promises accompanied him always, and went down with him even into the deep dungeon, and brought him up again, and never forsook him, till all that was promised was fulfilled. These are examples written for our learning (as Paul saith),[40] to teach us to trust in God in the strong fire of tribulation and purgatory of our flesh. And that they which submit themselves to follow God, should note and mark such things; for their learning and comfort is the fruit of the Scripture and the cause why it was written. And with such a purpose to read it is the way to everlasting life, and to those joyful blessings that are promised unto all nations in the seed of Abraham; which seed is Jesus Christ our Lord, to whom be honour and praise for ever and unto God our Father through him. Amen.

---

[37] Genesis 34:1-31.
[38] Genesis 37:4,8,11.
[39] Genesis 37:5-11.
[40] Romans 15:4.

3. Coverdale's Dedication and Preface to the Bible, 1535

Unto the most victorious Prince and our most gracious sovereign Lord, king Henry the eighth, king of England and of France, lord of Ireland, etc. Defender of the Faith, and under God the chief and supreme head of the Church of England. The right and just administration of the laws that God gave unto Moses and unto Joshua: the testimony of faithfulness that God gave of David: the plenteous abundance of wisdom that God gave unto Solomon: the lucky and prosperous age with the multiplication of seed which God gave unto Abraham and Sarah his wife, be given unto you most gracious Prince, with your dearest just wife, and most virtuous Princess, Queen Anne, Amen.

01. Caiaphas being bishop of that year, like a blind prophet (not understanding what he said) prophesied,[1] that it was better to put Christ unto death, than that all the people should perish: he meaning, that Christ was an heretic, a deceiver of the people, and a destroyer of the law, and that it was better therefore to put Christ unto death, than to suffer him for to live, and to deceive the people. &c. where in very deed Christ was the true prophet, the true Messiah, and the only true Saviour of the world, sent of his heavenly Father to suffer the most cruel, most shameful, and most necessary death for our redemption: according to the meaning of the prophesy truly understood. Even after the same manner the blind bishop of Rome, (that blind Balaam I say) not understanding what he did, gave unto your grace this title: Defender of the Faith, only because your highness suffered your bishops to burn God's word the rule of faith, and to persecute the lovers and ministers of the same. Where in very deed the blind bishop (though he knew not what he did) prophesied, that by the righteous administration and continual diligence of your grace, the faith should so be defended, that God's word, the mother of faith with the fruits thereof, should have his free course throughout all Christendom, but specially in your realm.

---

[1] John 11:49-50.

02. If your highness now of your princely benignity will pardon me to compare these two bishops (I mean bishop Caiaphas and the bishop of Rome) and their prophesies together, I doubt not but we shall find them agree like brethren, though the one be a Jew and the other a counterfeit Christian. First, Caiaphas prophesied that it was better to put Christ unto death, than that the people should perish. The bishop of Rome also, not knowing what he prophesied, gave your grace this title: Defender of the Faith. The truth of both these prophesies is of the Holy Ghost (as was Balaam's prophecy) though they that spake them knew not what they said. The truth of Caiaphas' prophecy is, that it was necessary for man's salvation, that Christ by his death should overcome death, and redeem us.[2] And the truth of our Balaam's prophecy is, that your grace in very deed should defend the faith, yea even the true faith of Christ, no dreams, no fables, no heresy, no papistical inventions, but the uncorrupted faith of God's most holy word, which to set forth (praised be the goodness of God, and increase your gracious purpose) your highness with your most honorable council, applieth all his study and endeavor. These two blind bishops now agree in the understanding of their prophesies: for Caiaphas taketh Christ for an heretic, our Balaam taketh the word of Christ for heresy. Caiaphas judgeth it to be a good deed to put Christ unto death, that he should not deceive the people, our Balaam calleth defending of the faith, the suppressing, keeping secret, and burning of the word of faith: lest the light thereof should utter his darkness: lest his own decretals and decrees, his own laws and constitutions, his own statutes and inventions should come to none effect: lest his intolerable exactions and usurpations should lose their strength: lest it should be known what a thief and murderer he is in the cause of Christ, and how heinous a traitor to God and man in defrauding all Christian kings and princes of their due obedience: lest we your grace's subjects should have eyes in the word of God, at the last to spy out his crafty conveyances and jugglings: and lest men should see, how sore he and his false apostles have deceived all Christendom, specially your noble realm of England.

03. Thus your grace seeth how brotherly the Jewish bishop and our Balaam agree together, not only in mitre and outward appearance:

---

[2] Numbers 24:17.

but as the one persecuted the Lord Jesus in his own person, so doth the other persecute his word and resisteth his holy ordinance in the authority of his anointed kings. For so much now as the word of God is the only truth that driveth away all lies, and discloseth all juggling and deceit, therefore is our Balaam of Rome so loathe that the Scripture should be known in the mother tongue: lest if kings and princes (specially above all other) were exercised therein, they should reclaim and challenge again their due authority, which he falsely hath usurped so many years, and so to tie him shorter: and lest the people being taught by the word of God, should fall from the false feigned obedience of him and his disguised apostles, unto the true obedience commanded by God's own mouth: as namely, to obey their prince, to obey father and mother, etc., and not to step over father and mother's belly to enter into his painted religions, as his hypocrites teach: For he knoweth well enough, that if the clear Son of God's word come once to the heat of the day, it shall drive away all the foul mist of his devilish doctrines. Therefore were it more to the maintenance of Antichrist's kingdom, that the world were still in ignorance and blindness, and that the scripture should never come to light. For the Scripture (both in the Old Testament and in the New) declareth most abundantly that the office, authority and power given of God unto kings is in earth above all other powers: let them call themselves popes, cardinals, or whatsoever they will,[3] the word of God declareth them (yea and commandeth them under pain of damnation) to be obedient unto the temporal sword, as in the Old Testament all the prophets, priests and levites were.[4]

04. And in the New Testament Christ and his apostles both were obedient themselves, and taught obedience of all men unto their princes and temporal rulers: which here unto us in the world present the person of God, and are called gods in the scripture, because of the excellency of their office. And though there were no more authorities but the same, to prove the pre-eminence of the temporal sword, yet by this the scripture declareth plainly, that as there is nothing above God, so is there no man above the king in his realm but that he only under God is the chief head of all the

---

[3] Romans 13:1.
[4] See Matthew 17:25; Titus 3:1; Exodus 22:28; Psalm 81[82]:1.

congregation and church of the same. And in token that this is true, there hath been of old antiquity (and is yet unto this day) a long ceremony used in your realm of England, that when your grace's subjects read your letters, or begin to talk or come of your highness, they [re]move their bonnets for a sign and token of reverence unto your grace, as to their most sovereign lord and head under God, which thing no man useth to do to any bishop, whereby (if our understanding were not blinded) we might evidently perceive, that even very nature teacheth us the same, that Scripture commandeth us: and that like as it is against God's word that a king should not be the chief head of this people, even so (I say) is it against kind that we should know any other head above him under God. And that no priest nor bishop is exempt (nor can be lawfully) from the obedience of his prince, the scripture is full both of straight commandments and practices of the holiest men.[5]

05. Aaron was obedient unto Moses, and called him his lord, though he was his own brother.[6] Eleazar and Phineas were under the obedience of Joshua.[7] Nathan the prophet fell down to the ground before king David, he had his prince in such reverence.[8] (He made not the king for to kiss his foot as the bishop of Rome maketh emperors to do); notwithstanding he spared not to rebuke him, and that right sharply when he fell from the word of God to adultery and manslaughter.[9] For he was not afraid to reprove him of his sins, no more than Elijah the prophet stood in fear to say unto king Ahab: 'It is thou and thy father's house that trouble Israel, because ye have forsaken the commandments of the Lord, and walk after Baal.'[10] And as John the Baptist durst say unto king Herod: 'It is not lawful for thee to take thy brother's wife.'[11] But to my purpose I pass over innumerable more examples both of the Old Testament and of the New, for fear lest I be too tedious unto your grace. In sum, in all godly regiments of old time the king and temporal judge was obeyed of every man, and was always

---

[5] See Numbers 12:11; Joshua 4:16-17; 1 Kings 18:1-16; Leviticus 18:1-5; Matthew 14:1-12.
[6] Numbers 12:11.
[7] Joshua 17:4; 22:13-20. The evidence for Coverdale's claim is ambiguous.
[8] There is no evidence for this.
[9] 2 Samuel 12:1-15.
[10] 1 Kings 18:18.
[11] Matthew 14:4.

under God the chief and supreme head of the whole congregation, and deposed even priests when he saw an urgent cause, as Solomon did unto Abiathar.[12] Who could then stand against the godly obedience of his prince (except he would be at defiance with God and all his holy ordinances) that were well acquainted with the Holy Scripture, which so earnestly commendeth unto every one of us the authority and power given of God unto kings and temporal rulers? Therefore doth Moses so straitly forbid the Israelites to speak so much as an evil word against the prince of the people, much less than to disobey him, or to withstand him.[13] Doth not Jeremy the prophet and Baruch also exhort the people in captivity, to pray for the prosperous welfare of the king of Babylon, and to obey him, though he was an infidel?[14]

06. In the New Testament when our Saviour Christ (being yet free and Lord of all kings and princes) showed his obedience in paying the tribute to our example, did he not a miracle there in putting the piece of money in the fish's mouth (that Peter might pay the customer therewith) and all to stablish the obedience due unto princes?[15] Did not Joseph and Mary the mother of our Saviour Christ depart from Nazareth unto Bethlehem so far from home, to show their obedience in paying the tax to the prince?[16] And would not our Saviour be born in the same obedience? Doth not Paul pronounce him to resist God himself, that resisteth the authority of his prince?[17] And (to be short) the Apostle Peter doth not only stablish the obedience unto princes and temporal rulers but affirmeth plainly the king (and no bishop) to be the chief head.[18] Innumerable places more are there in Scripture, which bind us to the obedience of our prince, and declare unto us, that no man is nor can be lawfully exempt from the same, but that all the ministers of God's word are under the temporal sword, and princes only to owe obedience unto God and his word. And whereas Antichrist unto your grace's time did thrust his head into

---

[12] 1 Kings 2:26.
[13] Exodus 22:28.
[14] Jeremiah 29:7; Baruch 2:21-2.
[15] Matthew 17:24-7.
[16] Luke 2:1-4.
[17] Romans 13:1-10.
[18] 1 Peter 2:13-14.

the imperial crown of your highness (as he doth yet with other noble princes more) that learned he of Satan the author of pride, and therein doth he both against the doctrine and also against the example of Christ, which because his kingdom was not of this world, meddled with no temporal matters, as it is evident both by his words and practice,[19] where he that hath eyes to see, may see, and he that hath ears to hear, may hear, that Christ's administration was nothing temporal, but plain spiritual, as he himself affirmeth and proveth in the fourth chapter of saint Luke out of the prophet Isaiah,[20] where all bishops and priests may see, how far their binding and loosing extendeth, and wherein their office consisteth, namely in preaching the Gospel. etc. wherefore (most gracious prince) there is no tongue I think, that can fully express and declare the intolerable injuries, which have been done unto God, to all princes and to the communities of all Christian realms, since they which should be only the ministers of God's word, became lords of the world, and thrust the true and just princes out of their rooms.

07. Whose heart would not pity it (yea even with lamentation) to remember but only the intolerable wrong done by that Antichrist of Rome unto your grace's most noble predecessor king John?[21] I pass over his pestilent picking of Peter pence out of your realm;[22] his stealing away of your money for pardons, benefices and bishoprics; his deceiving of your subject's souls with his devilish doctrines and sects of his false religions; his bloodshedding of so many of your grace's people, for books of the scripture. Whose heart would not be grieved (yea and that out of measure) to call to remembrance how obstinate and disobedient, how presumptuous and stubborn that Antichrist made the bishops of your realm against your grace's noble predecessors in times past, as it is manifest in the chronicles? I trust verily there be no such now within your realm: if there be, let them remember these words of scripture: *Presumptuousness goeth before destruction, and after a*

---

[19] Luke 1214; Matthew 26:52; Jn 6:27; 18:11.
[20] Luke 4:18-19, citing Isaiah 61:1-2.
[21] This refers to the papal interdict against John (1199-1216) in 1207.
[22] 'Peter's pence' was the name given to the tax imposed on every household for the support of the Roman church. It was so called because it was levied annually on 1 August, the feast of St Peter *ad Vincula*. It was abolished in 1533.

proud stomach there followeth a fall.[23] What is now the cause of all these intolerable and no more to be suffered abominations? Truly even the ignorance of the Scripture of God. For how had it else been possible, that such blindness should have come into the world, had not the light of God's word been extinct? How could men (I say) have been so far from the true service of God, and from the due obedience of their prince, had not the law of God been clean shut up, depressed, cast aside, and put out of remembrance?

08. As it was afore the time of that noble king Josiah, and as it hath been also among us unto your grace's time: by whose most righteous administration (through the merciful goodness of God) it is now found again as it was in the days of that most virtuous king Josiah.[24] And praised be the Father, the Son, and the Holy Ghost world without end, which so excellently hath endued your princely heart with such ferventness to his honour, and to the wealth of your loving subjects, that I may righteously (by just occasions in your person) compare your highness unto that noble and gracious king, that lantern of light among princes, that fervent protector and defender of the laws of God: which commanded straightly (as your grace doth) that the law of God should be read and taught unto all the people, set the priests to their office in the word of God, destroyed idolatry and false idols, put down all evil customs and abuses, set up the true honour of God, applied all his study and endeavor to the righteous administration of the most uncorrupted law of God, etc. O what felicity was among the people of Jerusalem in his days! And what prosperous health both of soul and body followeth the like ministration in your highness, we begin now (praised be God) to have experience. For as false doctrine is the original cause of all evil plagues and destruction, so is the true executing of the law of God and the preaching of the same, the mother of all godly prosperity.[25]

09. The only word of God (I say) is the cause of all felicity, it bringeth all goodness with it, it bringeth learning, it gendereth understanding, it causeth good works, it maketh children of

---

[23] Proverbs 16:18.
[24] 2 Kings 22:11-20; 2 Chronicles 34:8-21.
[25] Jeremiah 44:24-30.

obedience; briefly, it teacheth all estates their office and duty.[26] Seeing then that the Scripture of God teacheth us every thing sufficiently, both what we ought to do, and what we ought to leave undone; whom we are bound to obey, and whom we should not obey; therefore (I say) it causeth all prosperity, and setteth every thing in frame; and where it is taught and known, it lighteneth all darknesses, comforteth all sorry hearts, leaveth no poor man unhelped, suffereth nothing amiss unamended, letteth no prince be disobeyed, permitteth no heresy to be preached; but reformeth all things, amendeth that is amiss, and setteth every thing in order. And why? because it is given by the inspiration of God, therefore is it ever bringing profit and fruit, by teaching, by improving, by amending and reforming all them that will receive it, to make them perfect and meet unto all good works.[27] Considering now (most gracious prince) the inestimable treasure, fruit and prosperity everlasting, that God giveth with his word, and trusting in his infinite goodness that he would bring my simple and rude labour herein to good effect, therefore as the holy ghost moved other men to do the cost hereof, so was I boldened in God, to labour in the same. Again, considering your imperial majesty not only to be my natural sovereign liege lord and chief head of the church of England, but also the true defender and maintainer of God's laws, I thought it my duty and to belong unto my allegiance, when I had translated this Bible, not only to dedicate this translation unto your highness, but wholly to commit it unto the same: to the intent that if anything therein be translated amiss (for in many things we fail, even when we think to be sure) it may stand in your grace's hands, to correct it, to amend it, to improve it, yea and clean to reject it, if your godly wisdom shall think it necessary.

10. And as I do with all humbleness submit mine understanding and my poor translation unto the spirit of truth in your grace, so make I this protestation (having God to record in my conscience) that I have never wrested nor altered so much as one word for the maintenance of any manner of sect: but have with a clear conscience purely and faithfully translated this out of five sundry

---

[26] Wisdom of Solomon 7:8-12.
[27] 2 Timothy 3:16.

interpreters,[28] having only the manifest truth of the scripture before mine eyes, trusting in the goodness of God, that it shall be unto his worship; quietness and tranquility unto your highness; a perfect stablishment of all God's ordinances within your grace's dominion; a general comfort to all Christian hearts, and a continual thankfulness both of old and young unto God, and to your grace, for being our Moses, and for bringing us out of this old Egypt from the cruel hands of our spiritual Pharaoh. For where were the Jews (by ten thousand parts) so much bound unto king David for subduing of great Goliath and all their enemies,[29] as we are to your grace, for delivering us out of our old Babylonian captivity? For that which deliverance and victory I beseech our only mediator Jesus Christ, to make such means for us unto his heavenly Father, that we never be unthankful unto him nor unto your grace, but that we ever increase in the fear of him, in obedience unto your highness, in love unfeigned unto our neighbors, and in all virtue that cometh of God. To whom for the defending of his blessed word (by your grace's most rightful administration) be honour and thanks, glory and dominion, world without end, Amen. Your grace's humble subject and daily orator, Miles Coverdale.

A prologue. Miles Coverdale unto the Christian reader.

11. Considering how excellent knowledge and learning an interpreter of scripture ought to have in the tongues, and pondering also mine own insufficiency therein, and how weak I am to perform the office of a translator, I was the more loath to meddle with this work. Notwithstanding when I considered how great pity it was that we should want it so long, and called to my remembrance the adversity of them, which were not only of ripe knowledge, but would also with all their hearts have performed that they began, if they had not had impediment: considering (I say) that by reason of their adversity it could not so soon have been brought to an end, as our most prosperous nation would fain have had it: these and other reasonable causes considered, I was the more bold to

---

[28] These were the Latin Vulgate, William Tyndale's translations, Martin Luther's German Bible, a Swiss-German translation done by Huldrych Zwingli and Leo Juda (1524-9) and a Latin Old Testament published by Sanctes Pagninus in 1528.
[29] 1 Samuel 17:31-54.

take it in hand. And to help me herein, I have had sundry translations, not only in Latin, but also of the Dutch[30] interpreters: whom (because of their singular gifts and special diligence in the Bible) I have been the more glad to follow for the most part, according as I was required. But to say the truth before God, it was neither my labour nor desire, to have this work put in my hand: nevertheless it grieved me that other nations should be more plenteously provided for with the Scripture in their mother tongue, than we: therefore when I was instantly required, though I could not do so well as I would, I thought it yet my duty to do my best, and that with a good will. Whereas some men think now that many translations make division in the faith and in the people of God, that is not so: for it was never better with the congregation of God, than when every church almost had the Bible of a sundry translation.

12. Among the Greeks had not Origen a special translation?[31] Had not Vulgarius one peculiar,[32] and likewise Chrysostom? Beside the seventy interpreters, is there not the translation of Aquila, of Theodotion, of Symmachus, and of sundry other? Again among the Latin men, thou findest that every one almost used a special and sundry translation: for in so much as every bishop had the knowledge of the tongues, he gave his diligence to have the Bible of his own translation. The doctors, as Irenaeus, Cyprian, Tertullian, St Jerome, St Augustine, Hilary and St Ambrose upon diverse places of the scripture, read not the text all alike. Therefore ought it not to be taken as evil, that such men as have understanding now in our time, exercise themselves in the tongues, and give their diligence to translate out of one language into another. Yea we ought rather to give God high thanks therefore, which through his spirit stirreth up men's minds, so to exercise themselves therein. Would God it had never been left off after the time of St Augustine, then should we never have come

---

[30] 'German.'
[31] This seems to be a reference to the fact that Origen composed a *Hexapla*, containing six different versions of the Old Testament. The first was the Hebrew text, the second was the same text in Greek characters, the third was that of Aquila of Sinope, the fourth that of Symmachus, the fifth his own recension of the Septuagint and the sixth that of Theodotion. Origen felt free to edit the Septuagint using the other Greek translations and the Hebrew original to correct and supplement it.
[32] This seems to mean Jerome, who translated the Latin Vulgate using the Greek version of Symmachus as a guide.

into such blindness and ignorance, into such errors and delusions. For as soon as the Bible was cast aside, and no more put in exercise, then began every one of his own head to write whatsoever came into his brain and that seemed to be good in his own eyes: and so grew the darkness of men's traditions. And this same is the cause that we have had so many writers, which seldom made mention of the scripture of the Bible: and though they sometime alleged it, yet was it done so far out of season and so wide from the purpose, that a man may well perceive, how that they never saw the original. Seeing then that this diligent exercise of translating doth so much good and edifieth in other languages, why should it do evil in ours?

13. Doubtless like as all nations in the diversity of speeches may know one God in the unity of faith, and be one in love: even so may diverse translations understand one another, and that in the head articles and ground of our most blessed faith, though they use sundry words. Wherefore methinks we have great occasion to give thanks unto God, that he hath opened unto his church the gift of interpretation and of printing, and that there are now at this time so many, which with such diligence and faithfulness interpret the scripture to the honour of God and edifying of his people, whereas (like as when many are shooting together) everyone doth his best to be nearest the mark. And though they cannot all attain thereto, yet shooteth one nearer than another, and hitteth it better then another, yea one can do it better than another. Who is now then so unreasonable, so despiteful, or envious, as to abhor him that doth all his diligence to hit the prick,[33] and to shoot nearest it, though he miss and come not nearest the mark? Ought not such one rather to be commended, and to be helped forward, that he may exercise himself the more therein? For the which cause (according as I was desired) I took the more upon me to set forth this special translation, not as a checker, not as a reprover, or despiser of other men's translations (for among many as yet I have found none without occasion of great thanksgiving unto God) but lowly and faithfully have I followed mine interpreters, and that under correction. And though I have failed anywhere (as there is no man but he misseth in some thing) love shall construe all to the best without any

---

[33] 'Target.'

perverse judgment. There is no man living that can see all things, neither hath God given any man to know everything. One seeth more clearly than another, one hath more understanding than another, one can utter a thing better than another, but no man ought to envy, or despise another. He that can do better than another, should not set him at naught that understandeth less: yea he that hath the more understanding, ought to remember that the same gift is not his but God's, and that God hath given it him to teach and inform the ignorant. If thou hast knowledge therefore to judge where any fault is made, I doubt not but thou wilt help to amend it, if love be joined with thy knowledge. Howbeit wherein so ever I can perceive by myself, or by the information of other, that I have failed (as it is no wonder), I shall now by the help of God overlook it better and amend it.

14. Now will I exhort thee (whosoever thou be that readest Scripture) if thou find ought therein that thou understandest not, or that appeareth to be repugnant, give no temeritous nor hasty judgment thereof: but ascribe it to thine own ignorance, not to the Scripture, think that thou understandest it not, or that it hath some other meaning, or that it is haply overseen of the interpreters, or wrongly printed. Again, it shall greatly help thee to understand Scripture, if thou mark not only what is spoken or written, but of whom, and unto whom, with what words, at what time, where, to what intent, with what circumstance, considering what goeth before, and what followeth after. For there be some things which are done and written, to the intent that we should do likewise: as when Abraham believeth God, is obedient unto his word, and defendeth Lot his kinsman from violent wrong.[34] There be some things also which are written, to the intent that we should eschew such like. As when David lieth with Uriah's wife, and causeth him to be slain.[35] Therefore (I say) when thou readest Scripture, be wise and circumspect: and when thou comest to such strange manners of speaking and dark sentences, to such parables and similitudes, to such dreams or visions as are hid from thy understanding, commit them unto God or to the gift of his Holy Spirit in them that are better learned than thou.

15. As for the commendation of God's Holy Scripture, I would fain

---

[34] Genesis 14:1-16.
[35] 2 Samuel 11:1-27.

magnify it as it is worthy, but I am far insufficient thereto, and therefore I thought it better for me to hold my tongue, than with few words to praise or commend it: exhorting that (most dear reader) so to love it, so to cleave unto it, and so to follow it in thy daily conversation, that other men seeing thy good works and the fruits of the Holy Ghost in thee, may praise the Father of heaven, and give his word a good report: for to live after the law of God, and to lead a virtuous conversation, is the greatest praise that thou canst give unto his doctrine. But as touching the evil report and dispraise that the good word of God hath by the corrupt and evil conversation of some, that daily hear it and profess it outwardly with their mouths, I exhort thee (most dear reader) let not that offend thee nor withdraw thy mind from the love of the truth, neither move thee to be partaker in like unthankfulness: but seeing that light is come into the world, love no more the works of darkness, receive not the grace of God in vain. Call to thy remembrance how loving and merciful God is unto thee, how kindly and fatherly he helpeth thee in all trouble, teacheth thine ignorance, healeth thee in all thy sickness, forgiveth thee all thy sins, feedeth thee, giveth thee drink, helpeth thee out of prison, nourisheth thee in strange countries, careth for thee, and seeth that thou want nothing. Call this to mind (I say) and that earnestly, and consider how thou hast received of God all these benefits (yea and many more than thou canst desire) how thou art bound likewise to show thyself unto thy neighbour as far as thou canst, to teach him if he be ignorant, to help him in all his trouble, to heal his sickness, to forgive him his offenses, and that heartily, to feed him, to cherish him, to care for him, and to see that he want nothing.

16. And on this behalf I beseech thee (thou that hast the riches of this world, and lovest God with thy heart) to lift up thine eyes, and see how great a multitude of poor people run through every town: have pity on thine own flesh, help them with a good heart, and do with thy counsel all that ever thou canst, that this unshamefast begging may be put down, that these idle folks may be set to labor, and that such as are not able to get their living, may be provided for. At the least thou that art of counsel with such as are in authority, give them some occasion to cast their heads together, and to make provision for the poor. Put them in remembrance of those noble cities in other countries, that by the authority of their princes have so richly and well provided for their poor people, to

the great shame and dishonesty[36] of us, if we likewise receiving the word of God, show not such like fruits thereof. Would God that those men (whose office is to maintain the commonwealth) were as diligent in this cause as they are in other. Let us beware betimes, for after unthankfulness there followeth ever a plague: the merciful hand of God be with us, and defend us that we be not partakers thereof.

17. Go to now (most dear reader) and sit thee down at the Lord's feet and read his words, and as Moses teacheth the Jews, take them into thine heart, and let thy talking and communication be of them when thou sittest in thine house, or goest by the way, when thou lyest down, and when thou riseth up.[37] And above all things fashion thy life and conversation according to the doctrine of the Holy Ghost therein, that thou mayest be partaker of the good promises of God in the Bible, and be heir of his blessing in Christ. In whom if thou put thy trust, and be an unfeigned reader or hearer of his word with thy heart, thou shalt find sweetness therein, and spy wondrous things, to thy understanding, to the avoiding of all seditious sects, to the abhorring of thy old sinful life, and to the stablishing of thy godly conversation. In the first book of Moses (called Genesis) thou mayest learn to know the almighty power of God in creating all of naught, his infinite wisdom in ordering the same, his righteousness in punishing the ungodly, his love and fatherly mercy in comforting the righteous with his promises. In the second book (called Exodus) we see the mighty arm of God, in delivering his people from so great bondage out of Egypt, and what provision he maketh for them in the wilderness, how he teacheth them with his wholesome word and how the tabernacle was made and set up. In the third book (called Leviticus) is declared what sacrifices the priests and Levites used, and what their office & ministration was. In the fourth book (called Numbers) is declared how the people are numbered and mustered, how the captains are chosen after the tribes and kindreds, how they went forth to the battle, how they pitched their tents, and how they brake up. The fifth book (called Deuteronomy) showeth how that Moses now being old, rehearseth the law of God unto the people, putteth them in

---

[36] 'Dishonour.'
[37] Deuteronomy 6:1-9.

remembrance again of all the wonders and benefices that God had showed for them, and exhorteth them earnestly to love the Lord their God, to cleave unto him, to put their trust in him and to hearken unto his voice.

18. After the death of Moses doth Joshua bring the people into the land of promise where God doth wondrous things for his people by Joshua, which distributeth the land unto them, unto every tribe their possession. But in their wealth they forgot the goodness of God, so that oft times he gave them over into the hand of their enemies. Nevertheless whensoever they called faithfully upon him, and converted, he delivered them again, as the book of Judges declareth. In the books of the kings, is described the regiment of good and evil princes, how the decay of all nations cometh by evil kings. For in Jeroboam thou seest what mischief, what idolatry and such like abomination followeth, when the king is a maintainer of false doctrine, and causeth the people to sin against God, which falling away from God's word, increased so sore among them, that it was the cause of all their sorrow and misery, and the very occasion why Israel first and then Judah, were carried away into captivity. Again, in Jehoshaphat, in Hezekiah and in Josiah thou seest the nature of a virtuous king.[38] He putteth down the houses of idolatry, seeth that his priests teach nothing but the law of God, commandeth his lords to go with them, and to see that they teach the people. In these kings (I say) thou seest the condition of a true defender of the faith, for he spareth neither cost nor labor, to maintain the laws of God, to seek the wealth and prosperity of his people, and to root out the wicked. And where such a prince is, thou seest again, how God defendeth him and his people, though he have never so many enemies. Thus went it with them in the old time, and even after the same manner goeth it now with us: God be praised therefore, and grant us of his fatherly mercy, that we be not unthankful, lest where he now giveth us a Jehoshaphat, an Hezekiah, yea a very Josiah, he send us a Pharaoh, a Jeroboam, or an Ahab.

19. In the two first books of Ezra[39] and in Esther thou seest the deliverance of the people, which though they were but few, yet is it unto us all a special comfort, for so much as God is not

---

[38] 2 Chronicles 17:1-6.
[39] Ezra and Nehemiah in our modern Bibles.

forgetful of his promises, but bringeth them out of captivity, according as he had told them before. In the book of Job we learn comfort and patience, in that God not only punisheth the wicked, but proveth and trieth the just and righteous (howbeit there is no man innocent in his sight) by diverse troubles in this life, declaring thereby, that they are not his bastards, but his dear sons, and that he loveth them. In the Psalms we learn how to resort only unto God in all our troubles, to seek help at him, to call only upon him, to settle our minds by patience, and how we ought in prosperity to be thankful unto him. The Proverbs and the Preacher [Ecclesiates] of Solomon teach us wisdom, to know God, our own selves, and the world, and how vain all things are, save only to cleave unto God. As for the doctrine of the prophets, what is it else, but an earnest exhortation to eschew sin, and to turn unto God? A faithful promise of the mercy and pardon of God, unto all them that turn unto him, and a threatening of his wrath to the ungodly? Saving that here and there they prophesy also manifestly of Christ, of the expulsion of the Jews, and calling of the heathen. Thus much thought I to speak of the Old Testament, wherein almighty God openeth unto us his mighty power, his wisdom, his loving mercy and righteousness: for the which cause it ought of no man to be abhorred, despised, or lightly regarded, as though it were an old Scripture that nothing belonged unto us, or that now were to be refused. For it is God's true Scripture and testimony, which the Lord Jesus commandeth the Jews to search.[40] Whosoever believeth not the scripture, believeth not Christ, and whoso refuseth it, refuseth God also.

20. The New Testament or Gospel, is a manifest and clear testimony of Christ how God performeth his oath and promises made in the Old Testament, how the New is declared and included in the Old, and the Old fulfilled and verified in the New. Now whereas the most famous interpreters of all give sundry judgments of the text (so far as it is done by the spirit of knowledge in the Holy Ghost) methink no man should be offended thereat, for they refer their doings in meekness to the spirit of truth in the congregation of God; and sure I am, that there cometh more knowledge and understanding of the scripture by their sundry translations, than by all the glosses of our sophistical doctors. For that one

---

[40] John 5:39.

interpreteth something obscurely in one place, the same translateth another (or else he himself) more manifestly by a more plain vocable of the same meaning in another place. Be not thou offended therefore (good reader) though one call a scribe, that another calleth a lawyer; or elders, that another calleth father and mother; or repentance, that another calleth penance or amendment. For if thou be not deceived by men's traditions, thou shalt find no more diversity between these terms than between four pence and a groat.[41] And this manner have I used in my translation, calling it in some place penance, that in another place I call repentance, and that not only because the interpreters have done so before me, but that the adversaries of the truth may see, how that we abhor not this word penance (as they untruly report of us) no more than the interpreters of Latin abhor *paenitere*, when they read *resipiscere*. Only our heart's desire unto God, is, that his people be not blinded in their understanding, lest they believe penance to be aught save a very repentance, amendment, or conversion unto God, and to be an unfeigned new creature in Christ, and to live according to his law. For else shall they fall into the old blasphemy of Christ's blood, and believe, that they themselves are able to make satisfaction unto God for their own sins, from the which error God of his mercy and plenteous goodness preserve all his.

21. Now to conclude: for so much as all the Scripture is written for thy doctrine and ensample, it shall be necessary for thee to take hold upon it while it is offered thee, yea and with ten hands thankfully to receive it. And though it be not worthily ministered unto thee in this translation (by reason of my rudeness) yet if thou be fervent in thy prayer, God shall not only send it thee in a better shape, by the ministration of other that began it afore, but shall also move the hearts of them which as yet meddled not withal, to take it in hand, and to bestow the gift of their understanding thereon, as well in our language as other famous interpreters do in other languages. And I pray God, that through my poor ministration herein, I may give them that can do better, some occasion so to do: exhorting thee (most dear reader) in the meanwhile on God's behalf, if thou be a head, a judge, or ruler of the people that thou let not the book of this law depart out of thy

---

[41] A groat was worth four pence.

mouth,[42] but exercise thyself therein both day and night, and be ever reading in it as long as thou livest: that thou mayest learn to fear the Lord thy God, and not to turn aside from the commandment, neither to the right hand nor to the left: lest thou be a knower of persons in judgment, and wrest the right of the stranger, of the fatherless or of the widow, and so the curse to come upon thee.[43] But what office soever thou hast wait upon it, and execute it, to the maintenance of peace, to the wealth of thy people, defending the laws of God, and the lovers thereof, and to the destruction of the wicked. If thou be a preacher, and hast the oversight of the flock of Christ, awake and feed Christ's sheep with a good heart and spare no labour to do them good, seek not thyself, and beware of filthy lucre, but be unto the flock an ensample, in the word, in conversation, in love, in ferventness of the spirit, and be ever reading, exhorting, and teaching in God's word, that the people of God run not unto other doctrines and lest thou thyself (when thou shouldest teach other) be found ignorant therein.[44]

22. And rather than thou wouldest teach the people any other thing than God's word take the book in thine hand, and read the words even as they stand therein (for it is no shame so to do, it is more shame to make a lie). This I say for such as are not yet expert in the Scripture, for I reprove no preaching without the book as long as they say the truth. If thou be a man that hast wife and children first love thy wife, according to the ensample of the love wherewith Christ loved the congregation, and remember that so doing, thou lovest even thyself: if thou hate her, thou hatest thine own flesh: if thou cherish her and make much of her, thou cherishest and makest much of thyself, for she is bone of thy bones, and flesh of thy flesh.[45] And whosoever thou be that hast children, bring them up in the nurture and information of the Lord.[46] And if thou be ignorant, or art otherwise occupied lawfully that thou canst not teach them thyself, then be even as diligent to seek a good master for thy children, as thou wast to seek a mother to bear them: for there lieth as great weight in the one as in the

---

[42] Joshua 1:8; Deuteronomy 17:19-20.
[43] Deuteronomy 24:1-22, Romans 12:20-1, 1 Peter 4:1-6.
[44] Acts 20:28-31; 1 Peter 5:2-5; 1 Timothy 4:1-16, Titus 2:1-15.
[45] Ephesians 5:22-33.
[46] Ephesians 6:4.

other. Yea better it were for them to be unborn, than not to fear God, or to be evil brought up; which thing (I mean bringing up well of children) if it be diligently looked to, it is the upholding of all commonwealths: and the negligence of the same, the very decay of all realms.

23. Finally, whosoever thou be, take these words of Scripture into thy heart, and be not only an outward hearer, but a doer thereafter, and practice thyself therein, that thou mayest feel in thine heart, the sweet promises thereof for thy consolation in all trouble, and for the sure stablishing of thy hope in Christ, and have ever an eye to the words of Scripture, that if thou be a teacher of other thou mayest be within the bounds of the truth, or at the least, though thou be but an hearer or reader of another man's doings, thou mayest yet have knowledge to judge all spirits, and be free from every error, to the utter destruction of all seditious sects and strange doctrines, that the Holy Scripture may have free passage, and be had in reputation, to the worship of the author thereof, which is even God himself: to whom for his most blessed word be glory and dominion now and ever. Amen.

4. Cranmer's Preface to the Great Bible, 1540

01. For two sundry sorts of people, it seemeth much necessary that something be said in the entry of this book, by the way of a preface or prologue; whereby hereafter it may be both the better accepted of them which hitherto could not well bear it, and also the better used of them which heretofore have misused it. For truly some there are that be too slow, and need the spur; some other seem too quick, and need more of the bridle: some lose their game by short shooting, some by overshooting: some walk too much on the left hand, some too much on the right. In the former sort be all they that refuse to read, or to hear read the Scripture in the vulgar tongues; much worse they that also let or discourage the other from the reading thereof. In the latter sort be they, which by their inordinate reading, undiscreet speaking, contentious disputing, or otherwise, by their licentious living, slander and hinder the Word of God most of all other, whereof they would seem to be greatest furtherers. These two sorts, albeit they be most far unlike the one to the other, yet they both deserve in effect like reproach. Neither can I well tell whether of them I may judge the more offender, him that doth obstinately refuse so godly and goodly knowledge, or him that so ungodly and so ungoodly doth abuse the same.

02. And as touching the former, I would marvel much that any man should be so mad as to refuse in darkness light; in hunger, food; in cold, fire: for the Word of God is light: *lucerna pedibus meis Verbum tuum* (Thy Word is a light unto my feet);[1] food, *non in solo pane vivit homo, sed in omni Verbo Dei* (not on bread alone does man live, but in the whole Word of God);[2] fire, *ignem veni mittere in terram, et quid volo, nisi ut ardeat?* (I have come to put fire in the earth, and what do I desire, except that it burn?).[3] I would marvel (I say) at this, save that I consider how much custom and usage may do. So that if there were a people, as some write *de Cimmeriis*,[4] which never saw the sun by reason that they

---

[1] Psalm 19:105.
[2] Matthew 4:4.
[3] Luke 12:49.
[4] Cf. Marcus Tullius Cicero, *Academica* II, 19 (61).

be situated far toward the North Pole, and be enclosed and overshadowed with high mountains; it is credible and like enough that if, by the power and will of God, the mountains should sink down and give place, that the light of the sun might have entrance to them, at the first some of them might be offended therewith. And the old proverb affirmeth, that after tillage of corn was first found, many delighted more to feed of mast[5] and acorns, wherewith they had been accustomed, than to eat bread made of good corn. Such is the nature of custom, that it causeth us to bear all things well and easily, wherewith we have been accustomed, and to be offended with all things thereunto contrary. And therefore I can well think them worthy pardon, which at the coming abroad of Scripture doubted and drew back. But such as will persist still in their wilfulness, I must needs judge, not only foolish, froward and obstinate, but also peevish, perverse and indurate.

03. And yet, if the matter should be tried by custom, we might also allege custom for the reading of the Scripture in the vulgar tongues, and prescribe the more ancient custom. For it is not much above one hundred years ago, since Scripture hath not been accustomed to be read in the vulgar tongues within this realm; and many hundred years before that it was translated and read in the Saxons' tongue, which at that time was our mother's tongue; whereof there remaineth yet divers copies found lately in old abbeys, of such antique manners of writing and speaking, that few men now be able to read and understand them. And when this language waxed old and out of common usage, because folk should not lack the fruit of reading, it was again translated in the newer language. Whereof yet also many copies remain and be daily found.

04. But now to let pass custom, and to weigh, as wise men ever should, the thing in his own nature: let us here discuss, what availeth Scripture to be had and read of the lay and vulgar people. And to this question I intend here to say nothing but that was spoken and written by the noble doctor and most moral divine, St John Chrysostom, in his third sermon, *De Lazaro*: albeit I will be something shorter, and gather the matter into fewer words and less room than he doth there, because I would not be tedious. He

---

[5] 'Nuts'.

exhorteth there his audience, that every man should read by himself at home in the mean days and time, between sermon and sermon, to the intent they might both more profoundly fix in their minds and memories that he had said before upon such texts, whereupon he had already preached; and also that they might have their minds the more ready and better prepared to receive and perceive that which he should say from thenceforth in his sermons, upon such texts as he had not yet declared and preached upon: therefore saith he there: 'My common usage is to give you warning before, what matter I intend after to entreat upon, that you yourselves, in the mean days, may take the book in hand, read, weigh and perceive the sum and effect of the matter, and mark what hath been declared, and what remaineth yet to be declared: so that thereby your mind may be the more furnished, to hear the rest that shall be said. And that I exhort you,' saith he, 'and ever have and will exhort you, that ye (not only here in the church) give ear to that that is said by the preacher, but that also, when ye be at home in your houses, ye apply yourselves from time to time to the reading of Holy Scriptures, which thing also I never linn[6] to beat into the ears of them that be my familiars, and with whom I have private acquaintance and conversation. Let no man make excuse and say,' saith he, ''I am busied about matters of the commonwealth'; 'I bear this office or that'; 'I am a craftsman, I must apply mine occupation'; 'I have a wife, my children must be fed, my household must I provide for'; briefly, 'I am a man of the world, it is not for me to read the Scriptures, that belongeth to them that hath bidden the world farewell, which live in solitariness and contemplation, that hath been brought up and continually nosylled[7] in learning and religion.'[8]

05. To this answering, 'What sayest thou, man?' saith he: 'Is it not for thee to study and to read the Scripture, because thou art encumbered and distract with cures and business? So much the more it is behoveful for thee to have defence of Scriptures, how much thou art the more distressed in worldly dangers. They that be free and far from trouble and intermeddling of worldly things, liveth in safeguard and tranquillity, and in the calm, or within a

---

[6] 'Cease.'
[7] 'Nurtured.'
[8] John Chrysostom, *De Lazaro* III, 1. (PG 48, 991-2).

sure haven. Thou art in the midst of the sea of worldly wickedness, and therefore thou needest the more of ghostly succour and comfort; they sit far from the strokes of battle, and far out of gunshot, and therefore they be but seldom wounded; thou that standest in the forefront of the host and nighest to thine enemies, must needs take now and then many strokes, and be grievously wounded. And therefore thou hast more need to have thy remedies and medicines at hand. Thy wife provoketh thee to anger, thy child giveth thee occasion to take sorrow and pensiveness, thine enemies lieth in wait for thee, thy friend (as thou takest him) sometime envieth thee, thy neighbour misreporteth thee, or pricketh quarrels against thee, thy mate or partner undermineth thee, thy lord judge or justice threateneth thee, poverty is painful unto thee, the loss of thy dear and well-beloved causeth thee to mourn; prosperity exalteth thee, adversity bringeth thee low. Briefly, so divers and so manifold occasions of cares, tribulations and temptations besetteth thee and besiegeth thee round about. Where canst thou have armour or fortress against thine assaults? Where canst thou have salve for thy sores, but of Holy Scripture? Thy flesh must needs be prone and subject to fleshly lusts, which daily walkest and art conversant amongst women, seest their beauties set forth to the eye, hearest their nice and wanton words, smellest their balm, civet and musk, with other like provocations and stirrings, except thou hast in a readiness wherewith to suppress and avoid them, which cannot elsewhere be had, but only out of the Holy Scriptures. Let us read and seek all remedies that we can, and all shall be little enough. How shall we then do, if we suffer and take daily wounds, and when we have done, will sit still and search for no medicines? Dost thou not mark and consider how the smith, mason or carpenter, or any other handy-craftsman, what need soever he be in, what other shift soever he make, he will not sell nor lay to pledge the tools of his occupation; for then how should he work his feat, or get a living thereby? Of like mind and affection ought we to be towards Holy Scripture; for as mallets, hammers, saws, chisels, axes and hatchets be the tools of their occupation, so be the books of the prophets and apostles, and all Holy Writ inspired by the Holy Ghost, the instruments of our salvation. Wherefore, let us not stick[9] to buy and provide us the Bible, that is to say, the

---

[9] 'Hesitate'.

books of Holy Scripture. And let us think that to be a better jewel in our house than either gold or silver. For like as thieves be loth to assault a house where they know to be good armour and artillery; so wheresoever these holy and ghostly books be occupied, there neither the Devil nor none of his angels dare come near. And they that occupy them be in much safeguard, and having great consolation, and be the readier unto all goodness, the slower to all evil; and if they have done anything amiss, anon, even by the sight of the books, their consciences be admonished, and they wax sorry and ashamed of the fact.'

06. 'Peradventure they will say unto me, How and if we understand not that we read that is contained in the books? What then? Suppose thou understand not the deep and profound mysteries of Scripture; yet can it not be but that much fruit and holiness must come and grow unto thee by the reading: for it cannot be that thou shouldest be ignorant in all things alike. For the Holy Ghost hath so ordered and attempered the Scriptures, that in them as well publicans, fishers and shepherds may find their edification, as great doctors their erudition: for those books were not made to vainglory, like as were the writings of the Gentile philosophers and rhetoricians, to the intent the makers should be had in admiration for their high styles and obscure manner of writing, whereof nothing can be understand [*sic*] without a master or an expositor. But the apostles and prophets wrote their books so that their special intent and purpose might be understood and perceived of every reader, which was nothing but the edification or amendment of the life of them that readeth or heareth it. Who is that reading or hearing read in the Gospel 'Blessed are they that be meek, blessed are they that be merciful, blessed are they that be of clean heart,' and such other like places, can perceive nothing, except he have a master to teach him what it meaneth? Likewise the signs and miracles with all other histories of the doings of Christ or his apostles, who is there of so simple wit and capacity, but he may be able to perceive and understand them? These be but excuses and cloaks for the rain, and coverings of their own idle slothfulness. 'I cannot understand it.' What marvel? How shouldest thou understand, if thou wilt not read nor look upon it? Take the books into thine hands, read the whole story, and that thou understandest keep it well in memory; thou that understandest not, read it again and again: if thou can neither so come by it, counsel with some other that is better

learned. Go to thy curate and preacher; show thyself to be desirous to know and learn: and I doubt not but God, seeing thy diligence and readiness (if no man else teach thee), will himself vouchsafe with his Holy Spirit to illuminate thee, and to open unto thee that which was locked from thee.'

07. 'Remember the eunuch of Candace, Queen of Ethiopia, which, albeit he was a man of a wild and barbarous country, and one occupied with worldly cures and businesses, yet riding in his chariot, he was reading the Scripture.[10] Now consider, if this man passing in his journey, was so diligent as to read the Scripture, what thinkest thou of like was he wont to do sitting at home? Again, he that letted not to read[11], albeit he did not understand, what did he then, trowest[12] thou, after that, when he had learned and gotten understanding? For that thou may well know that he understood not what he read, hearken what Philip there saith unto him: 'Understandest thou what thou readest?' And he, nothing ashamed to confess his ignorance, answereth, 'How should I understand, having nobody to show me the way?' Lo, when he lacked one to show him the way and to expound to him the Scriptures, yet did he read; and therefore God the rather provided for him a guide of the way, that taught him to understand it. God perceived his willing and toward mind; and therefore he sent him a teacher by and by. Therefore let no man be negligent about his own health and salvation: though thou have not Philip always when thou wouldest, the Holy Ghost, which then moved and stirred up Philip, will be ready and not to fail thee if thou do thy diligence accordingly. All these things be written to us to our edification and amendment, which be born towards the latter end of the world. The reading of Scriptures is a great and strong bulwark or fortress against sin; the ignorance of the same is the greater ruin and destruction of them that will not know it. That is the thing that bringeth in heresies, that it is that causeth all corrupt and perverse living; that it is that bringeth all things out of good order.'

08. Hitherto, all that I have said, I have taken and gathered out of the foresaid sermon of this holy doctor, St John Chrysostom. Now if I

---

[10] Acts 8:26-38.
[11] 'Letted not to read' means 'did not give up reading'.
[12] 'Believest.'

should in like manner bring forth what the selfsame doctor speaketh in other places, and what other doctors and writers say concerning the same purpose, I might seem to you to write another Bible rather than to make a preface to the Bible. Wherefore, in few words to comprehend the largeness and utility of the Scripture, how it containeth fruitful instruction and erudition for every man; if any things be necessary to be learned, of the Holy Scripture we may learn it. If falsehood shall be reproved, thereof we may gather wherewithal. If anything be to be corrected and amended, if there need any exhortation or consolation, of the Scripture we may well learn. In the Scriptures be the fat pastures of the soul; therein is no venomous meat, no unwholesome thing; they be the very dainty and pure feeding. He that is ignorant shall find there what he should learn. He that is a perverse sinner shall there find his damnation to make him to tremble for fear. He that laboureth to serve God shall find there his glory, and the promissions of eternal life, exhorting him more diligently to labour. Herein may princes learn how to govern their subjects; subjects obedience, love and dread to their princes; husbands, how they should behave them unto their wives; how to educate their children and servants; and contrary the wives, children and servants may know their duty to their husbands, parents and masters. Here may all manner of persons, men, women, young, old, learned, unlearned, rich, poor, priests, laymen, lords, ladies, officers, tenants, and mean men, virgins, wives, widows, lawyers, merchants, artificers, husbandmen, and all manner of persons, of what estate or condition soever they be, may in this book learn all things what they ought to believe, what they ought to do, and what they should not do, as well concerning Almighty God, as also concerning themselves and all other. Briefly, to the reading of the Scripture none can be enemy, but that either be so sick that they love not to hear of any medicine, or else that be so ignorant that they know not Scripture to be the most healthful medicine.

09. Therefore, as touching this former part, I will here conclude and take it as a conclusion sufficiently determined and approved, that it is convenient and good the Scripture to be read of all sorts and kinds of people, and in the vulgar tongue, without further allegations and probations for the same; which shall not need, since that this one place of John Chrysostom is enough and sufficient to persuade all of them that be not frowardly and

perversely set in their own wilful opinion; specially now that the King's Highness, being Supreme Head next under Christ of this Church of England, hath approved with his royal assent the setting forth hereof, which only to all true and obedient subjects ought to be a sufficient reason for the allowance of the same, without farther delay, reclamation or resistance, although there were no preface nor other reason herein expressed.

10. Therefore now to come to the second and latter part of my purpose. There is nothing so good in this world, but it may be abused, and turned from fruitful and wholesome to hurtful and noisome. What is there above better than the sun, the moon, the stars? Yet was there that took occasion by the great beauty and virtue of them to dishonour God, and to defile themselves with idolatry, giving the honour of the living God and Creator of all things to such things as he had created. What is there here beneath better than fire, water, meats, drinks, metals of gold, silver, iron and steel? Yet we see daily great harm and much mischief done by every one of these, as well for lack of wisdom and providence of them that suffer evil, as by the malice of them that worketh the evil. Thus to them that be evil of themselves everything setteth forward and increaseth their evil, be it of his own nature a thing never so good; like as contrarily, to them that studieth and endeavoureth themselves to goodness, everything prevaileth them and profiteth unto good, be it of his own nature a thing never so bad. As St Paul saith: *His qui diligant Deum, omnia cooperantur in bonum* (To them that love God, everything works together for good)[13]; even as out of most venomous worms is made treacle, the most sovereign medicine for the preservation of man's health in time of danger. Wherefore I would advise you all, that cometh to the reading or hearing of this book, which is the Word of God, the most precious jewel, and most holy relic that remaineth upon earth, that ye bring with you the fear of God, and that ye do it with all due reverence, and use your knowledge thereof, not to vainglory of frivolous disputation, but to the honour of God, increase of virtue and edification both of yourselves and other.

11. And to the intent that my words may be the more regarded, I will use in this part the authority of St Gregory Nazianzene, like as in

---

[13] Romans 8:28

the other I did of St John Chrysostom. It appeareth that in his time there were some (as I fear me, there be also now at these days a great number) which were idle babblers and talkers of the Scripture out of season and all good order, and without any increase of virtue or example of good living. To them he writeth all his first book, *De theologia*;[14] whereof I shall briefly gather the whole effect, and recite it here unto you. 'There be some,' saith he, 'whose not only ears and tongues, but also their fists, be whetted and ready bent all to contention and unprofitable disputation; whom I would wish, as they be vehement and earnest to reason the matter with tongue, so they were also ready and practise to do all good deeds. But forasmuch as they, subverting the order of all godliness, have respect only to this thing, how they may bind and loose subtle questions, so that now every market-place, every alehouse and tavern, every feast-house, briefly, every company of men, every assembly of women, is filled with such talk; since the matter is so,' saith he, 'and that our faith and holy religion of Christ beginneth to wax nothing else, but as it were a sophistry or a talking-craft, I can no less do but say something thereunto. It is not fit,' saith he, 'for every man to dispute the high questions of divinity, neither is it to be done at all times, neither in every audience must we discuss every doubt; but we must know when, to whom, and how far we ought to enter into such matters.'

12. 'First, it is not for every man, but it is for such as be of exact and exquisite judgements, and such as have spent their time before in study and contemplation; and such as before have cleansed themselves as well in soul and body, or at the least, endeavoured themselves to be made clean. For it is dangerous,' saith he, 'for the unclean to touch that thing that is most clean; like as the sore eye taketh harm by looking upon the sun. Secondarily, not at all times, but when we be reposed and at rest from all outward dregs and trouble, and when that our heads be not encumbered with other worldly and wandering imaginations: as if a man should mingle balm and dirt together. For he that shall judge and determine such matters and doubts of Scriptures, must take his time when he may apply his wits thereunto, that he may thereby

---

[14] Gregory of Nazianzus, *Oratio* XXVII (PG 36, coll. 12-25), here paraphrased and abridged.

the better see and discern what is truth. Thirdly, where, and in what audience? There and among those that be studious to learn, and not among such as have pleasure to trifle with such matters as with other things of pastime, which repute for their chief delicates the disputation of high questions, to show their wits, learning and eloquence in reasoning of high matters.'

13. 'Fourthly, it is to be considered how far to wade in such matters of difficulty. No further,' saith he, 'but as every man's own capacity will serve him; and again, no further than the weakness or intelligence of the other audience may bear. For like as too great noise hurteth the ear, too much meat hurteth a man's body, too heavy burdens hurteth the bearers of them, too much rain doth more hurt than good to the ground; briefly, in all things too much is noyous;[15] even so weak wits and weak consciences may soon be oppressed with over-hard questions. I say not this to dissuade men from the knowledge of God, and reading or studying of the Scripture. For I say that it is as necessary for the life of man's soul, as for the body to breathe. And if it were possible so to live, I would think it good for a man to spend all his life in that, and to do no other thing. I commend the law which biddeth to meditate and study the Scriptures always, both night and day, and sermons and preachings to be made both morning, noon and eventide; and God to be lauded and blessed in all times, to bedward, from bed, in our journeys and all our other works. I forbid not to read, but I forbid to reason. Neither forbid I to reason so far as is good and godly. But I allow not that this is done out of season, and out of measure and good order. A man may eat too much of honey, be it never so sweet, and there is time for everything; and that thing that is good is not good, if it be ungodly done; even as a flower in winter is out of season and as a woman's apparel becometh not a man, neither contrarily, the man's the woman; neither is weeping convenient at a bridal, neither laughing at burial. Now if we can observe and keep that is comely and timely in all other things, shall not we then the rather do the same in the Holy Scriptures? Let us not run forth as it were wild horse, that can suffer neither bridle in their mouths nor sitter on their backs. Let us keep us in our bounds, and neither let us go too far on the one side, lest we return into Egypt, neither too far over the other, lest we be carried

---

[15] 'Harmful.'

away to Babylon. Let us not sing the song of our Lord in a strange land; that is to say, let us not dispute the Word of God at all adventures, as well where it is not to be reasoned as where it is, and as well in the ears of them that be not fit therefore as of them that be. If we can in no wise forbear but that we must needs dispute, let us forbear thus much at the least, to do it out of time and place convenient. And let us entreat of those things which be holy holily; and upon those things that be mystical, mystically; and not to utter the divine mysteries in the ears unworthy to hear them; but let us know what is comely as well in our silence and talking, as in our garments' wearing, in our feeding, in our gesture, in our goings and in all our other behaving. This contention and debate about Scriptures and doubts thereof (specially when such as pretend to be the favourers and students thereof cannot agree within themselves) dost most hurt to ourselves, and to the furthering of the cause and quarrels that we would have furthered above all things. And we in this,' saith he, 'be not unlike to them that, being mad, set their own houses on fire, and that slay their own children, or beat their own parents. I marvel much,' saith he, 'to recount whereof cometh all this desire of vainglory, whereof cometh all this tongue-itch, that we have so much delight to talk and clatter? And wherein is our communication? Not in the commendations and virtuous and good deeds of hospitality, of love between Christian brother and brother, of love between man and wife, of virginity and chastity, and of alms towards the poor; not in psalms and godly songs, not in lamenting for our sins, not in repressing the affections of the body, not in prayers to God. We talk of Scripture, but in the meantime we subdue not our flesh by fasting, waking and weeping; we make not this life a meditation of death; we do not strive to be lords of our appetites and affections; we go not about to pull down our proud and high minds, to abate our fumish and rancorous stomachs, to restrain our lusts and bodily delectations, our undiscreet sorrows, our lascivious mirth, our inordinate looking, our insatiable hearing of vanities, our speaking without measure, our inconvenient thoughts, and briefly, to reform our life and manners. But all our holiness consisteth in talking. And we pardon each other from all good living, so that we may stick fast together in argumentation; as though there were no more ways to heaven but this alone, the way of speculation and knowledge (as they take it); but in very deed it is rather the way of superfluous contention and sophistication.'

14. Hitherto have I recited the mind of Gregory Nazianzene in that book which I spake of before. The same author saith also in another place, that 'the learning of a Christian man ought to begin of the fear of God, to end in matters of high speculation; and not contrarily, to begin with speculation, and to end in fear. For speculation,' saith he, 'either high cunning or knowledge, if it be not stayed with the bridle of fear to offend God, is dangerous and enough to tumble a mean headlong down the hill. Therefore,' saith he, 'the fear of God must be the first beginning, and as it were an ABC, or an introduction to all them that shall enter to the very true and most fruitful knowledge of Holy Scriptures. Where as is the fear of God, there is,' saith he, 'the keeping of the commandments, there is the cleansing of the flesh, which flesh is a cloud before the soul's eye, and suffereth it not purely to see the beam of the heavenly light. Where as is the cleansing of the flesh, there is the illumination of the Holy Ghost, the end of all our desires, and the very light whereby the verity of Scriptures is seen and perceived.'[16] This is the mind and almost the words of Gregory Nazianzene, doctor of the Greek Church, of whom St Jerome saith, that unto his time the Latin Church had no writer able to be compared and to make an even match with him.

15. Therefore, to conclude this latter part, every man that cometh to the reading of this holy book ought to bring with him first and foremost this fear of Almighty God, and then next a firm and stable purpose to reform his own self according thereunto; and so to continue, proceed, and prosper from time to time, showing himself to be a sober and fruitful hearer and learner. Which if he do, he shall prove at the length well able to teach, though not with his mouth, yet with his living and good example, which is sure the most lively and most effectuous form and manner of teaching. He that otherwise intermeddleth with this Book, let him be assured at once he shall make account therefore, when he shall have said to him, as it is written in the prophet David, *Peccatori dicit Deus* etc.: 'Unto the ungodly saith God, Why dost thou preach my laws, and takest my testament in thy mouth? Whereas thou hatest to be reformed, and hast been partakers with advoutrers.'[17] Thou hast let thy mouth speak wickedness, and with thy tongue thou hast set

---

[16] Gregory of Nazianzus, *Oratio* XXXIX, 8 (PG 36, col. 344).
[17] 'Adulterers.'

forth deceit. Thou sattest and spakest against thy brother; and hast slandered thine own mother's son. These things hast thou done, and I held my tongue, and thou thoughtedst (wickedly) that I am even such a one as thyself. But I will reprove thee, and set before thee the things that thou hast done. O consider this, ye that forget God; lest I pluck you away, and there be none to deliver you. Whoso offereth me thanks and praise, he honoureth me: and to him that ordereth his conversation right will I show the salvation of God."[18]

God save the King.

---

[18] Psalm 50:16-23.

5. A Fruitful Exhortation to the Reading and Knowledge of Holy Scripture, 1547

By Thomas Cranmer

01. Unto a Christian man there can be nothing either more necessary or profitable that the knowledge of Holy Scripture, forasmuch as in it is contained God's true Word, setting forth his glory and also man's duty. And there is no truth nor doctrine necessary for our justification and everlasting salvation but that is, or may be, drawn out of that fountain and well of truth. Therefore, as many as be desirous to enter into the right and perfect way unto God, must apply their minds to know Holy Scripture, without the which they can neither sufficiently know God and his will, neither their office and duty. And as drink is pleasant to them that be dry and meat to them that be hungry, so is the reading, hearing, searching and studying of Holy Scripture to them that be desirous to know God, or themselves, and to do his will. And their stomachs do only loathe and abhor the heavenly knowledge and food of God's Word that be so drowned in worldly vanities that they neither savour God, nor any godliness; for that is the cause why they desire such vanities rather than the true knowledge of God. As they that are sick of an ague, whatsoever they eat and drink, though it be never so pleasant, yet it is as bitter to them as wormwood, not for the bitterness of the meat but for the corrupt and bitter humour that is in their own tongue and mouth; even so is the sweetness of God's Word bitter, not of itself, but only unto them that have their minds corrupted with long custom of sin and love of this world.

02. Therefore, forsaking the corrupt judgment of fleshly men, which care not but for their carcase, let us reverently hear and read Holy Scripture, which is the food of the soul. Let us diligently search for the well of life in the books of the Old and New Testament, and not run to the stinking puddles of men's traditions, devised by men's imagination, for our justification and salvation. For in Holy Scripture is fully contained what we ought to do and what to eschew, what to believe, what to love and what to look for at God's hands at length. In these books we shall find the Father from whom, the Son by whom and the Holy Ghost in whom all things have their being and conservation, and these three persons to be

but one God and one substance. In these books we may learn to know ourselves, how vile and miserable we be, and also to know God, how good he is of himself, and how he communicateth his goodness unto us and to all creatures. We may learn also in these books to know God's will and pleasure, as much as for this present time is convenient for us to know. And as the great clerk and godly preacher Saint John Chrysostom saith: 'Whatsoever is required to the salvation of man is fully contained in the Scripture of God. He that is ignorant may there learn and have knowledge. He that is hard-hearted and an obstinate sinner shall there find everlasting torments, prepared of God's justice, to make him afraid and to mollify or soften him. He that is oppressed with misery in this world shall there find relief in the promises of everlasting life, to his great consolation and comfort. He that is wounded by the devil unto death shall find there medicine whereby he may be restored again unto health.'[1] 'If it shall require to teach any truth or reprove false doctrine, to rebuke any vice, to commend any virtue, to give good counsel, to comfort or to exhort, or to do any other thing requisite for our salvation; all those things,' saith Saint Chrysostom, 'we may learn plentifully of the Scripture.'[2] 'There is,' saith Fulgentius, 'abundantly enough both for men to eat and children to suck. There is whatsoever is convenient for all ages and for all degrees and sorts of men.'[3]

03. These books therefore ought to be much in our hands, in our eyes, in our ears, in our mouths, but most of all in our hearts. For the Scripture of God is the heavenly meat of our souls.[4] The hearing and keeping of it maketh us blessed, sanctifieth us, and maketh us holy.[5] It converteth our souls, it is a light lantern to our feet,[6] it is a sure, a constant and a perpetual instrument of salvation, it giveth wisdom to the humble and lowly hearts, it comforteth, maketh glad, cheereth and cherisheth our conscience, it is a more excellent jewel or treasure than any gold or precious

---

[1] *Homiliae in Matthaeum* XLI, (PG 56, col. 859). This is from the *Opus imperfectum*, whose true author is unknown.
[2] John Chrysostom, *Homiliae in 2 Timotheum* IX, (PG 62, coll. 649-50).
[3] Fulgentius of Ruspe, *Sermones* I, 1. (PL, 65, coll. 719-21).
[4] Matthew 4:4; Luke 11:28.
[5] John 17:17.
[6] Psalm 119:105.

stone, it is more sweet than honey or honeycomb,[7] it is called the best part which Mary did choose, for it hath in it everlasting comfort.[8] The words of Holy Scripture be called words of everlasting life for they be God's instrument, ordained for the same purpose.[9] They have power to convert, through God's promise and they be effectual through God's assistance, and being received in a faithful heart they have ever an heavenly spiritual working in them.[10] They are lively, quick and mighty in operation, and sharper than any two-edged sword, and enter through, even unto the dividing asunder of the soul and the spirit, of the joints and the marrow.[11] Christ calleth him a wise builder that buildeth upon his Word, upon his sure and substantial foundation.[12] By this Word of God we shall be judged, for 'the word that I speak,' saith Christ, 'is it that shall judge in the last day.'[13] He that keepeth the Word of Christ is promised the love and favour of God, and that he shall be the dwelling-place or temple of the blessed Trinity.[14]

04. This Word, whosoever is diligent to read and in his heart to print that he readeth, the great affection to the transitory things of this world shall be minished in him, and the great desire of heavenly things that be therein promised of God, shall increase in him. And there is nothing that so much establisheth our faith and trust in God, that so much conserveth innocency and pureness of the heart, and also of outward godly life and conversation, as continual reading and meditation of God's Word. For that thing which by perpetual use of reading of Holy Scripture, and diligent searching of the same, is deeply printed and graven in the heart, at length turneth almost into nature. And moreover, the effect and virtue of God's Word is to illuminate the ignorant and to give more light unto them that faithfully and diligently read it, to comfort their hearts and to encourage them to perform that which of God is commanded. It teacheth patience in all adversity, in

---

[7] Psalm 19:7-10, 119:105, 130.
[8] Luke 10:39, 42.
[9] John 6:68.
[10] Colossians 1:5-6, 25-8.
[11] Hebrews 4:12.
[12] Matthew 7:24.
[13] John 12:48.
[14] John 14:23.

prosperity humbleness, what honour is due unto God, what mercy and charity to our neighbour.[15]

05. It giveth good counsel in all doubtful things. It showeth of whom we shall look for aid and help in all perils, and that God is the only giver of victory in all battles and temptations of our enemies, bodily and ghostly. And in reading of God's Word he not always most profiteth that is most ready in turning of the book, or in saying of it without the book, but he that is most turned into it, that is most inspired with the Holy Ghost, most in his heart and life altered and transformed into that thing which he readeth, he that is daily less and less proud, less ireful, less covetous and less desirous of worldly and vain pleasures; he that daily forsaking his old vicious life, increaseth in virtue more and more. And to be short, there is nothing that more maintaineth godliness of the mind and expelleth ungodliness than doth the continual reading or hearing of God's Word, if it be joined with a godly mind and a good affection to know and follow God's will. For without a single eye, pure intent and good mind, nothing is allowed for good before God. And on the other side, nothing more obscureth Christ and the glory of God, nor induceth more blindness and all kinds of vices, than doth the ignorance of God's Word.[16]

06. In the first part of this sermon, which exhorteth to the knowledge of Holy Scripture, was declared: 'Wherefore the knowledge of the same is necessary and profitable to all men, and that by the true knowledge and understanding of Scripture, the most necessary points of our duty towards God and our neighbours are also known.' Now as concerning the same matter you shall hear what followeth.[17] If we profess Christ, why be we not ashamed to be ignorant in his doctrine, seeing that every man is ashamed to be ignorant in that learning which he professeth? That man is ashamed to be called a philosopher which readeth not the books of philosophy, and to be called a lawyer, an astronomer or a physician that is ignorant in the books of law, astronomy and physic. How can any man then say that he professeth Christ and his religion if he will not apply himself as far forth as he can or may conveniently, to read and hear, and so to know the books of

---

[15] 1 Samuel 14:6-23; 2 Chronicles 20:1-30; 1 Corinthians 15:57; 1 John 5:4.
[16] Isaiah 5:13, 24; Matthew 22: 29; 1 Corinthians 14.
[17] Added in 1549.

Christ's gospel and doctrine? Although other sciences be good and to be learned, yet no man can deny but this is the chief and passeth all other incomparably. What excuse shall we therefore make at the last day, before Christ, that delight to hear men's fantasies and inventions more than his most holy gospel? And will find no time to do that which chiefly, above all things, we should do, and will rather read other things than that for the which we ought rather to leave reading of all other things? Let us therefore apply ourselves as far forth as we can have time and leisure, to know God's Word by diligent hearing and reading thereof, as many as profess God and have faith in him.

07. But they that have no good affection to God's Word, to colour this their fault, allege commonly two vain and feigned excuses. Some go about to excuse them by their own frailness and fearfulness, saying that they dare not read Holy Scripture, lest through their ignorance they should fall into any error. Others pretend that the difficulty to understand it and the hardness thereof is so great that it is meet to be read only of clerks and learned men.

08. As touching the first, ignorance of God's Word is the cause of all error, as Christ himself affirmed to the Sadducees, saying that they erred because they knew not the Scripture.[18] How should they then eschew error, that will be still ignorant? And how should they come out of ignorance that will not read nor hear that thing which should give them knowledge? He that now hath most knowledge was at the first ignorant, yet he forbare not to read, for fear he should fall into error; but he diligently read lest he should remain in ignorance, and through ignorance in error. And if you will not know the truth of God – a thing most necessary for you – lest you fall into error, by the same reason you may then lie still and never go, lest, if you go, you fall into the mire; nor eat any good meat, lest you take a surfeit; nor sow your corn, nor labour in your occupation, nor use your merchandise for fear you lose your seed, your labour, your stock; and so by that reason it should be best for you to live idly and never to take in hand to do any manner of good thing, lest peradventure some evil thing may chance thereof. And if you be afraid to fall into error by reading of Holy Scripture I shall show you how you may read it without danger of error. Read it humbly, with a meek and a lowly heart, to

---

[18] Matthew 22:29.

the intent you may glorify God and not yourself, with the knowledge of it; and read it not without daily praying to God that he would direct your reading to good effect, and take upon you to expound it no further than you can plainly understand it. For as Saint Augustine saith, the knowledge of Holy Scripture is a great, large and a high palace, but the door is very low so that the high and arrogant man cannot run in, but he must stoop low and humble himself, that shall enter into it.[19] Presumption and arrogancy is the mother of all error and humility needeth to fear no error. For humility will only search to know the truth; it will search and will confer one place with another, and where it cannot find the sense it will pray; it will inquire of others that know and will not presumptuously and rashly define anything which it knoweth not. Therefore the humble man may search any truth boldly in the Scripture, without any danger of error. And if he be ignorant, he ought the more to read and to search Holy Scripture, to bring him out of ignorance. I say not nay, but a man may profit with only hearing, but he may much more profit with both hearing and reading.

09. This have I said as touching the fear to read, through ignorance of the person. And concerning the difficulty of Scripture, he that is so weak that he is not able to brook strong meat, yet he may suck the sweet and tender milk and defer the rest until he wax stronger and come to more knowledge.[20] For God receiveth the learned and unlearned and casteth away none, but is indifferent[21] to all. And the Scripture is full, as well of low valleys, plain ways and easy for every man to use and to walk in, as also of high hills and mountains, which few men can ascend unto. And 'whosoever giveth his mind to Holy Scriptures with diligent study and fervent desire, it cannot be,' saith Saint John Chrysostom, 'that he should be destitute of help. For either God Almighty will send him some godly doctor to instruct him – as he did to instruct the eunuch, a nobleman of Ethiopia and treasurer unto Queen Candace, who having a great affection to read the Scripture, although he understood it not, yet for the desire that he had unto God's Word, God sent his apostle Philip to declare unto him the true sense of

---

[19] Augustine, *Confessiones*, III, 5 (PL 32, col. 686); *Sermones* LI, 6 (PL 38, col. 358).
[20] 1 Corinthians 3:2; Hebrews 5:12-14.
[21] 'Impartial'

the Scripture that he read"[22] – or else, if we lack a learned man to instruct and teach us, yet God himself from above will give light unto our minds and teach us those things which are necessary for us, and wherein we be ignorant.'[23] And in another place Chrysostom saith that man's human and worldly wisdom or science is not needful to the understanding of Scripture, but the revelation of the Holy Ghost who inspireth the true sense unto them that with humility and diligence do search therefore. He that asketh shall have and he that seeketh shall find and he that knocketh shall have the door opened.[24] If we read once, twice or thrice and understand not, let us not cease so, but still continue reading, praying, asking of others, and so, by still knocking, at the last the door shall be opened, as Saint Augustine saith.[25] Although many things in the Scripture be spoken in obscure mysteries, yet there is nothing spoken under dark mysteries in one place, but the selfsame thing in other places is spoken more[26] familiarly and plainly, to the capacity both of learned and unlearned.[27] And those things in the Scripture that be plain to understand and necessary for salvation, every man's duty is to learn them, to print them in memory and effectually to exercise them, and as for the obscure mysteries, to be contented to be ignorant in them until such time as it shall please God to open those things unto him. In the mean season, if he lack either aptness or opportunity, God will not impute it to his folly, but yet it behoveth not that such as be apt should set aside reading, because some others be unapt to read; nevertheless, for the difficulty of such places the reading of the whole ought not to be set apart. And briefly to conclude, as Saint Augustine saith: 'By the Scripture all men be amended; weak men be strengthened and strong men be comforted.'[28] So that surely none be enemies to the reading of God's Word but such as either be so ignorant that they know not how wholesome a thing it is, or else be so sick that they hate the most comfortable medicine that

---

[22] Acts 8:30-5.
[23] John Chrysostom, *Homiliae in Genesim* XXXV, 1-2 (PG 53, coll. 321-3).
[24] Matthew 7:8.
[25] Augustine, *Sermones* CCLXX *In die Pent.* 5 (PL 38, coll. 1237-45). Cf. *idem*, *Enarrationes in Psalmos* 33, 1 (PL 36, col. 300); 93, 1 (PL 37, coll. 1189-91); 146, 12 (PL 37, col. 1907).
[26] This word was added in the second edition of 1547.
[27] Augustine, *De doctrina Christiana*, II, 8 (PL 34, coll. 40-1).
[28] Augustine, *Epistulae* CXXXVII, 18 (PL 33, col. 524).

should heal them, or so ungodly that they would wish the people still to continue in blindness and ignorance of God.

10. Thus we have briefly touched some part of the commodities of God's holy Word, which is one of God's chief and principal benefits given and declared to mankind here on earth. Let us thank God heartily for this his great and special gift, beneficial favour and fatherly providence. Let us be glad to revive this precious gift of our heavenly Father.[29] Let us hear, read and know these holy rules, injunctions and statutes of our Christian religion, and upon that we have made profession to God at our baptism. Let us with fear and reverence lay up in the chest of our hearts these necessary and fruitful lessons. Let us night and day muse and have meditation and contemplation in them;[30] let us ruminate and, as it were, chew the cud, that we may have the sweet juice, spiritual effect, marrow, honey, kernel, taste, comfort and consolation of them. Let us stay, quiet and certify our consciences with the most infallible certainty, truth and perpetual assurance of them. Let us pray to God, the only author of these heavenly meditations, that we may speak, think, believe, live and depart hence, according to the wholesome doctrine and verities of them. And by that means, in this world we shall have God's protection, favour and grace, with the unspeakable solace of peace and quietness of conscience, and after this miserable life, we shall enjoy the endless bliss and glory of heaven, which he grant us all that died for us all, Jesus Christ, to whom with the Father and Holy Ghost be all honour and glory, both now and everlastingly. Amen.

---

[29] 2 Timothy 1:6.
[30] Psalm 1:2.

6. Preface to the Geneva New Testament, 1557

By William Whittingham

To the reader, mercy and peace through Christ our Saviour.

01. As the life of a true Christian is most subject to the reprehension of the world, so all his actions and enterprises, be they never so commendable, move the wicked rather to grudge and murmur, than to glorify God who is [the] author of the same. Which evil God hath left to his church as a necessary exercise, as well that man should not be puffed up with opinion of the gifts that he receiveth of his heavenly Father, as also that seeing how he ever maintaineth the same in despite of all outrageous tyranny, he might be more assured of God's divine providence and lovingkindness towards his elect.

02. For this cause we see that in the church of Christ there are three kinds of men. Some are malicious despisers of the word and graces of God, who turn all things into poison and a farther hardening of their hearts. Others do not openly resist and contemn the Gospel because they are stroken, as it were, in a trance with the majesty thereof, yet either they quarrel and cavil, or else deride and mock at whatsoever thing is done for the advancement of the same. The third sort are the simple lambs which partly are already in the fold of Christ and so hear willingly their shepherd's voice, and partly wandering astray by ignorance, tarry the time till the shepherd find them and bring them unto his flock. To this kind of people in this translation I chiefly had respect, as moved with zeal, counselled by the godly and drawn by occasion, both of the place where God hath appointed us to dwell and also of the store of heavenly learning and judgement which so aboundeth in this city of Geneva, that justly it may be called the patron and mirror of true religion and godliness. To these therefore which are of the flock of Christ, which know their Father's will and are affectioned to the truth, I render a reason of my doing in few lines.

03. First, as touching the perusing of the text, it was diligently revised by the most approved Greek examples and conference of translations in other tongues, as the learned may easily judge both by the faithful rendering of the sentence and also by the propriety

of the words and perspicuity of the phrase. Furthermore, that the reader might be by all means profited, I have divided the text into verses and sections, according to the best editions in other languages, and also, as to this day the ancient Greek copies mention, it was wont to be used. And because the Hebrew and Greek phrases which are strange to render in other tongues, and also short, should not be too hard, I have sometime interpreted them without any whit diminishing the grace of the sense, as our language doth use them, and sometime have put to that word, which lacking made the sentence obscure, but have set it in such letters as may easily be discerned from the common text.

04. As concerning the annotations whereunto these letters a, b, c etc. lead us, I have endeavoured do to profit all thereby that both the learned and others might be holpen, for to my knowledge I have omitted nothing unexpounded whereby he that is in anything exercised in the Scriptures of God might justly complain of hardness, and also in respect of them that have more profited in the same, I have explicat[ed] all such places by the best learned interpreters, as either were falsely expounded by some or else absurdly applied by others, so that by this means both they which have not ability to buy the commentary upon the New Testament, and they also which have not opportunity and leisure to read them because of their prolixity¹, may use this book instead thereof, and sometime where the place is not greatly hard, I have noted with this mark ", that which may serve to the edification of the reader, adding also such commonplaces as may cause him better to take heed of the doctrine.

05. Moreover, the diverse readings according to diverse Greek copies which stand but in one word may be known by this note ', and if the books do alter in the sentence then it is noted with this star *, as the quotations are. Last of all remain the arguments, as well they which contain the sum of every chapter as the other which are placed before the books and epistles, whereof the commodity is so great that they may serve instead of a commentary to the reader. For many read the Scriptures with minds to profit, but because they do not consider the scope and purpose wherefore the Holy Ghost so writeth and to what end (which thing the arguments do faithfully express) they either bestow their time

---

¹ 'Great length and number'.

without fruit or else defraud themselves of a great deal which they might attain unto otherwise.

06. To the intent therefore that not only they which are already advanced in the knowledge of the Scriptures, but also the simple and unlearned might be furthered hereby, I have so moderat[ed] them with plainness and brevity that the very ignorant may easily understand them and bear them in memory. And for this cause I have applied but one argument to the four evangelists, chiefly for because that all writing one matter, though by every one diversely handled, they required no diversity of arguments. Thus in few words I have declared as touching the chief points, beseeching God so to inflame our hearts with the desire to know his genuine will that we may meditate in his holy word both day and night,[2] wherein he hath revealed it, and having attained thereunto so practise it in all our actions that, as we grow in the ripeness of our Christian age, so we may glorify him more and more, rendering to him eternal thanks and praises for his heavenly and inestimable gifts, bestowed upon his church, that although Satan, Antichrist and all his enemies rage and burst, yet are they not able to suppress them, neither will he diminish them, for seeing he doth not only bridle his enemies' fury, but causeth them to defend and preserve his gifts for the use of his church (as we see the Jews, Christ's professed enemies, preserve the Old Testament in most integrity), what should we doubt of his bountiful liberality towards us? Or why do we not rather with all humility and submission of mind obey him, love and fear him which is God blessed for ever? To whom with the Son and Holy Ghost be praise, honour and glory. Amen.

---

[2] Cf. Psalm 1:2.

7. Preface to the Geneva Bible, 1560

To the most virtuous and noble Queen Elizabeth, Queen of England, France and Ireland, etc., Your humble subjects of the English Church at Geneva, with grace and peace from God the Father through Christ Jesus our Lord.

01. How hard a thing it is, and what great impediments let, to enterprise any worthy act, not only daily experience sufficiently showeth (most noble and virtuous Queen), but also that notable proverb doth confirm the same, which admonisheth us that all things are hard which are fair and excellent. And what enterprise can there be of greater importance, and more acceptable unto God, or more worthy of singular commendation, than the building of the Lord's temple, the house of God, the Church of Christ, whereof the Son of God is the head and perfection?

02. When Zerubbabel went about to build the material temple, according to the commandment of the Lord, what difficulties and stays daily arose to hinder his worthy endeavours, the books of Ezra and Esdras[1] plainly witness; how that not only he and the people of God were sorely molested with foreign adversaries (whereof some maliciously warred against them and corrupted the King's officers, and others craftily practised under pretence of religion) but also at home with domestical enemies, as false prophets, crafty worldlings, faint-hearted soldiers and oppressors of their brethren, who as well by false doctrine and lies as by subtle counsel, cowardice and extortion, discouraged the hearts almost of all, so that the Lord's work was not only interrupted and left off for a long time, but scarcely at the length with great labour and danger after a sort brought to pass.

03. Which thing when we weigh aright, and consider earnestly how much greater charge God hath laid upon you in making you a builder of his spiritual temple, we cannot but partly fear, knowing the craft and force of Satan our spiritual enemy and the weakness and inability of this our nature; and partly be fervent in our prayers toward God that he would bring to perfection this noble

---

[1] Nehemiah. In the Greek Old Testament, Ezra is 1 Esdras and Nehemiah is 2 Esdras.

work which he hath begun by you, and therefore we endeavour ourselves by all means to aid, and to bestow our whole force under your grace's standard, whom God hath made as our Zerubbabel for the erecting of this most excellent temple, and to plant and maintain his holy Word to the advancement of his glory, for your own honour and salvation of your soul, and for the singular comfort of that great flock which Christ Jesus the great shepherd hath bought with his precious blood, and committed unto your charge to be fed both in body and soul.

04. Considering therefore how many enemies there are, which by one means or other, as the adversaries of Judah and Benjamin went about to stay the building of that temple, so labour to hinder the course of this building (whereof some are Papists, who under pretence of favouring God's Word, traitorously seek to erect idolatry and to destroy your Majesty; some are worldlings, who as Demas have forsaken Christ for the lord of this world;[2] others are ambitious prelates, who as Amaziah and Diotrephes can abide none but themselves, and as Demetrius may practise sedition to maintain their errors),[3] we persuaded ourselves that there was no way so expedient and necessary for the preservation of the one, and destruction of the other, as to present unto your Majesty the Holy Scriptures faithfully and plainly translated according to the languages wherein they were first written by the Holy Ghost. For the Word of God is an evident token of God's love and our assurance of his defence, wheresoever it is obediently received; it is the trial of the spirits, and as the prophet saith, it is a fire and hammer to break the stony hearts of them that resist God's mercies offered by the preaching of the same.[4] Yea it is sharper than any two-edged sword to examine the very thoughts and to judge the affections of the heart, and to discover whatsoever lieth hid under hypocrisy and would be secret from the face of God and his Church. So that this must be the first foundation and groundwork, according whereunto the good stones of this building must be framed, and the evil tried out and rejected.

05. Now as he that goeth about to lay a foundation surely, first taketh

---

[2] 2 Timothy 4:10.
[3] For Amaziah, see 2 Kings 14:11. Diotrephes is in 3 John 9 and Demetrius in Acts 19:24-38.
[4] Jeremiah 23:29.

away such impediments as might justly either hurt, let or deform the work; so it is necessary that your grace's zeal appear herein, that neither the crafty persuasion of man, neither worldly policy, or natural fear dissuade you to root it out, cut down and destroy these weeds and impediments which do not only deface your building, but utterly endeavour, yea and threaten the ruin thereof. For when the noble Josiah enterprised the like kind of work, among other notable and many things, he destroyed not only, with utter confusion, the idols with their appurtenances, but also burnt (in sign of detestation) the idolatrous priests' bones upon their altars, and put to death the false prophets and sorcerers, to perform the words of the law of God; and therefore the Lord gave him good success and blessed him wonderfully, so long as he made God's Word his line and rule to follow, and enterprised nothing before he had enquired at the mouth of the Lord.[5]

06. And if these zealous beginnings seem dangerous and to breed disquietness in your dominions, yet by the story of King Asa it is manifest that the quietness and peace of the kingdoms standeth in the utter abolishing of idolatry, and in advancing of true religion; for in his days Judah lived in rest and quietness for the space of five and thirty years, till at length he began to be cold in the zeal of the Lord, feared the power of man, imprisoned the prophet of God and oppressed the people; then the Lord sent him wars and at length took him away by death.[6]

07. Wherefore great wisdom, not worldly, but heavenly, here is required, which your grace must earnestly crave of the Lord, as did Solomon, to whom God gave an understanding heart to judge his people aright, and to discern between good and bad. For if God for the furnishing of the old temple gave the Spirit of wisdom and understanding to them that should be the workmen thereof, as to Bezaleel, Aholiab and Hiram;[7] how much more will he indue your grace and other godly princes and chief governors with a principal spirit, that you may procure and command things necessary for this most holy temple, foresee and take heed of things that might hinder it, and abolish and destroy whatsoever might impair and overthrow the same?

---

[5] 2 Chronicles 34:3-5.
[6] 2 Chronicles 15-16.
[7] Exodus 31:1-11. For Hiram, see 1 Kings 7:40.

08. Moreover the marvellous diligence and zeal of Jehoshaphat, Josiah and Hezekiah are by the singular providence of God left as an example to all godly rulers to reform their countries and to establish the Word of God with all speed, lest the wrath of the Lord fall upon them for the neglecting thereof. For these excellent kings did not only embrace the Word promptly and joyfully, but also procured earnestly and commanded the same to be taught, preached and maintained through all their countries and dominions, binding them and all their subjects both great and small with solemn protestations and covenants before God to obey the word, and to walk after the ways of the Lord. Yea and in the days of King Asa it was enacted that whosoever would not seek the Lord God of Israel, should be slain, whether he were small or great, man or woman.[8] And for the establishing hereof and performance of this solemn oath, as well priests and judges were appointed and placed through all the cities of Judah to instruct the people in the true knowledge and fear of God, and to minister justice according to the Word, knowing that, except God by his Word did reign in the hearts and souls, all man's diligence and endeavours were of none effect, for without this Word we cannot discern between justice and injury, protection and oppression, wisdom and foolishness, knowledge and ignorance, good and evil. Therefore the Lord, who is the chief governor of his Church, willeth that nothing be attempted before we have inquired thereof at his mouth. For seeing he is our God, of duty we must give him this pre-eminence, that of ourselves we enterprise nothing but that which he hath appointed, who only knoweth all things and governeth them as may best serve to his glory and our salvation. We ought not therefore to prevent him, or do anything without his Word, but as soon as he hath revealed his will, immediately to put it in execution.

09. Now as concerning the manner of this building, it is not according to man, nor after the wisdom of the flesh, but of the Spirit, and according to the Word of God, whose ways are divers from man's ways. For if it was not lawful for Moses to build the material tabernacle after any other sort than God had showed him by a pattern, neither to prescribe any other ceremonies and laws than such as the Lord had expressly commanded; how can it be

---

[8] 2 Chronicles 15:13.

lawful to proceed in this spiritual building any other ways, than Jesus Christ the Son of God, who is both the foundation, head and chief cornerstone thereof[9], hath commanded by his Word? And forasmuch as he hath established and left an order in his Church for the building up of his body, appointing some to be apostles, some prophets, others evangelists, some pastors and teachers[10], he signifieth that every one according as he is placed in this body which is the Church, ought to enquire of his ministers concerning the will of the Lord, which is revealed in his Word. For they are, saith Jeremiah, as the mouth of the Lord;[11] yea, and he promiseth to be with their mouth, and that their lips shall keep knowledge, and that the truth and the law shall be in their mouth. For it is their office chiefly to understand the Scriptures and teach them. For this cause the people of Israel in matters of difficulty used to ask the Lord either by the prophets or by the means of the high priest, who bare *urim* and *thummim*, which were tokens of light and knowledge, of holiness and perfection, which should be in the high priest. Therefore when Jehoshaphat took this order in the church of Israel, he appointed Amariah to be the chief concerning the Word of God, because he was most expert in the law of the Lord and could give counsel and govern according unto the same.[12] Else there is no degree or office which may have that authority and privilege to decide concerning God's Word, except withal he have the Spirit of God, and sufficient knowledge and judgement to define according thereunto. And as everyone is indued of God with greater gifts, so ought he to be herein chiefly heard, or at least that without the express word none be heard; for he that hath not the Word speaketh not by the mouth of the Lord. Again, what danger it is to do anything, seem it never so godly or necessary, without consulting with God's mouth, the examples of the Israelites, deceived hereby through the Gibeonites;[13] and of Saul, whose intention seemed good and necessary,[14] and of Josiah also, who for great considerations was moved for the defence of true religion and his people, to fight against Pharaoh Necho King

---

[9] Ephesians 2:20
[10] Ephesians 4:11
[11] Jeremiah 15:19.
[12] 2 Chronicles 19:11.
[13] Joshua 9:1-27.
[14] See 1 Samuel 11:1-11.

of Egypt,[15] may sufficiently admonish us.

10. Last of all (most gracious Queen) for the advancement of this building and rearing up of the work, two things are necessary; first, that we have a lively and steadfast faith in Christ Jesus, who must dwell in our hearts as the only means and assurance of our salvation; for he is the ladder that reacheth from the earth to heaven; he lifteth up his Church and setteth it in the heavenly places; he maketh us lively stones and buildeth us upon himself; he joineth us to himself as the members and body to the head; yea he maketh himself and his Church one Christ. The next is that our faith bring forth good fruits, so that our godly conversation may serve us as a witness to confirm our election, and be an example to all others to walk as appertaineth to the vocation whereunto they are called; lest the Word of God be evil spoken of, and this building be stayed to grow up to a just height, which cannot be without the great provocation of God's just vengeance and discouraging of many thousands through all the world, if they should see that our life were not holy and agreeable to our profession. For the eyes of all that fear God in all places behold your countries as an example to all that believe, and the prayers of all the godly at all times are directed to God for the preservation of your Majesty. For considering God's wonderful mercies toward you at all seasons, who hath pulled you out of the mouth of the lions, and how that from your youth you have been brought up in the Holy Scriptures, the hope of all men is so increased that they cannot but look that God should bring to pass some wonderful work by your grace to the universal comfort of his Church. Therefore even above strength you must show yourself strong and bold in God's matters; and though Satan lay all his power and craft together to hurt and hinder the Lord's building, yet be you assured that God will fight from heaven against this great dragon, the ancient serpent, which is called the devil and Satan, till he have accomplished the whole work and made his Church glorious to himself, without spot or wrinkle[16]. For albeit all other kingdoms and monarchies, as the Babylonians, Persians, Grecians and Romans have fallen and taken end; yet the Church of Christ even under the cross hath from the beginning of the world been

---

[15] 2 Kings 23:28-30.
[16] Ephesians 5:27

victorious, and shall be everlastingly. Truth it is, that sometime it seemeth to be shadowed with a cloud or driven with a stormy persecution, yet suddenly the beams of Christ the sun of justice shine and bring it to light and liberty. If for a time it lie covered with ashes, yet it is quickly kindled again by the wind of God's Spirit, though it seem drowned in the sea, or parched and pined in the wilderness, yet God giveth ever good success, for he punisheth the enemies and delivereth his, nourisheth them and still preserveth them under his wings. This Lord of lords and King of kings who hath ever defended his, strengthen, comfort and preserve your Majesty, that you may be able to build up the ruins of God's house to his glory, the discharge of your conscience, and to the comfort of all them that love the coming of Christ Jesus our Lord. From Geneva, 10 April 1560.

To our beloved in the Lord, the brethren of England, Scotland, Ireland, etc. Grace, mercy and peace, through Christ Jesus.

11. Besides the manifold and continual benefits which Almighty God bestoweth upon us, both corporal and spiritual, we are especially bound (dear brethren) to give him thanks without ceasing for his great grace and unspeakable mercies, in that it hath pleased him to call us unto this marvellous light of his Gospel, and mercifully to regard us after so horrible backsliding and falling away from Christ to Antichrist, from light to darkness, from the living God to dead and dumb idols, and that after so cruel murther of God's saints, as alas hath been among us, we are not altogether cast off, as were the Israelites and many others for the like, or not so manifest wickedness, but received again to grace with most evident signs and tokens of God's especial love and favour. To the intent therefore that we may not be unmindful of these great mercies, but seek by all means (according to our duty) to be thankful for the same, it behoveth us so to walk in his fear and love, that all the days of our life we may procure the glory of his holy name. Now forasmuch as this thing chiefly is attained by the knowledge and practising of the Word of God (which is the light to our paths, the key of the kingdom of heaven, our comfort in affliction, our shield and sword against Satan, the school of all wisdom, the glass wherein we behold God's face, the testimony of his favour, and the only food and nourishment of our souls) we thought that we could bestow our labours and study in nothing which could be more acceptable to God and comfortable to his

Church than in the translating of the Holy Scriptures into our native tongue; the which thing, albeit that divers heretofore have endeavoured to achieve, yet considering the infancy of those times and the imperfect knowledge of the tongues, in respect of this ripe age and clear light which God hath now revealed, the translations required greatly to be perused and reformed. Not that we vindicate anything to ourselves above the least of our brethren (for God knoweth with what fear and trembling we have been now, for the space of two years and more day and night occupied herein) but being earnestly desired and by divers, whose learning and godliness we reverence, exhorted and also encouraged by the ready wills of such, whose hearts God likewise touched, not to spare any charges for the furtherance of such a benefit and favour of God toward his Church (though the time then was most dangerous and the persecution sharp and furious) we submitted ourselves at length to their godly judgements, and seeing the great opportunity and occasions which God presented unto us in this Church, by reason of so many godly and learned men, and such diversities of translations in divers tongues; we undertook this great and wonderful work (with all reverence, as in the presence of God, as intreating the Word of God, whereunto we think ourselves insufficient), which now God according to his divine providence and mercy hath directed to a most prosperous end. And this we may with good conscience protest, that we have in every point and word, according to the measure of that knowledge which it pleased Almighty God to give us, faithfully rendered the text, and in all hard places most sincerely expounded the same. For God is our witness that we have by all means endeavoured to set forth the purity of the Word and right sense of the Holy Ghost for the edifying of the brethren in faith and charity.

12. Now as we have chiefly observed the sense, and laboured always to restore it to all integrity, so have we most reverently kept the propriety of the words, considering that the apostles who spake and wrote to the Gentiles in the Greek tongue, rather constrained them to the lively phrase of the Hebrew than enterprised far by mollifying their language to speak as the Gentiles did. And for this and other causes we have in many places reserved the Hebrew phrases, notwithstanding that they may seem somewhat hard in their ears that are not well practised, and also delight in the sweet-sounding phrases of the Holy Scriptures. Yet lest either

the simple should be discouraged, or the malicious have any occasion of just cavillation, seeing some translations read after one sort and some after another, whereas all may serve to good purpose and edification, we have in the margin noted that diversity of speech or reading which may also seem agreeable to the mind of the Holy Ghost and proper for our language with this mark: '.

13. Again whereas the Hebrew speech seemed hardly to agree with ours, we have noted it in the margin after this sort: ", using that which was more intelligible. And albeit that many of the Hebrew names be altered from the old text and restored to the true writing and first original, whereof they have their signification, yet in the usual names little is changed for fear of troubling the simple readers. Moreover, whereas the necessity of the sentence required anything to be added (for such is the grace and propriety of the Hebrew and Greek tongues, that it cannot but either by circumlocution, or by adding the verb or some word, be understand [sic] of them that are not well practised therein) we have put it in the text with another kind of letter, that it may easily be discerned from the common letter. As touching the division of the verses, we have followed the Hebrew examples, which have so even from the beginning distinct them. Which thing as it is most profitable for memory, so doth it agree with the best translations and is most easy to find out both by the best concordances, and also by the quotations which we have diligently herein perused and set forth by this star: *. Besides this, the principal matters are noted and distinguished by this mark: ¶. Yea and the arguments both for the book and for the chapters with the number of the verse are added, that by all means the reader might be holpen.[17] For the which cause also we have set over the head of every page some notable word or sentence which may greatly further as well for memory, as for the chief point of the page. And considering how hard a thing it is to understand the Holy Scriptures, and what errors, sects and heresies grow daily for lack of the true knowledge thereof, and how many are discouraged (as they pretend) because they cannot attain to the true and simple meaning of the same, we have also endeavoured both by the diligent reading of the best commentaries, and also by the

---

[17] 'Helped.'

conference with the godly and learned brethren, to gather brief annotations upon all the hard places, as well for the understanding of such words as are obscure, and for the declaration of the text, as for the application of the same as may most appertain to God's glory and the edification of his Church. Furthermore, whereas certain places in the books of Moses, of the Kings and Ezekiel, seemed so dark that by no description they could be made easy to the simple reader, we have to set them forth with figures and notes for the full declaration thereof, that they which cannot by judgement, being holpen by the annotations noted by the letters a b c etc., and attain thereunto, yet by the perspective, and as it were by the eye may sufficiently know the true meaning of all such places. Whereunto also we have added certain maps of cosmography which necessarily serve for the perfect understanding and memory of divers places and countries, partly described, and partly by occasion touched, both in the Old and New Testament. Finally, that nothing might lack which might be bought by labours, for the increase of knowledge and the furtherance of God's glory, we have adjoined two more profitable tables, the one serving for the interpretation of the Hebrew names and the other containing all the chief and principal matters of the whole Bible; so that nothing (as we trust) that any could justly desire, is omitted. Therefore, as brethren that are partakers of the same hope and salvation with us, we beseech you, that this rich pearl and inestimable treasure may not be offered in vain, but as sent from God or the people of God, for the increase of his kingdom, the comfort of his Church, and discharge of our conscience, whom it hath pleased him to raise up for this purpose, so you would willingly receive the Word of God, earnestly study it and in all your life practise it, that you may now appear indeed to be the people of God, not walking any more according to this world, but in the fruits of the Spirit, that God in us may be fully glorified through Christ Jesus our Lord, who liveth and reigneth for ever. Amen. From Geneva, 10 April 1560.

8. Preface to the Bishops' Bible, 1568

01. Of all the sentences pronounced by our Saviour Christ in his whole doctrine, none is more serious or more worthy to be borne in remembrance, than that which he spake openly in his Gospel, saying: *Scrutamini Scripturas, quia vos putatis in ipsis vitam aeternam habere, et illae sunt qui testimonium perhibent de me.* 'Search ye the Scriptures, for in them ye think to have eternal life, and those they be which bear witness of me.'[1] These words were first spoken unto the Jews by our Saviour, but by him in his doctrine meant to all; for they concern all, of what nation, of what tongue, of what profession soever any man be. For to all belongeth it to be called unto eternal life, so many as by the witness of the Scriptures desire to find eternal life. No man, woman or child is excluded from this salvation, and therefore to every of them is this spoken proportionately yet, and in their degrees and ages, and as the reason and congruity of their vocation may ask. For not so lieth it in charge to the worldly artificer to search, or to any other private man so exquisitely to study, as it lieth to the charge of the public teacher to search in the Scriptures, to be the more able to walk in the house of God (which is the church of the living God, the pillar and ground of truth)[2] to the establishing of the true doctrine of the same, and to the impugning of the false. And though whatsoever difference there may be betwixt the preacher in office and the auditor in his vocation, yet to both it is said: 'Search ye the Scriptures, whereby ye may find eternal life and gather witness of that salvation which is in Christ Jesus our Lord.

02. For although the prophet of God Moses biddeth the king when he is once set on the throne of his kingdom to describe before his eyes the volume of God's law, according to the example which he should receive of the priests of the levitical tribe, to have it with him and to read in it all the days of his life, to the end that he might learn to fear the Lord his God and to observe his laws, that his heart be not advanced in pride over his brethren, nor to

---

[1] John 5:39.
[2] 1 Timothy 3:15.

swerve either on the right hand or on the left,³ yet the reason of this precept, for that it concerneth all men, may reasonably be thought to be commanded to all men, and all men may take it to be spoken to themself in their degree. Though Almighty God himself spake to his captain Joshua in precise words: *Non recedat volumen legis huius ab ore tuo, sed meditaberis in eo diebus ac noctibus etc.* 'let not the volume of this book depart from thy mouth, but muse therein both days and nights, that thou mayest keep and perform all things which be written in it, that thou mayest direct well thy way and understand the same;⁴ yet as well spake Almighty God this precept to all his people in the directions of their ways to himward, as he meant it to Joshua; for that he hath care for all, he accepteth no man's person,⁵ his will is that all men should be saved,⁶ his will is that all men should come to the way of truth.⁷ How could this be more conveniently declared by God to man, than when Christ his well-beloved Son our most loving Saviour, the way, the truth and the life of us all,⁸ did bid us openly: 'Search the Scriptures,' assuring us herein to find eternal life, to find full testification of all his graces and benefits towards us in the treasure thereof? Therefore it is most convenient that we should all suppose that Christ spake to us all in this his precept of searching the Scriptures.

03. If this celestial doctor (so authorised by the Father of heaven and commanded as his only Son to be heard of us all)⁹ biddeth us busily to search the Scriptures, of what spirit can it proceed to forbid the reading and studying of the Scriptures? If the gross Jews used to read them, as some men think that our Saviour Christ did show by such kind of speaking, their usage, with their opinion they had therein to find eternal life, and were not of Christ rebuked or disproved, either for their searching or for the opinion they had, how superstitiously or superficially soever some of them used to expend the Scriptures? How much more unadvisedly do such as boast themself to be either Christ's vicars

---

³ Deuteronomy 17:20.
⁴ Joshua 1:7-8.
⁵ Ephesians 6:9.
⁶ 2 Peter 3:9.
⁷ 1 Timothy 2:4.
⁸ John 14:6.
⁹ Matthew 17:5.

or be of his guard, to lothe[10] Christian men from reading, by their covert, slanderous reproaches of the Scriptures, or in their authority by law or statute to contract this liberty of studying the word of eternal salvation? Christ calleth them not only to the single reading of Scriptures (saith Chrysostom) but sendeth them to the exquisite searching of them, for in them is eternal life to be found, and they be (saith himself) the witness of me[11]; for they declare out his office, they commend his benevolence towards us, they record his whole works wrought for us to our salvation. Antichrist therefore he must be, that under whatsoever colour would give contrary precept or counsel to that which Christ did give unto us. Very little do they resemble Christ's loving Spirit moving us to search for our comfort, that will discourage us from such searching, or that would wish ignorance and forgetfulness of his benefit to reign in us, for that they might by our ignorance reign the more frankly in our consciences, to the danger of our salvation. Who can take the light from us in this miserable vale of blindness and mean not to have us stumble in the paths of perdition to the ruin of our souls? Who will envy us this bread of life prepared and set on the table for our eternal sustenance, and mean not to famish us, or instead thereof, with their corrupt traditions and doctrines of man, to infect us?[12] All the whole Scripture, saith the holy apostle St Paul, inspired from God above, is profitable to teach, to reprove, to reform, to instruct in righteousness, that the man of God may be sound and perfect, instructed to every good work.[13]

04. Search therefore, good reader (on God's name) as Christ biddeth thee, the Holy Scripture, wherein thou mayest find thy salvation. Let not the volume of this book (by God's own warrant) depart from thee, but occupy thyself therein in the whole journey of this they worldly pilgrimage, to understand thy way how to walk rightly before him all the days of thy life. Remember that the prophet David pronounceth him the blessed man which will muse in the law of God both day and night;[14] remember that he calleth him blessed which walketh in the way of the Lord, which

---

[10] 'Forbid.'
[11] John 5:39
[12] Psalm 22:29.
[13] 2 Timothy 3:16.
[14] Psalm 1:1.

will search diligently his testimonies, and will in their whole heart seek the same.[15] Let not the covert, suspicious insinuations of the adversaries drive thee from the search of the Holy Scripture, either for the obscurity which they say is in them, or for the inscrutable hidden mysteries they talk to be comprised in them, or for the strangeness and homeliness of the phrases they would charge God's book with. Christ exhorteth thee therefore the rather for the difficulty of the same, to search them diligently. St Paul willeth thee to have thy senses exercised in them, and not to be a child in thy senses, but in malice.[16] Though many things may be difficult to thee to understand, impute it rather to they dull hearing and reading, than to think that the Scriptures be insuperable to them which with diligent searching labour to discern the evil from the good. Only search with an humble spirit, ask in continual prayer, seek with purity of life, knock with perpetual perseverance, and cry to that good Spirit of Christ the Comforter, and surely to every such asker it will be given, such searchers must needs find, to them it will be opened.[17] Christ himself will open the sense of the Scriptures, not to the proud or to the wise of the world, but to the lowly and contrite in heart[18], for he hath the key of David, who openeth and no man shutteth, who shutteth and no man openeth[19]. For as this Spirit is a benign and liberal spirit[20], and will be easily found of them which will early in carefulness rise to seek him[21], and as he promiseth, he will be the comforter from above to teach us and to lead us into all the ways of truth, if that in humility we bow unto him, denying our own natural senses, our carnal wits and reasons[22]; so he is the spirit of purity and cleanness and will recede from him whose conscience is subject to filthiness of life.[23] Into such a soul this heavenly wisdom will not enter, for all perverse cogitations will separate us from God, and then, how busily soever we search this holy table of the Scripture, yet will it then be a table to such to their own

---

[15] Psalm 119:2-4.
[16] Hebrews 5:12-14; 1 Corinthians 14:20.
[17] Matthew 7:7.
[18] Matthew 11:25; Isaiah 61:1.
[19] Revelation 3:7.
[20] 1 Corinthians 12:4-11.
[21] Psalm 63:1.
[22] John 16:13.
[23] Job 14:4; Wisdom of Solomon 1:1-16.

snare, a trap, a stumbling stock and a recompense to themself.[24]

05. We ought therefore to search to find out the truth, not to oppress it, we ought to seek Christ, not as Herod did, under the pretence of worshipping him to destroy him,[25] or as the Pharisees searched the Scriptures to disprove Christ and to discredit him, and not to follow him; but to embrace the salvation which we may learn by them. Nor yet is it enough so to acknowledge the Scriptures as some of the Jews did, of the holiest of them who used such diligence that they could number precisely, not only every verse but every word and syllable, how oft every letter of the alphabet was repeated in the whole Scriptures. They had some of them such reverence to that book that they would not suffer in a great heap of books any other to lay over them. They would not suffer that book to fall to the ground as nigh as they could, they would costly bind the books of Holy Scriptures and cause them to be exquisitely and ornately written. Which devotion, yet though it was not to be discommended, yet was it not for that intent, why Christ commended the Scriptures, nor they thereof allowed before God. For they did not call upon God in a true faith, they were not charitable to their neighbours, but in the midst of all this devotion they did steal, they were adulterers, they were slanderers and backbiters, even much like many of our Christian men and women nowadays, who glory much that they read the Scriptures, that they search them and love them, that they frequent the public sermons in an outward show of all honesty and perfection, yea they can pick out of the Scriptures virtuous sentences and godly precepts to lay before other men. And though these manner of men do not much err for such searching and studying, yet they see not the scope and the principal state of the Scriptures, which is as Christ declareth it, to find Christ as their Saviour, to cleave to his salvation and merits, to be brought to the low repentance of their lives, and to amend themself, to raise up their faith to our Saviour Christ, so to think of him as the Scriptures do testify of him. These be the principal causes why Christ did send the Jews to search the Scriptures, for to this end were they written, saith St John: *Haec scripta sunt ut credatis, et ut credentes vitam habeatis aeternam*, 'these were written to this intent, that ye should

---

[24] Psalm 68:1-2.
[25] Matthew 2:8.

believe, and that through your belief ye should have everlasting life.'[26]

06. And here, good reader, great cause we have to extol the wondrous wisdom of God, and with great thanks to praise his providence, considering how he hath preserved and renewed from age to age by special miracle, the incomparable treasure of his church. For first he did inspire Moses, as John Chrysostom doth testify, to write the stony tables, and kept him in the mountain forty days to give him his law;[27] after him, he sent the prophets, but they suffered many thousand adversities, for battles did follow, all were slain, all were destroyed, books were brent[28] up. He then inspired another man to repair these miraculous Scriptures, Ezra I mean, who of their leavings set them again together.[29] After that, he provided that the seventy interpreters should take them in hand. At the last came Christ himself, the apostles did receive them and spread them throughout all nations. Christ wrought his miracles and wonders and what followed after these great volumes the apostles also did write, as St Paul doth say: 'These be written to the instruction of us that be come to the end of the world'[30] and Christ doth say: 'Ye therefore err, because ye know not the Scriptures nor the power of God.'[31] And Paul did say: 'Let the word of Christ be plentiful among you'[32] and again saith David: 'Oh how sweet be thy words to my throat.'[33] He said not 'to my hearing' but 'to my throat, above the honey or the honeycomb to my mouth.' Yea, Moses saith: 'Thou shalt meditate in them evermore when thou risest, when thou sittest down, when thou goest to sleep, continue in them' he saith;[34] and a thousand places more. And yet after so many testimonies thus spoken, there be some persons that do not yet so much as know what the Scriptures be, whereupon nothing is in good state amongst us, nothing worthily is done amongst us. 'In this which pertain to this life we make very great haste, but of spiritual goods we have

---

[26] John 20:31.
[27] Hebrews 3:5.
[28] 'Burnt.'
[29] II (IV) Esdras 94:18; Clement of Alexandria, *Stromateis* I, 22, 148. 3 (PG 8, col. 893).
[30] 1 Corinthians 10:6.
[31] Matthew 22:29.
[32] Colossians 3:16.
[33] Psalm 119:103; Psalm 19:10.
[34] Deuteronomy 11:19.

no regard.' Thus far John Chrysostom.

07.   It must needs signify some great thing to our understanding, that Almighty God hath had such care to prescribe these books thus unto us; I say not to prescribe them only, but to maintain them and defend them against the malignity of the devil and his ministers, who always went about to destroy them, and yet could these never be so destroyed, but that he would have them continue whole and perfect to this day, to our singular comfort and instruction, where other books of mortal wise men have perished in great numbers. It is recorded that Ptolemy Philadelphus, king of Egypt,[35] had gathered together in one library at Alexandria by his great cost and diligence, seven hundred thousand books, whereof the principal were the books of Moses, which reserved not much more than by the space of two hundred years, were all brent[36] and consumed in that battle when Caesar restored Cleopatra again after her expulsion.[37] At Constantinople perished under Zeno by one common fire, one hundred and twenty thousand books.[38] At Rome, when Lucius Aurelius Antoninus did reign,[39] his notable library by a lightning from heaven was quite consumed; yea, it is recorded that Gregory I did cause a library of Rome, containing only certain pagans' works, to be burned, to the intent the Scriptures of God should be more read and studied.[40] What other great libraries have been consumed but of late days? And what libraries have of old throughout this realm almost in every abbey of the same, been destroyed at sundry ages, besides the loss of other men's private studies, it were too long to rehearse. Whereupon seeing Almighty God by his divine providence hath preserved these books of the Scriptures safe and sound, and that in their native languages they were first written in the great ignorance that reigned in these

---

[35] Ptolemy II Philadelphus reigned from 285-246 BC.
[36] 'Burnt.'
[37] Cleopatra VII reigned from 51-30 BC, but had to compete with her brother Ptolemy XIII for power until Julius Caesar intervened. The fire occurred in February 47 BC, but did not consume the entire library.
[38] Zeno (474-91) was challenged by Basiliscus, who seized the throne in 475-6. The fire probably occurred at that time.
[39] Marcus Aurelius (161-80) is meant. The confusion is with his brother and co-emperor, Lucius Aurelius Verus (161-9).
[40] Gregory I the Great was pope from 590-604. For this story, which is apocryphal, see John of Salisbury, *Polycraticus*, VIII, 19 (PL 199, coll. 798-93).

tongues, and contrary to all other casualties, chanced upon all other books in mauger[41] of all worldly wits, who would so fain have had them destroyed; and yet he, by his mighty hand, would have them extant as witnesses and interpreters of his will toward mankind; we may soon see cause most reverently to embrace these divine testimonies of his will, to study them and to search them, to instruct our blind nature so sore corrupted and fallen from the knowledge in which first we were created.

08. Yet having occasion given somewhat to recover our fall and to return again to that divine nature wherein we were once made, and at the last to be inheritors in the celestial habitation which God Almighty, after the end of our mortality here brought to his dust again; these books I say being of such estimation and authority, so much reverenced of them who had any mean taste of them, could never be put out of the way, neither by the spite of any tyrant, as that tyrant Maximian[42] destroyed all the Holy Scriptures wheresoever they could be found, and burnt them in the midst of the market, neither the hatred of any Porphyrian[43] philosopher or rhetorician, neither by the envy of the Romanists and of such hypocrites who from time to time did ever bark against them, some of them not in open sort of condemnation but more cunningly under false pretences, for that as they say, they were so hard to understand, and specially for that they affirm it to be a perilous matter to translate the text of the Holy Scripture, and therefore it cannot be well translated. And here we may behold the endeavour of some men's cavillations, who labour all they can to slander the translators, to find fault in some words of the translation, but themself will never set pen to the book, to set out any translation at all. They can in their constitutions provincial under pain of excommunication inhibit all other men to translate them without the ordinaries or the provincial council agree thereunto,[44] but they will be well ware never to agree or to give

---

[41] 'Spite.'
[42] Co-emperor with Diocletian (286-305) and again (306-8), he was a noted persecutor of Christians.
[43] Porphyry (234-305) was a Neoplatonist philosopher and disciple of Plotinus (204-70). He was noted for his hatred of Christianity and determined opposition to it. The Neoplatonists maintained their anti-Christian stance until their academy at Athens was dissolved in 529 and the remaining philosophers had to flee to Persia.
[44] The seventh canon of the council of Oxford, held in 1407. (See introduction.)

counsel to set them out. Which their subtle compass in effect tendeth but to bewray[45] what inwardly they mean, if they could bring it about, that is, utterly to suppress them, being in this their judgement far unlike the old fathers in the primitive church, who hath exhorted indifferently all persons, as well men as women, to exercise themselves in the Scriptures, which by St Jerome's authority be the Scriptures of the people.

09. Yea, they be far unlike their old forefathers that have ruled in this realm, who in their times and in divers ages did their diligence to translate the whole books of the Scriptures, to the erudition of the laity, as yet at this day to be seen divers books translated into the vulgar tongue, some by kings of the realm, some by bishops, some by abbots, some by other devout godly fathers, so desirous they were of old time to have the lay sort edified in godliness by reading in their vulgar tongue, that very many books be yet extant, though for the age of the speech and the strangeness of the charact[ers] of many of them, almost worn out of knowledge. In which books may be seen evidently how it was used among the Saxons to have in their churches read the four Gospels, so distributed and picked out in the body of the Evangelists' books, that to every Sunday and festival day in the year, they were sorted out to the common ministers of the church in their common prayers to be read to their people. Now as of the most ancient fathers the prophets, St Peter testifieth that these holy men of God had the impulsion of the Holy Ghost, to speak out these divine testimonies,[46] so it is not to be doubted but that these latter holy fathers of the English church had the impulsion of the Holy Ghost to set out these sacred books in their vulgar language to the edification of the people, by the help whereof they might the better follow the example of the godly Christians, in the beginning of the church, who not only received the word with all readiness of heart but also did search diligently in the Scriptures, whether the doctrine of the apostles were agreeable to the same Scriptures.[47] And these were not of the rascal sort (saith the divine story) but they were of the best and of most noble birth among the Thessalonians, Birrhenses [Beroeans] by name.[48] Yea, the

---

[45] 'Betray'.
[46] 2 Peter 1:21.
[47] Acts 17:11.
[48] This is a mistake, of course, as Beroea was another city.

prophets themselves in their days, writeth St Peter, were diligent searchers to inquire out this salvation by Christ, searching when and at what article of time this grace of Christ's dispensation should appear to the world.[49]

10. What meant the fathers of the church in their writings but the advancing of these holy books, where some do attribute no certainty of undoubted verity but to the canonical Scriptures? Some do affirm it to be a foolish, rash boldness to believe him who proveth not by the Scriptures that which he affirmeth in his word. Some do accurse all that is delivered by tradition not found in the legal and evangelical Scriptures. Some say that our faith must needs stagger if it be not grounded upon the authority of the Scripture. Some testifieth that Christ and his church ought to be advouched[50] out of the Scriptures, and do contend in disputation that the true church cannot be known, but only by the Holy Scriptures. For all other things (saith the same author) may be found among the heretics. Some affirm it to be a sinful tradition that is obtruded without the Scripture. Some plainly pronounce that not to know the Scriptures is not to know Christ.[51] Wherefore let men extol out the church practices as highly as they can, and let them set out their traditions and customs, their decisions in synods and councils, with vaunting the presence of the Holy Ghost among them really, as some doth affirm it in their writing, let their grounds and their demonstrations, their foundations be as stable and as strong as they blaze them out, yet we will be bold to say with St Peter: *Habemus nos firmiorem sermonem propheticum.*[52] We have for our part a more stable ground, the prophetical words (of the Scriptures) and doubt not to be commended therefore of the same St Peter with these words: *Cui dum attenditis cum lucerne apparenti in obscuro loco, recte facitis donec dies illucescat, etc.* 'Whereunto,' saith he, while ye do attend as to a light shining in a dark place, ye do well until the

---

[49] 1 Peter 1:5.
[50] 'Proved'.
[51] Jerome, *Epistula* XVIII, 6 (PL 22, col. 364); Tertullian, *De praescriptione haereticorum*, 9 (PL 2, coll. 22-3); Augustine, *De doctrina Christiana* II, 11 (PL 34, coll. 42-3); Pseudo-John Chrysostom, *Homiliae in Matthaeum* XLIX (PG 56, col. 909), [the anonymous *Opus Imperfectum*]; Basil of Caesarea, *In psalmum* I, 1 (PG 29, coll. 209-12).
[52] 2 Peter 1:19.

daylight appear and till the bright star do arise in our hearts.'[53] For this we know, that all the prophetical Scripture standeth not in any private interpretation of vain names, of several churches, of catholic and universal sees, of singular and wilful heads which will challenge by custom all decision to pertain to them only, who be working so much for their vain superiority that they be not ashamed now to be of that number *qui dixerunt linguam nostram magnificabimus, labia nostra a nobis sunt, quis noster dominus est?* 'Which have said, with our tongue we will prevail, we are they that ought to speak, who is lord over us?'[54]

11. And while they shall thus contend for their strange claimed authority, we will proceed in the reformation begun and doubt no more by the help of Christ his grace of the true unity to Christ's catholic church and of the uprightness of our faith in this province, than the Spanish clergy once gathered together in council (only by the commandment of their king, before which time the pope was not so acknowledged in his authority which he now claimeth), I say as surely dare we trust as they did trust of their faith and unity.[55] Yea, no less confidence have we to profess that which the fathers of the universal council at Carthage in Africa as they write themself did profess in their epistle written to pope Celestine, laying before his face the foul corruption of himself (as two other of his predecessors did the like error) in falsifying the canons of the Nicene council, for his wrong challenge of his new-claimed authority. Thus writing: *Prudentissime enim iustissimeque providerunt [Nicaena et Africana decreta] quaecunque negotia in suis locis (ubi orta sunt) finienda, nec unicuique provinciae gratiam Sancti Spiritus defuturam, qua aequitas a Christi sacerdotibus et prudenter videatur et constantissime teneatur, maxime quia unicuique concessum est, si iudicio offensus fuerit cognitorum, ad concila suae provinciae vel etiam universale provocare.* 'That (the Nicene and African decrees) have most prudently and justly provided for all manner of matters to be ended in their territories where they had their beginning, and they trusted that not to any one province should want the grace of the Holy Ghost, whereby both the truth

---

[53] 2 Peter 1:19.
[54] Psalm 12:4.
[55] This seems to refer to the third council of Braga (Portugal), summoned by King Wamba in 675.

or equity might prudently be seen of the Christian prelates of Christ, and might be also by them most prudently defended, specially for that it is granted to every man (if he be grieved) by the judgement of the cause once known, to appeal to the councils of his own province, or else to the universal.'[56] Except there may be any man which may believe that our Lord God would inspire the righteousness of examination to any one singular person and to deny the same to priests gathered together into council without number, etc. And there they do require the bishop of Rome to send none of his clerks to execute such provincial causes, lest else they say, mought[57] be brought in the vain pride of the world into the church of Christ.

12. In this antiquity may we in this Christian catholic church of England repose ourself, knowing by our own annals of ancient record that king Lucius, whose conscience was much touched with the miracles which the servants of Christ wrought in divers nations, thereupon being in great love with the true faith, sent unto Eleutherius, then bishop of Rome,[58] requiring of him the Christian religion. But Eleutherius did readily give over that care to king Lucius in his epistle, for that the king as he writeth, the vicar of God in his own kingdom, and for that he had received the faith of Christ. And for that he had also both Testaments in his realm, he willed him to draw out of them by the grace of God and by the counsel of his wise men, his laws, and by that law of God to govern his realm of Britain, and not so much to desire the Roman and emperor's laws, in the which some default might be found, saith he, but in the laws of God nothing at all. With which answer the king's legates, Eluanus and Medwinus, sent as messengers by the king to the pope, returned to Britain again, Eluanus being made a bishop and Medwinus allowed a public teacher, who for the eloquence and knowledge they had in the Holy Scriptures, they repaired home again to king Lucius, and by their holy

---

[56] Celestine I was pope from 422-32. The council that sent this letter to him met in 424.
[57] 'Might.'
[58] Eleutherius was supposedly pope from 175-89. This entire account is completely fictitious, but it may reflect the fact that Christianity was probably established in Roman Britain about this time. Certainly there were at least three bishops already in post when Christianity was legalised in 313, because they attended the council held at Arles in the following year. See William of Malmesbury, *Gesta reum Anglorum* I, 19 (PL 179, col. 978).

preachings Lucius and the noble men of the whole Britain received their baptism, etc. Thus far in the story.[59] Now therefore, knowing and believing with St Paul: *Quod quaecunque praescripta sunt, ad nostram doctrinam praescripta sunt, ut per patientiam et consolationem Scripturarum spem habeamus* 'Whatsoever is afore written, is written before for our instruction, that we through the patience and comfort of Scriptures might have hope,'[60] the only surety to our faith and conscience is to stick to the Scriptures. Whereupon while this eternal word of God be our rock and anchor to stick unto, we will have patience with all the vain inventions of men who labour so highly to magnify their tongues, to exalt themselves above all that is God. We will take comfort by the Holy Scriptures against the maledictions of the adversaries and doubt not to nourish our hope continually therewith, so to live and die in this comfortable hope and doubt not to pertain to the elect number of Christ's church, how far soever we be excommunicated out of the synagogue of such who suppose themselves to be the universal lords of all the world, lords of our faith and consciences, at pleasure.

13. Finally, to commend further unto thee, good reader, the cause in part before intreated, it shall be the less needful, having so nigh following that learned preface which sometime was set out by the diligence of that godly father Thomas Cranmer, late bishop in the see of Canterbury, which he caused to be prefixed before the translation of that Bible that was then set out. And for that the copies thereof be so wasted[61] that very many churches do want their convenient Bibles, it was thought good to some well-disposed men to recognise the same Bible again into this form as it is now come out, with some further diligence in that printing and with some more light added, partly in the translation and partly in the order of the text, not as condemning the former translation, which was followed mostly of any other translation, excepting the original text from which as little variance was made

---

[59] A marginal note reads: 'And yet may it be true that William of Malmesbury writeth, that Phaganus and Dervutanus were sent after (as coadjutors) with these learned men to the preaching of the Gospel, which was never extinguished in Britain from Joseph of Arimathea his time, as to Dominus Austen [Augustine] the first bishop of Canterbury, they do openly avouch.'

[60] Romans 15:4.

[61] 'Worn out'.

as was thought meet to such as took pains therein, desiring thee, good reader, if aught be escaped, either by such as had the expending of the books or by the oversight of the printer, to correct the same in the spirit of charity, calling to remembrance what diversity hath been seen in men's judgements in the translation of these books before these days, though all directed their labours to the glory of God, to the edification of the church, to the comfort of their Christian brethren, and always as God did further open unto them, so ever more desirous they were to reform their former human oversights rather than in a stubborn wilfulness to resist the gift of the Holy Ghost, who from time to time is resident as that heavenly teacher and leader into all truth, by whose direction the church is ruled and governed.

14. And let all men remember in themself how error and ignorance is created with our nature; let frail man confess with that great wise man that the cogitations and inventions of mortal men be very weak, and our opinions soon deceived.[62] For the body so subject to corruption doth oppress the soul, that it cannot aspire so high as of duty it ought. Men we be all, and that which we know is not a thousand part of that we know not. Whereupon saith St Austen [Augustine], otherwise to judge than the truth is, this temptation riseth of the frailty of man.[63] A man so to love and stick to his own judgement or to envy his brothers to the peril of dissolving the Christian communion, or to the peril of schism and of heresy, this is diabolical presumption, but so to judge in every matter as the truth is, this belongeth only to the angelical perfection. Notwithstanding, good reader, thou mayst be well assured nothing to be done in this translation either of malice or wilful meaning in altering the text, either by putting more or less to the same, as of purpose to bring in any private judgement by falsification of the words, as some certain men hath been overbold so to do, little regarding the majesty of God his Scripture, but so to make it serve to their corrupt error, as in alleging the sentence of St Paul to the Romans the 6,[64] one certain writer to prove his satisfaction, was bold to turn the word of *sanctificationem* into the word of *satisfactionem*, thus: *Sicut*

---

[62] Ecclesiasticus 11:1-10; Wisdom of Solomon 9:6.
[63] Augustine, *De doctrina Christiana*, I, 3 (PL 34, col. 20).
[64] Romans 6:19.

exhibuimus antea membra nostra servire immunditiae et iniquitati ad iniquitatem, ita deinceps membra nostra servire iustitiae in satisfactionem, that is: 'We have given our members to uncleanness, from iniquity to iniquity; even so from henceforth let us give our members to serve righteousness into satisfaction,' where the true word is 'into sanctification.'[65] Even so likewise for the advantage of his cause, to prove that men may have in their prayer faith upon saints, corruptly allegeth St Paul's text *Ad Philemonem* thus: *Fidem quam habes in Domino Iesu et in omnes sanctos*, leaving out the word *caritatem*, which would rightly have been distributed unto *omnes sanctos*, as *fidem* unto *in Domino Iesu*. Where the text is: *Audiens caritatem tuam et fidem quam habes in Domino Iesu et in omnes sanctos, etc.*[66]

15. It were too long to bring in many examples, as may be openly found in some men's writings in these days, who would be counted the chief pillars of the catholic faith, or to note how corruptly they abuse the text to the commodity of their cause. What manner of translation may men think to look for at their hands, if they should translate the Scriptures to the comfort of God's elect, which they never did, nor be not like to purpose it, but be rather studious only to seek quarrels in other men's well-doings, to pick fault where none is. And where any is escaped through human negligence, there to cry out with their tragical exclamations, but in no wise to amend by the spirit of charity and lenity[67] that which might be more aptly set. Whereupon for frail man (compassed himself with infirmity) it is most reasonable not to be too severe in condemning his brother's knowledge or diligence where he doth err, not of malice but of simplicity, and specially in handling of these so divine books, so profound in sense, so far passing our natural understanding. And with charity it standeth, the reader not to be offended with the diversity of translators, nor with the ambiguity of translations, for as St Austen [Augustine] doth witness, by God's providence it is brought about that the Holy Scriptures, which be the salves for every man's sore, though at the first they came from one language

---

[65] Hosius, Stanislaus (1504-79), *Confessio catholicae fidei* XLIV, 'De sacramento paenitentiae' (fos. 65v-66r) (Venice, 1573; first published at Antwerp, 1559).

[66] Philemon 5; Hosius, *Confessio* LVIII, 'De spe et oratione' (fos. 99v-107r). (Hearing [of your love and] of the faith that you have toward the Lord Jesus and all the saints).

[67] 'Leniency'.

and thereby might have been spread to the whole world, now by diversity of many languages, the translators should spread the salvation (that is contained in them) to all nations by such words of utterance as the reader might perceive the mind of the translator, and so consequently to come to the knowledge of God his will and pleasure.[68] And although many rash readers be deceived in the obscurities and ambiguities of their translations, while they take one thing for another, and while they use much labour to extricate themselves out of the obscurities of the same, yet I think (saith he) this is not wrought without the providence of God, both to tame the proud arrogancy of man by his such labour of searching as also to keep his mind from loathsomeness and contempt, where if the Scriptures universally were too easy, he would less regard them. And though (saith he) in the primitive church the late interpreters which did translate the Scriptures be innumerable, yet wrought this rather an help than an impediment to the readers, if they be not too negligent. For saith he, divers translations have made many times the harder and darker sentences the more open and plain, so that of congruence no offence can justly be taken for this new labour, nothing prejudicing any other man's judgement by this doing, nor yet hereby professing this to be so absolute a translation as that hereafter might follow no other that might see that which as yet was not understood.

16. In this point it is convenient to consider the judgement that John [Fisher], once bishop of Rochester was in, who thus wrote: 'It is not unknown but that many things hath been more diligently discussed and more clearly understanded by the wits of these latter days, as well concerning the Gospels as other Scriptures, than in old time they were.'[69] the cause whereof is (saith he) for that to the old men the use was not broken, or for that their age was not sufficient exquisitely to expend the whole main sea of the Scriptures, or else for that in this large field of the Scriptures a man may gather some ears untouched after the harvest men, how diligent soever they were. For there be yet (saith he) in the

---

[68] Augustine, *De doctrina Christiana* II, 5 (PL 34, col. 38).
[69] J. Fisher, *Sacri sacerdotii defensio contra Lutherum*, 17 (London, 1525). Fisher was bishop of Rochester from 24 November 1504 until his deprivation on 2 January 1535 and subsequent martyrdom on 22 June 1535. As he was put to death for having opposed Henry VIII, it is remarkable that he is quoted so explicitly in this preface.

Gospels very many dark places which without all doubt, to the posterity shall be made much more open. For why should we despair herein, seeing the Gospel (writeth he) was delivered to this intent, that it might be utterly understood of us, yea to the very inch. Wherefore, for as much as Christ showeth no less love to his church now than hitherto he hath done, the authority whereof is as yet no whit diminished, and for as much as that Holy Spirit, the perpetual keeper and guardian of the same church, whose gifts and graces do flow as continually and as abundantly as from the beginning, who can doubt but that such things as remain yet unknown in the Gospel shall be hereafter made open to the latter wits of our posterity, to their clear understanding. (Thus far this writer.)

17. Only, good readers, let us oft call upon the Holy Spirit of God our heavenly Father, by the mediation of our Lord and Saviour, with the words of the octonary psalm of David, who did so importunately crave of God to have the understanding of his laws and testament,[70] let us humbly on our knees pray to Almighty God with that wise king Solomon, in his very words, saying thus:

O God of my fathers and Lord of mercies (thou that hast made all things with thy word and didst ordain man through thy wisdom, that he should have dominion over thy creatures which thou hast made, and that he should order the world according to holiness and righteousness, and that he should execute judgement with a true heart) give me wisdom which is ever about thy seat, and put me not out from among thy children. For I thy servant and son of thy handmaiden am a feeble person, of a short time, and too weak to the understanding of thy judgements and laws. And though a man be never so perfect among the children of men, yet if thy wisdom be not with him, he shall be of no value. O send her out therefore from thy holy heavens and from the throne of thy majesty, that she may be with me and labour with me, that I may know what is acceptable in thy sight; for she knoweth and understandeth all things, and she shall lead me soberly in my works, and preserve me in her power.[71]

So shall my works be acceptable by Christ our Lord, to whom with

---

[70] Psalm 119:34,73,125,144,169.
[71] Wisdom of Solomon 9:1-6, 10-11.

the Father and the Holy Ghost be all honour and glory, world without end. Amen.

9. Preface to the Revised Geneva New Testament, 1576

By Laurence Tomson

To the right honourable Mr Francis Walsingham, esquire, one of the principal secretaries to her excellent Majesty and of her highness, privy council, and to the right worshipful Mr Francis Hastings, L[aurence] T[omson] wisheth prosperity in this life and life everlasting in Christ our Saviour.[1]

01. If I had to render a reason for this my travail in rendering into our mother tongue that that hath been fruitfully laboured and put forth in the Latin, to the great commodity and profit of such to whom our good God hath given understanding therein, I might truly and justly say it was for my poor brethren's sake, which want the blessing beforesaid for the understanding of the Latin, and yet have great riches of the Lord in that he hath given them the benefit to understand and read their own. For as the sun which shineth upon the just and unjust was not made for the benefit of our country only but of all the world, nor the Son of God sent into the world for the Jews only but also for the Gentiles, part of whom we are (for he shut us all under unbelief that he might have mercy upon all), so neither were the Scriptures left for the Grecian only, but for the barbarian also, both for the wise and unwise, both for the learned and unlearned of what nation and tongue soever they were, that we altogether, through patience and comfort of the Holy Scripture might have hope.[2] For so far have the Scriptures of duty to go as the apostles had commandment to preach, and in so many tongues should the apostles preach as by their gift from above they might.[3] And as they themselves are in this sort to be applied to our use, through the gift of tongues which God doth still pour upon his church (though not after the same sort as at

---

[1] Laurence Tomson (1539-1608) translated Theodore Beza's revised version of the New Testament (1565), including the notes attached to it. This revision replaced the original New Testament in the Geneva Bible.
[2] Romans 15:4.
[3] Acts 1:8.

the first,)⁴ even so, whatsoever holy men have written upon them through his unspeakable mercies and by the working of his Holy Spirit in our tongue, ought likewise, by the same gift, to be divided to the profit of the brethren elsewhere which differ in tongue but agree in unity of faith.

02. For so it cometh to pass that we communicate one with another's benefits and become to have a fellowship in those things which otherwise seemed to be several⁵ to some one of us. This benefit of God for his part and consideration of every one of our duties for our parts, brought the Scriptures themselves, first out of Judaea and the Hebrew tongue into Grecia and the language of that country, though not so happily as might be wished⁶, from thence to the Romans and into the Latin tongue, and so through the loving visitation of our God, into Dutch,⁷ French, English, Italian and so forth, which no man repineth at, (that Antichrist of Rome only except, who hateth the light because he is not of the light, but of darkness as his father, the prince of darkness, the devil is) but all that love God and fear God, most humbly thank him for, as obedient and dutiful children, showing their obedience toward him in studying in his law both day and night.

03. And as our brethren and saints of God have done for our behoof⁸ in this point touching the Scriptures, so have they done for the works of good fathers and prophets, causing them to speak familiarly to us as home born children with us, which otherwise were plants of Palestina and grafts of Graecia and citizens of the Latins. All this I say for our profit, that we might taste and see how loving and merciful our God is, and what in part this communion of saints is, which we so oft recite and so constantly believe at this present, and shall I trust to the end, when belief shall cease and God shall be all in all.⁹ For this we confess and believe all, and wheresoever we are and into how many countries

---

⁴ Acts 2:4.
⁵ 'Disparate'.
⁶ It was generally believed that the many differences between the Hebrew and the Greek were due to faulty translation. That was sometimes true, but we now have access to more early Hebrew manuscripts, which occasionally support the Greek variants.
⁷ 'German.'
⁸ 'Sake.'
⁹ 1 Corinthians 15:28.

of the world soever we are scattered, we are but one church, we make but one body, we have but one head and but one Spirit. If God raise up a prophet in our country as he did at the first in Judaea, his mind is that the words of this his own prophet shall be profitable to the whole body, as well the foot which is the furthest part as the heart that is the nearer shall receive nourishment and increase of strength by it. And for this end and purpose he divideth divers gifts unto this body, that the nourishment which seemeth to be so far off may be brought nearer, yea and so near that each member may live thereby. So that the gift received layeth a burden upon him that hath received it and it is no more in his power to do or not to do, but he must of necessity do for the profit of God's church according to the measure of that gift which God hath given him, remembering always with himself that our God is a wary and heedy giver and looketh for an account because he tendereth his children. He made us not for ourselves but for our brethren and so long shall we be here as he hath appointed our brethren to reap commodity by us, if we will seem to make a property of that which ought to be common and keep it to ourselves as our own, which is not ours but our brethren's, the Lord is faithful, who will not be slack to punish our unfaithfulness and to render us the recompense of our faithless dealing both towards him and them.

04. This was one reason, no doubt, and not the least, which moved the fathers in old time and our good fathers of this our blessed age, yet living amongst us, to do as they did and do still, by publishing those things which they have received of God for us and not for themselves. And hereupon was this our godly brother and father whom we think worthy all reverence in the Lord, not only satisfied to put these his notes forth in the Latin tongue, but desired also some of our godly brethren to communicate them with his countrymen in their own language, which as it hath been godly intended, so I am sure it will be performed as the Lord will. Which thing was no small moving to me, considering as great want in mine own countrymen and as great profit which may I trust rise unto them by it, if they can be as content to take pains to read as I have taken the labour to write, only for conscience sake and in the fear of God, to make them partakers of that commodity which I myself and many mo[re] of my learned brethren have felt by this so singular blessing of our merciful Father and Lord God, through the tender care that this most reverend father and loving

brother Theodore Beza had of us.[10] This I thought myself of duty bound unto, being no otherways so presently able to help them, not minding to prevent any other men's doing, for I heard not of any that was or would go about it, but tendering only the profit of the more simple and unlearned which are as desirous of instruction as I would instruction were ready for them, and respecting that, that I must be called to an account for in the day of our Lord Jesus. This reason of my doing, I say, I have to give and testify to all the world, if it be not so much as I might have done, as happily some will say. I stay myself upon the testimony of a good conscience before God, being assured that herein I have not done amiss, craving pardon at the Lord's hands for all my wants, as well of duty as of other things in what other respects and parts of my life soever. What profit shall come of it? I leave that to the Lord, for neither the planter nor the waterer is anything, but God that giveth the increase,[11] and yet I doubt not but it shall do that good which the Lord hath appointed it for.

05. The enemies will take occasion to stumble at it and that is one profit, for Christ was made for the fall of many,[12] other I trust shall receive comfort by it, for the same is a Saviour to his. As all men have not faith, so all men shall not receive it,[13] and therein as no man can marvel, so I cannot be grieved, for they that are such are prepared to destruction.[14] Only my purpose was, and mine earnest prayer to God is, that if not all, yet many may receive comfort of it to their immortality; as for the rest, if the Lord hath so appointed it, that I should be a savour of death unto death to them,[15] and this my pains taken should be a furtherance to their hardening, as I go not about to seek out his unspeakable counsel, so all laud and praise be to his name for it. Howbeit I determine of none but unto them that have this sign of reprobation, this I say, and I call heaven and earth to witness against them this day, that if they go forward in this striving against God they shall

---

[10] (1519-1605). He was John Calvin's successor at Geneva (from 1564) and the greatest Biblical scholar of his age. Tomson translated the notes that he prepared for his 1565 edition of the New Testament and updated the English text of the Geneva Bible to correspond with Beza's emendations.

[11] 1 Corinthians 3:6.

[12] Luke 2:34.

[13] See 1 Timothy 4:1; Matthew 17:20 and Matthew 25:26-30.

[14] Philippians 3:9; 2 Thessalonians 1:9; Matthew 7:13; 2 Peter 3:16; Jude 13.

[15] 2 Corinthians 2:16.

undoubtedly perish, and this my labour shall be a witness against them in that day. For he that refuseth to hear the word preached and will not read it, if God have given him that gift that he may read it, pronounceth sentence against himself, that he is none of the children of God, that he is none of the sheep of Christ, that he hath no part of inheritance in that kingdom which was prepared for us before the beginning of the world. For doth not Christ say: *'My sheep hear my voice,'*[16] and doth not Paul say: *'Faith is by hearing, and hearing by the word of God?'*[17] We are not Christ's then if we will not hear and we cannot have faith if the word do not sound under us, and look – where faith is not, there is no Christianity, there is no life, there is no salvation, and if no life, if no salvation, then no Christ, no God, for God is not the God of the dead but of the living,[18] and live without faith we cannot, and to have faith without the word it is impossible,[19] as the Apostle speaketh of the ordinary way of our salvation; if it otherways fall out by way of revelation, it is rather by way of miracle and of a special grace which may not cause us to tempt the Lord in forsaking his appointed way.

06. David, speaking of the blessedness of the happy man (and there is no happy man but the child of God) setteth down this (we know) as a chiefest point of his happiness, that he studieth upon the law of the Lord both day and night.[20] And this is not left unto us as a point to be ordered at our discretion, as who would say we may be happy with it and we may be blessed without it; no, not so, it is a thing very requisite and necessary for them which have the gift, as without which they shall not be blessed. For how can we receive a gift of the Lord and not give an account for it? And what is he so void of the Spirit of God that knoweth not how he must repent him of his slackness in using any good blessing of God and call for pardon and mercy, that his negligence may not be imputed to him? And is there any repentance without a sin? Can I crave pardon at God's hands for that wherein I have not offended? Thy very calling for mercy (O man) whatsoever thou art, argueth and telleth thy conscience thou hast sinned therein, and if thou see, it

---

[16] John 10:27.
[17] Romans 10:17.
[18] Matthew 22:23.
[19] Romans 10:17.
[20] Psalm 1:1-2.

must be so as thy latter end, if God give thee space and grace to repent, consider it betime with thyself, make thy reckoning now, that if thou wilt be blessed, thou must meditate and study in the Scriptures of thy Lord and God both day and night. If thou remember the recreation of thy body with some lawful pleasures, forget not the refreshing of thy soul with this heavenly food. Let not God's goodness towards thee in giving thee some liberty cause thee to become unmindful and ungrate to him, and deadly enemy to thyself.

07. Our dutifulness herein, and how much God requireth at our hands, is set forth herein, that in the law written by Moses all fathers are commanded to teach it their children, to speak of it, sitting at home and going abroad, to write it upon the posts of their houses, to make them frontlets of it and hems of their garments.[21] And shall we think that this law perished with them? Because we are not Jews, are we not therefore God's people? No doubt it is written for our instruction, for all things that are written, saith the Apostle, are written for our learning.[22] And what then shall we learn hereby, yea, what thing must we learn hereby, but as we have heard and read in David, that if we will be blessed, we must meditate in it both day and night, both for ourselves and for our children, for our brethren, for our families. Hereupon also the Apostle reneweth the commandment and refresheth the charge to all Christians of what estate, order, calling, condition soever they be, saying: 'Let the word of God dwell in you plenteously in all wisdom.'[23] Harken, you loathsome hearts, and give ear, you that will needs bear about with you this open mark of reprobation, think you that this is spoken to you? For if you be not within the compass of this saying of the Apostle, you are not within the compass of everlasting life. Are you, or do you take yourselves to be of the number of them, in whom the word of God must dwell plenteously? How shall it come to dwell in you? How shall it take possession of you? Can you tell what dwelling meaneth? It is to have full possession and a mansion house in you, to sit and rest there, to rule and govern there, as you do in your houses and places of your own abode. And how shall this be

---

[21] Deuteronomy 11:18-20.
[22] 2 Timothy 3:16.
[23] Colossians 3:16.

but by that ordinary means which God hath appointed you, which is by reading and hearing? It cometh not by idleness and worldly vanities, it cometh not by dicing and carding, dancing and dalliance, it cometh not by chambering and wantonness; this is not the way to have the word of God to dwell in you. You must search the Scriptures. Do you think to have eternal life? You must look into them, '*search the Scriptures*,' saith Christ, '*for they bear witness of me.*'[24] But you pass[25] not for him; if you did, you would never be so careless of yourselves and careful to serve the devil. I say you are careful to serve the devil when you rise up early and go late to bed, when you leave no labour nor pains to seek after the pleasures of the flesh and cannot abide to hear of the word, you cannot abide, I say, once to look upon it, it is death to you to hear a preacher once in a twelvemonth.

08. And yet you will be called Abraham's children. He that should say otherways of you should have the defiance given him, but the truth is, you are not his children unless you follow his steps. And what saith the Scripture of him? I know that he will command his sons and his household after him that they keep the way of the Lord.[26] Which of you hath a care to that? Or how can you have a care to it, if you know them not? And how can you know them without reading or preaching? Cornelius was a true child of Abraham, he feared God and all his household.[27] So was Eunice, Timothy's mother and Lois his grandmother, and see what her practice was.[28] Being but a woman, she nourished up her son in the words of faith and of good doctrine. Which of you can bring up his child in doctrine and knoweth none himself? Or how wilt thou have thy child follow that which thou hatest thyself? It cannot be. Such grapes cannot be gathered of such thorns, nor such figs of these thistles[29]. They of Beroea were right children of Abraham and famous fellows, so saith the Scriptures, and what for? 'For they received the word with all readiness and searched the Scriptures daily, whether those things were so.[30] Why then are

---

[24] John 5:39.
[25] 'Care'.
[26] Genesis 18:19.
[27] Acts 10:1-2.
[28] 2 Timothy 1:5.
[29] Matthew 7:16.
[30] Acts 17:11.

you but bastards and no children, shameful in your name and hateful to all the world? For where is your readiness in receiving the word, where is your daily searching the Scriptures? '*Give attendance to reading*,'[31] saith Paul to Timothy, and again: '*Continue in learning, for in doing this thou shalt both save thy life and them that hear thee.*'[32] And this is not a precept for ministers only, but generally for all men. '*For thou shalt save thyself,*' saith he; other I am sure will be partakers of salvation as well as they, it is not proper to them only to be saved, no more is it to them also to read the Scriptures.

09. So then, if it be a commandment to him, it is to us all because we will all be saved. Wilt thou be saved then? Then must thou read and hear the Scriptures. Thou must have it dwell plenteously in thee[33]. By dwelling plenteously, the Apostle meaneth thou must be cunning and persist in it, both for the knowledge of it to instruct thyself and other and also for the framing of thy life after it. To you it is, to you, I say, which are not ministers, whom the Apostle speaketh unto, to you that are troubled with worldly affairs, you especially must read the Scriptures and read them with great diligence. The more enemies a man hath, the better he ought to be armed. None have more enemies than the worldly men. Which of you goeth forth to battle and putteth not on his armour? The armed commonly overcome and are saved, and not the unarmed. And who needeth the physician more than he that is most wounded? I will not enter into comparison, whether of you is in most danger, the minister I mean or the other that is no minister. I would rather with you to consider it yourselves, that so by entering into yourselves, you might feel what need of armour you have, what need of a physician. But this I will say, because you feel it to your smart, where it pleaseth God to visit you. When any temptation falleth upon you, as if it please the Lord to strike you with sickness, with lameness, to take away your children, your goods and those things which you love best, instead of comforting yourselves and humbly submitting yourselves to the mighty hand of God, you fall to murmuring against him, you fall to desperation, you remain comfortless, you cannot raise up your

---

[31] 1 Timothy 4:13.
[32] 1 Timothy 4:16.
[33] Colossians 3:16.

own hearts nor the hearts of your brethren which are proved with the like temptation.

10. What a lamentable case is it to see one of your haters and despisers of the word of God, to come to a sick man to comfort him, yea, to your own wives and children, to your friends and acquaintances, miserable is the comfort God wot[34] that you give him, you stand like blocks and stocks, not knowing how to direct him, thus showing forth your condemnation, being nearer to hell than he is to the grave and to everlasting death than he is to this bodily death. You can pretend[35] no excuse but only that you are not learned, and why are you not learned (I speak to you that can read) seeing you have the Scriptures in your own tongue? Your common pretence in former times hath been because they were hard, though that excuse be none, for some of you that can read have travailed in harder, I am sure, and for the rest, this I say, that the harder it is the more pains you ought to have bestowed in it. For if you be resolved as you ought to be, that you are bound to know your Father's will, the hardness of it will not cause you to forsake your duty. I will refer you but to your own judgements. What is he amongst you that if, in his father's last will and testament, by the benefit whereof he looketh to enjoy his father's lands, there were some one clause hard, would not you be diligent in searching it out by reading and reading again, by conferring with other more learned than himself, by having the judgement of the best lawyers? So that in our causes or earthly matters hardness cannot but cause us to use more diligence.

11. So should it be, yea, so would it be in this will and testament, whereby our hope is to come to the inheritance of everlasting life, if any one clause of it should be hard, that should not cause an hardness of heart to cast off the care of the whole, and utterly to surcease from looking upon it. But this showeth, as I said, what we are. For if we were children and not bastards, we would have as great a care to it, for all the hardness, as we have to an earthly will. Well it hath pleased God in this our latter age to remove this cloak. The Scriptures are made plain unto us and this New Testament, by these notes of Beza, so plain both for the meaning itself of every sentence and for the plain light of every word and

---

[34] 'Knows'.
[35] 'Offer'.

kind of speech, that no man can pretend that former excuse. I dare avouch it, and who so readeth it shall so find it, that there is not one hard sentence nor dark speech nor doubtful word but is so opened and hath such light given it, that children may go through with it and the simplest that are, may walk without any guide, without wandering and going astray. So that if thou wilt not still harden thine own heart and purchase wrath unto thyself against the day of wrath, thou must now come and take better ways and show forth better fruits than thou hast done. But haply[36] thou wilt pretend corruption and say that the Scriptures are falsified with these corrections and marred with these glosses.

12. Thus indeed, Antichrist saith, but thou hast to follow the counsel of the Holy Ghost by the mouth of the apostles, try the spirits, whether they be of God or no[37]. Thou must examine them and confer them first with the Scriptures, before thou condemn them, for so did they of Beroea, and so did the Samaritans, as we read in John.[38] For unless thou hear Christ himself speak in his word and confer those things that are laid before thee with the Scripture, thou shalt be deceived. Thou knowest even in worldly affairs, for a man to condemn another before he have heard him is a great point of rashness and disallowed of all men, and he that will give his judgement upon a matter before he have well weighed it, carrieth about him the name of a fool. But if according to the hardness of thine heart which cannot repent, thou wilt not come to better ways and meanest to remain still in like loathing of the Scriptures, and for slacking thy duty therein as thou hast done in former times, I pronounce the wrath and vengeance of God against thee and tell thee from the Lord's mouth, thou shalt have no part in the inheritance of the righteous[39]. And as for you, my poor brethren, which have tasted and felt the loving mercies of our good and gracious Lord and Father, and have entered into a league with him, to take him to be your God as he hath taken you to be his people, receive you this benefit of the Lord as my trust is you will, with joyful hearts.

13. Be mindful to give thanks to the Lord for this worthy brother of

---

[36] 'Perhaps'.
[37] 1 John 4:1.
[38] John 4:19-25.
[39] Ephesians 5:5.

ours and pray for his continuance amongst us in his church, that we may be further enriched by his means and receive greater comforts of the Lord by the hands of his servant. I will not stand[40] to commend this work unto you, both for the faithfulness of the translation and for the singular profit of the notes, the commodity which I know undoubtedly you shall reap thereby will commend it sufficiently to your godly hearts. The thankfulness that you can show both to God for him, and to him for his pains, is the diligent and painful reading of that which he hath diligently and painfully written. If otherwise it should fall out, which I hope will not, you should fall into the condemnation of the wicked and turn this blessing of the Lord to your hurt and destruction. And as you shall think yourselves bound to him for thus opening the Scriptures of God unto you, so be you mindful to pray for them by whose godly means they come to your hands. This door hath been shut up a great while you know; be thankful therefore to God and pray for the long life and happy reign of our most dreadful[41] sovereign Elizabeth, by God's gracious and loving mercies towards this his church of England our most lawful and only prince, our true anointed of the Lord and mother of this Israel. As the Lord hath preserved her Majesty mightily these years past from the treacherous treasons of traitorous and bloodthirsty dissembling hypocrites' hearts, so it may please him to continue his fatherly protection towards her and discover all counterfeits and pluck away all visards[42] from their faces, that her Majesty may see indeed who are her enemies, and he through his mighty power confound and bring them to shame that either with heart or hand intend or mean anything against her.

14. And let all such as fear the Lord say with David touching God's enemies and her Majesty's: '*Pour out thy wrath O Lord upon the people that have not known thee, and upon the kingdoms that have not called upon thy name.*'[43] Be thankful also and pray for the honourable council by whose good means under her Majesty you enjoy this benefit and shall do greater, if with thankful hearts you turn unfeignedly to the Lord and pray for the increasing of his graces in them whom he hath placed as under-shepherds over

---

[40] 'Hesitate'.
[41] In the older sense of inspiring obedience.
[42] 'Visors, masks.'
[43] Psalm 79:6.

this his house of Israel.

15. And for mine own part, as I shall I trust remain mindful all the days of my life with earnest and hearty prayer, first for her Majesty and her long and blessed reign over us with all peace and quietness, to the destruction of all her enemies, both open and dissembling, which seek their own wealth more than her Majesty's health, and next for her most honourable council, that as good fathers they may rule over us as children and not as servants, so to your honour, as I am most bound, I present this testimony of mine hearty good will and meaning towards you, being ready to perform all the dutifulness to your honour which the Lord shall give me, both in prayer to him for your health and increase of zeal to the maintenance of his kingdom, which is the only project of your honour and the mark you have to shoot at. And as in duty I have and am bound to your worship for the great courtesies I have received of you not a few years, and for the fear of God which I see in you, which the Lord increase to the honour of his name and to be a light to the brethren, so I join you herein, in one poor and simple remembrance of my good will, being not able by several gifts to show how much I think myself in debt to you. The thing itself I know is great, but my labour but final, for my chiefest respect was to further and help the more simple sort. God grant that it may be profitable to them, and that his children may reap that commodity by it, which my prayer is they shall. Then shall I think myself blessed of the Lord and thank him heartily for his Fatherly goodness towards me, with earnest prayer to him for your honour and worship, that his peace may remain upon you for ever, and upon all the Israel of God.

10. Preface to the Reims New Testament, 1582

The preface to the reader, treating of these three points: of the translation of Holy Scriptures into the vulgar tongues, and namely into English, of the causes why this New Testament is translated according to the ancient vulgar Latin text, and of the manner of translating the same.

01. The Holy Bible long since translated by us into English, and the Old Testament lying by us for lack of good means to publish the whole in such sort as a work of so great charge and importance requireth, we have yet through God's goodness at length fully finished for thee (most Christian reader) all the New Testament, which is the principal, most profitable and comfortable piece of Holy Writ, and as well for all other institution of life and doctrine, as specially for deciding the doubts of these days, more proper and pregnant than the other part not yet printed.

02. Translation of the Scriptures into the vulgar tongues, not absolutely necessary or profitable, but according to the time.

    Which translation we do not for all that publish, upon erroneous opinion of necessity, that the Holy Scriptures should always be in our mother tongue, or that they ought, or were ordained by God, to be read indifferently of all, or could be easily understood of everyone that readeth or heareth them in a known language, or that they were not often through man's malice or infirmity, pernicious and much hurtful to many; or that we generally and absolutely deemed it more convenient in itself, and more agreeable to God's Word and honour, or edification of the faithful, to have them turned into vulgar tongues, than to be kept and studied only in the ecclesiastical learned languages; not for these nor any such like causes do we translate this sacred book, but upon special consideration of the present time, state and condition of our country, unto which divers things are either necessary, or profitable and medicinable now, that otherwise in the peace of the Church were neither much requisite, nor perchance wholly tolerable.

03. The Church's wisdom and moderation concerning vulgar translation.

    In this matter, to mark only the wisdom and moderation of holy

Church and the governors thereof on the one side, and the indiscreet zeal of the popular, and their factious leaders on the other, is a high point of prudence. These later, partly of simplicity, partly of curiosity, and specially of pride and disobedience, have made claim in this case for the common people, with plausible pretences many, but good reasons none at all. The other, to whom Christ hath given charge of our souls, the dispensing of God's mysteries and treasures (among which Holy Scripture is no small store) and the feeding his family in season with food fit for every sort, have neither of old nor of late ever wholly condemned all vulgar versions of Scripture, nor have at any time generally forbidden the faithful to read the same; yet they have not by public authority prescribed, commanded or authentically ever recommended any such interpretation to be indifferently used of all men.

04. The Scriptures in the vulgar languages of divers nations.

The Armenians say they have the Psalter and some other pieces translated by St John Chrysostom into their language, when he was banished among them. And George the Patriarch, in writing his life, signifieth no less.[1] The Slavonians affirm they have the Scriptures in their vulgar tongue, turned by St Jerome, and some would gather so much by his own words in his epistle to Sophronius, but the place indeed proveth it not.[2] Ulfilas [Wulfila] surely gave the Scriptures to the Goths in their own tongue, and that before he was an Arian.[3]

05. Ancient Catholic translations of the Bible into the Italian, French and English tongue.

It is almost three hundred years since James, Archbishop of Genoa, is said to have translated the Bible into Italian.[4] More than two hundred years ago, in the days of Charles V the French King, was it put forth faithfully in French, the sooner to shake out of the

---

[1] The life of St John Chrysostom attributed to Patriarch George of Alexandria (620-30) is of no historical value.
[2] Jerome, *Praefatio in librum Psalmorum iuxta Hebraicam veritatem* (PL 28, coll. 1124-5).
[3] Wulfila did produce a Gothic Bible in the fourth century, but he was already an Arian.
[4] Jacopo de Voragine was archbishop of Genoa (1292-8) but although he was reputed to have translated the Bible into Italian, there has never been any sign of it.

deceived people's hands the false heretical translations of the sect called Waldenses.⁵

06. An ancient provincial constitution in England concerning English translations.

In our own country, notwithstanding the Latin tongue was ever (to use Venerable Bede's words) common to all the provinces of the same for meditation or study of Scriptures,⁶ and no vulgar translation commonly used or occupied of the multitude, yet they were extant in English even before the troubles that Wycliffe and his followers raised in our church,⁷ as appeareth as well by the testimony of Malmesbury, recording that Venerable Bede translated divers parts into the vulgar tongue of his time, and by some pieces yet remaining,⁸ as by a provincial constitution of Thomas Arundel, Archbishop of Canterbury in a council holden at Oxford.⁹ Where straight provision was made that no heretical version set forth by Wycliffe, or his adherents, should be suffered, nor any other in or after his time be published or permitted to be read, being not approved and allowed by the diocesan before; alleging St Jerome for the difficulty and danger of interpreting the Holy Scripture out of one tongue into another, though by learned and Catholic men. So also it is there insinuated that neither the translations set forth before that heretic's time, nor other afterward being approved by the lawful ordinaries, were ever in our country wholly forbidden, though they were not (to say the truth) in quiet and better times (much less when the people were prone to alteration, heresy or novelty) either hastily admitted, or ordinarily read of the vulgar, but used only or specially of some devout religious and contemplative persons, in reverence, secrecy and silence, for their spiritual comfort.

07. The like Catholic and vulgar translations in many countries, since Luther's time.

Now since Luther's revolt also, divers learned Catholics, for the more speedy abolishing of a number of false and impious

---

⁵ The translation by Raoul de Presles done in 1377 and dedicated to King Charles V (1364-80).
⁶ Bede, *Historia ecclesiastica* I, 1 (PL 95, col. 26).
⁷ The Lollard movement. See the introduction.
⁸ William of Malmesbury, *Gesta regum Anglorum* I, 60 (PL 179, col. 1017).
⁹ In 1407. See the introduction.

translations put forth by sundry sects, and for the better preservation or reclaim of many good souls endangered thereby, have published the Bible in the several languages of almost all the principal provinces of the Latin Church, no other books in the world being so pernicious as heretical translations of the Scriptures, poisoning the people under colour of divine authority, and not many other remedies being more sovereign against the same (if it be used in order, discretion and humility) than the true, faithful and sincere interpretation opposed thereunto.

08. The Church's order and determination concerning the reading of Catholic translations of the Bible in vulgar tongues.

Which causeth the holy Church not to forbid utterly any Catholic translation, though she allow not the publishing or reading of any absolutely and without exception or limitation; knowing by her divine and most sincere wisdom how, where, when and to whom these her Master's and Spouse's gifts are to be bestowed to the most good of the faithful; and therefore neither generally permitteth that which must needs do hurt to the unworthy, nor absolutely condemneth that which may do much good to the worthy. Whereupon, the order which many a wise man wished for before, was taken by the deputies of the late famous Council of Trent in this behalf, and confirmed by supreme authority, that the Holy Scriptures, though truly and catholicly translated into vulgar tongues, yet may not be indifferently[10] read of all men, nor of any other than such as have express licence thereunto of their lawful ordinaries, with good testimony from their curates or confessors, that they be humble, discreet and devout persons, and likely to take much good and no harm thereby.[11] Which prescript, though in these days of ours it cannot be so precisely observed, as in other times and places where there is more due respect of the church's authority, rule and discipline; yet we trust all wise and godly persons will use the matter in the meanwhile, with such moderation, meekness and subjection of heart, as the handling of so sacred a book, the sincere senses of God's truth therein, and the holy canons, councils, reason and religion do require.

---

[10] 'Indiscriminately'.
[11] Council of Trent, session 4, 8 April 1546 (second decree).

09. The Holy Scriptures never read of all persons indifferently, at their pleasure.

Wherein, though for due preservation of this divine work from abuse and profanation, and for the better bridling of the intolerable insolency of proud, curious and contentious wits, the governors of the church, guided by God's Spirit, as ever before, so also upon more experience of the malady of this time than before, have taken more exact order both for the readers and translations in these later ages, than of old; yet we must not imagine that in the primitive church, either everyone that understood the learned tongues wherein the Scriptures were written, or other languages into which they were translated, might without reprehension read, reason, dispute, turn and toss the Scriptures; or that our forefathers suffered every schoolmaster, scholar or grammarian that had a little Greek or Latin, straight to take in hand the holy Testament; or that the translated Bibles into the vulgar tongues were in the hands of every husbandman, artificer, apprentice, boys, girls, mistress, maid, man; that they were sung, played, alleged, of every tinker, taverner, rhymer, minstrel; that they were for table talk, for ale benches, for boats and barges, and for every profane person and company. No, in those better times men were neither so ill, nor so curious of themselves, so to abuse the blessed book of Christ; neither was there any such easy means before printing was invented, to disperse the copies into the hands of every man, as now there is.

10. Where and in whose hands the Scriptures were in the primitive church.

They were then in libraries, monasteries, colleges, churches, in bishops', priests' and some other devout principal laymen's houses and hands; who used them with fear and reverence, and specially such parts as pertained to good life and manners, not meddling, but in pulpit and schools (and that moderately, too) with the hard and high mysteries and places of greater difficulty.

11. How the laity of those days did read them, with what humility and religion, and information of life and manners.

The poor ploughman could then, in labouring the ground, sing the hymns and psalms either in known or unknown languages, as they heard them in the holy Church, though they could neither read nor know the sense, meaning and mysteries of the same. Such holy persons of both sexes to whom St Jerome in divers epistles to them commendeth the reading and meditation of Holy Scriptures, were diligent to search all the godly histories and imitable examples of chastity, humility, obedience, clemency, poverty, penance, renouncing the world; they noted specially the places that did breed the hatred of sin, fear of God's judgement, delight in spiritual cogitations; they referred themselves in all hard places to the judgement of the ancient fathers and their masters in religion, never presuming to contend, control, teach or talk of their own sense and fantasy, in deep questions of divinity. Then the virgins did meditate upon the places and examples of chastity, modesty and demureness; the married, on conjugal faith and continency; the parents, how to bring up their children in faith and fear of God; the prince, how to rule; the subject, how to obey; the priest, how to teach; the people, how to learn.

12. The Fathers sharply reprehend as an abuse, that all indifferently should read, expound and talk of the Scriptures.

Then the scholar taught not his master, the sheep controlled not the pastor, the young student set not the doctor to school, nor reproved their fathers of error and ignorance. Or if any were in those better days (as in all times of heresy such must needs be) that had itching ears, tickling tongues and wits, curious and contentious disputers, hearers and talkers, rather than doers of God's Word; such the fathers did ever sharply reprehend, counting them unworthy and unprofitable readers of the Holy Scriptures. St Jerome, in his epistle to Paulinus,[12] after declaration that no handicraft is so base, nor liberal science so easy that can be had without a master (which St Augustine also affirmeth,)[13] nor that men presume in any occupation to teach that which they never learned, 'Only,' saith he, 'the art of Scripture is that which every man challengeth; this the chatting old wife, this the doting old man, this the brabling sophister, this on every hand, men presume to teach before they learn it.' Again: 'Some with poise of lofty words devise of Scripture matters among women; othersome (fie upon it!) learn of women what to teach men; and lest that be not enough, by facility of tongue or rather audacity, teach that to others which they understand never a whit themselves. To say nothing of such as be of my faculty; who stepping from secular

---

[12] Jerome, *Epistula* LIII, 7 (PL 22, col. 544).
[13] Augustine, *De utilitate credendi* 7 (PL 42, coll. 75-8).

learning to Holy Scriptures, and able to tickle the ears of the multitude with smooth tale[14], think all they speak to be the law of God.' This he wrote then, when this malady of arrogancy and presumption in divine matters was nothing so outrageous as now it is.

13. The Scriptures must be delivered in measure and discretion, according to each man's need and capacity.

St Gregory Nazianzene made an oration of the moderation that was to be used in these matters;[15] where he saith that some in his time thought themselves to have all the wisdom in the world, when they could once repeat two or three words, and them ill couched together, out of Scriptures; but he there divinely discourseth of the orders and differences of degrees; how in Christ's mystical body some are ordained to learn, some to teach; that all are not apostles, all doctors, all interpreters, all of tongues and knowledge, not all learned in Scriptures and divinity;[16] that the people went not up to talk with God in the mountain, but Moses, Aaron and Eleazar;[17] nor they neither, but by the difference of their callings; that they that rebel against this ordinance are guilty of the conspiracy of Korah and his accomplices;[18] that in Scripture there is both milk for babes and meat for men, to be dispensed, not according to everyone's greediness of appetite or wilfulness, but as is most meet for each one's necessity and capacity;[19] that as it is a shame for a bishop or priest to be unlearned in God's mysteries, so for the common people it is oftentimes profitable to salvation, not to be curious, but to follow their pastors in sincerity and simplicity; whereof excellently saith St Augustine: *Fidei simplicitate et sinceritate lactati nutriamur in Christo: et cum parvi sumus, maiorum cibos non appetamus*, that is: 'Being fed with the simplicity and sincerity of faith, as it were with milk, so let us be nourished in Christ, and when we are little ones, let us not covet the meats of the elder sort.'[20] Who in

---

[14] 'Talk'.
[15] Gregory of Nazianzus, *Oratio* XXXII (PG 36, coll. 173-212).
[16] 1 Corinthians 12:28-9; Ephesians 4:11
[17] Exodus 19:23-4; Numbers 20:25-9.
[18] Numbers 16:1-35.
[19] Hebrews 5:12-14.
[20] Augustine, *De agone Christiano* XXXIII, 35 (PL 40, coll. 309-10).

another place[21] testifieth that the Word of God cannot be preached, nor certain mysteries uttered to all men alike, but are to be delivered according to the capacities of the hearers; as he proveth both by St Paul's example, who gave not to every sort strong meat, but milk to many,[22] as being not spiritual, but carnal and not capable; and by our Lord's also, who spake to some plainly and to others in parables,[23] and affirmed that he had many things to utter which the hearers were not able to bear.[24]

How much more may we gather, that all things that be written, are not for the capacity and diet of every of the simple readers, but that very many mysteries of Holy Writ be very far above their reach, and may and ought to be (by as great reason) delivered them in measure and mean most meet for them? Which indeed can hardly be done, when the whole book of the Bible lieth before every man in his mother tongue, to make choice of what he list.[25]

14. The Jews' law for not reading certain books of Holy Scripture until a time.

For which cause the said Gregory Nazianzene wisheth the Christians had as good a law as the Hebrews of old had;[26] who, as St Jerome also witnesseth, took order among themselves that none should read the *Cantica Canticorum* [Song of Songs], nor certain other pieces of hardest Scriptures till they were thirty years of age.[27] And truly there is no cause why men should be more loth to be ordered and moderated in this point by God's Church and their pastors, than they are in the use of the holy sacraments; for which as Christ hath appointed priests and ministers at whose hands we must receive them, and not be our own carvers; so hath he given us doctors, prophets, expounders, interpreters, teachers and preachers, to take the law and our faith at their mouths; because our faith and religion cometh not to us properly or principally by reading of Scriptures, but (as the Apostle saith)[28] by

---

[21] Augustine, *De dono perseverantiae* XVI, 40 (PL 45, coll. 1017-18); *De Genesi ad litteram* VII, 9 (PL 34, col. 560); *Homiliae in Iohannem* XVIII, 5 (PL 35, col. 1545).
[22] 1 Corinthians 3:2.
[23] Luke 8:10.
[24] John 16:12.
[25] 'Wishes.'
[26] Gregory of Nazianzus, *Oratio* XXXII, 32 (PG 36, coll. 209-12).
[27] Jerome, *In Ezechielem prologus* (PL 25, coll. 15-17).
[28] Romans 10:17.

hearing of the preachers lawfully sent; though reading in order and humility, much confirmeth and advanceth the same. Therefore this holy book of the Scriptures is called of St Ambrose *liber sacerdotalis* (the book of priests), at whose hands and disposition we must take and use it.[29]

15. The popular objections of withholding the Scriptures from the people answered.

The wise will not here regard what some wilful people do mutter, that the Scriptures are made for all men, and that it is of envy that the priests do keep the holy book from them. Which suggestion cometh of the same serpent that seduced our first parents, who persuaded them that God had forbidden them that tree of knowledge, lest they should be as cunning as himself, and like unto the Highest.[30]

16. Why the church permitteth not everyone at their pleasure to read the Scripture.

No, no, the church doth it to keep them from blind ignorant presumption and from that which the Apostle calleth *falsi nominis scientiam*, 'knowledge falsely so called';[31] and not to embar them from the true knowledge of Christ. She would have all wise, but *usque ad sobrietatem*, 'unto sobriety,' as the Apostle speaketh;[32] she knoweth the Scriptures be ordained for every state, as meats, elements, fire, water, candle, knives, sword and the like; which are as needful (most of them) for children as old folks, for the simple as the wise; but yet would mar all, if they were at the guiding of other than wise men, or were in the hands of everyone, for whose preservation they be profitable.

17. The Holy Scriptures to carnal men and heretics, are as pearls to swine.

She forbiddeth not the reading of them in any language, envieth no man's commodity, but giveth order how to do it to edification and not destruction; how to do it without casting 'the holy to dogs'

---

[29] Ambrose, *De fide ad Gratianum* III, 15, 128 (PL 16, col. 615).
[30] Genesis 3:5.
[31] 1 Timothy 6:20.
[32] Romans 12:3.

or 'pearls to hogs';[33] (see St John Chrysostom, declaring these hogs and dogs to be carnal men and heretics, that take no good of the holy mysteries, but thereby do both hurt themselves and others;)[34] how to do it agreeably to the sovereign sincerity, majesty and depth of mystery contained in the same. She would have the presumptuous heretic, notwithstanding he allege them never so fast, flying as it were through the whole Bible, and quoting the Psalms, Prophets, Gospels, Epistles, never so readily for his purpose, as Vincentius Lirinensis [Vincent of Lérins] saith such men's fashion is;[35] yet she would, according to Tertullian's rule, have such mere usurpers quite discharged of all occupying and possession of the holy Testament, which is her old and only right of inheritance, and belongeth not to heretics at all,[36] whom Origen called *Scripturarum fures*, 'thieves of the Scriptures'.[37] She would have the unworthy repelled, the curious repressed, the simple measured, the learned humbled, and all sorts so to use them or abstain from them, as is most convenient for everyone's salvation; with this general admonition, that none can understand the meaning of God in the Scriptures except Christ open their sense (Luke 24:27,45), and make them partakers of his Holy Spirit in the unity of his mystical body; and for the rest, she committeth it to the pastor of every province and people, according to the difference of time, place and persons, how and in what sort the reading of the Scriptures is more or less to be procured or permitted.

18. St Chrysostom's exhortations to the reading of Holy Scriptures, and when the people is to be so exhorted.

Wherein, the variety of circumstances causeth them to deal diversely; as we see by St Chrysostom's people of Constantinople, who were so delicate, dull, worldly and so much given to dice, cards, specially stage plays or theatres (as St Gregory Nazianzene witnesseth;)[38] that the Scriptures and all holy lections of divine things were loathsome unto them; whereby their holy bishop was forced in many of his sermons to cry out against their extreme

---

[33] Matthew 7:6.
[34] John Chrysostom, *Homiliae in Matthaeum* XXIII/XXIV, 3 (PG 57, coll. 310-12).
[35] Vincent of Lérins, *Commonitorium* I, 25 (PL 50, col. 659).
[36] Tertullian, *De praescriptione haereticorum* 15-19 (PL 2, coll. 28-31).
[37] Origen, *Commentary on Romans*, II. 11.11. (PG 14, col. 897).
[38] Gregory of Nazianzus, *Oratio* XXI, 5 (PG 35, col. 1088).

negligence and contempt of God's Word, declaring that not only hermits and religious (as they alleged for their excuse) but secular men of all sorts might read the Scriptures, and often have more need thereof in respect of themselves than the other that live in more purity and contemplation; further insinuating that though divers things be high and hard therein, yet many godly histories, lives, examples, and precepts of life and doctrine be plain; and finally, that when the Gentiles were so cunning and diligent to impugn their faith, it were not good for Christians to be simple or negligent in the defence thereof, as (in truth) it is more requisite for a Catholic man in these days when our adversaries be industrious to impeach our belief, to be skilful in Scriptures, than at other times when the Church had no such enemies.[39]

19. St Chrysostom maketh nothing for the popular and licentious reading of Scriptures used among the Protestants nowadays.

To this sense said St Chrysostom divers things, not as a teacher in school, making exact and general rules to be observed in all places and times, but as a pulpit man, agreeably to that audience and his people's default.

20. Every simple artificer among them readeth much more the deepest and hardest questions of Holy Scripture, than the moral parts.

Not making it therefore (as some perversely gather of his words) a thing absolutely needful for every poor artificer to read or study Scriptures, nor any whit favouring the presumptuous, curious and contentious jangling and searching of God's secrets reproved by the foresaid fathers, much less approving the excessive pride and madness of these days, when every man and woman is become not only a reader but a teacher, controller, and judge of doctors, church, Scriptures and all; such as either contemn or easily pass over all the moral parts, good examples and precepts of life (by which as well the simple as learned might be much edified) and only in a manner, occupy themselves in dogmatical, mystical, high and hidden secrets of God's counsels, as of predestination, reprobation, election, prescience, forsaking of the Jews, vocation of the Gentiles and other incomprehensible

---

[39] Pseudo-John Chrysostom, *Homilia in Matthaeum* II, 5 (PG 56, col. 640). This is from the anonymous *Opus imperfectum*.

mysteries, 'languishing about questions'[40] of only faith, fiducy, new phrases and figures, 'ever learning' but 'never coming to knowledge,'[41] reading and tossing in pride of wit, conceit of their own cunning, and upon presumption of I can tell what spirit, such books especially and epistles, as St Peter foretold that the unlearned and instable would deprave to their own damnation.[42]

21. They presuppose[43] no difficulties, which all the learned Fathers felt to be in the Scriptures.

They delight in none more than the Epistle to the Romans, the *Cantica Canticorum* [Song of Songs], the Apocalypse, which have in them as many mysteries as words. They find no difficulty in the sacred book clasped with seven seals;[44] they ask for no expositor with the holy eunuch,[45] they feel no such depth of God's science in the Scriptures, as St Augustine did, when he cried out: *Mira profunditas eloquiorum tuorum, mira profunditas (Deus meus) mira profunditas: horror est intendere in eam, horror honoris, et tremor amoris*, that is: 'O wonderful profoundness of thy words; wonderful profoundness, my God, wonderful profoundness; it maketh a man quake to look on it, to quake for reverence, and to tremble for the love thereof.'[46] They regard not that which the same doctor affirmeth, that the depth and profundity of wisdom, not only in the words of Holy Scripture, but also in the matter and sense, is so wonderful, that, live a man never so long, be he of never so high a wit, never so studious, never so fervent to attain the knowledge thereof, yet when he endeth, he shall confess he doth but begin.[47] They feel not, with St Jerome, that the text hath a hard shell to be broken before we come to the kernel.[48] They will not stay themselves in only reading the sacred Scriptures thirteen years together, with St Basil and St Gregory Nazianzene, before they expound them, nor take the care (as they did) never otherwise to interpret them, than by the

---

[40] 1 Timothy 6:4.
[41] 2 Timothy 3:7.
[42] 2 Peter 3:16.
[43] 'Allow for'.
[44] Revelation 5:1.
[45] Acts 8:27-38.
[46] Augustine, *Confessiones* XII, 14 (PL 32, col. 832).
[47] Augustine, *Epistulae* 137.3 (PL 33, coll. 516-17).
[48] Jerome, *Epistulae* LVIII, 9 (PL 22, col. 585).

uniform consent of their forefathers and tradition apostolic.

22. Manners and life nothing amended; but much worse, since this licentious tossing of Holy Scriptures.

If our new ministers had had this cogitation and care that these and all other wise men have, and ever had, our country had never fallen to this miserable state in religion, and that under pretence, colour and countenance of God's Word; neither should virtue and good life have been so pitifully corrupted in time of such reading, toiling, trembling and translating the book of our life and salvation; whereof the more precious the right and reverent use is, the more pernicious is the abuse and profanation of the same; which every man of experience by these few years prove, and by comparing the former days and manners to these of ours, may easily try.

Look whether your men be more virtuous, your women more chaste, your children more obedient, your servants more trusty, your maids more modest, your friends more faithful, your laity more just in dealing, your clergy more devout in praying; whether there be more religion, fear of God, faith and conscience in all states now, than of old, when there was not so much reading, chatting and jangling of God's Word, but much more sincere dealing, doing and keeping the same. Look whether through this disorder, women teach not their husbands, children their parents, young fools their old and wise fathers, the scholars their masters, the sheep their pastor, and the people the priest.

23. Scriptures as profanely cited as heathen poets.

Look whether the most chaste and sacred sentences of God's holy Word be not turned of many into mirth, mockery, amorous ballets and detestable letters of love and lewdness; their delicate times, tunes and translations much increasing the same.

24. Scriptures erroneously expounded according to every wicked man's private fantasy.

This fall of good life and profaning the divine mysteries, everybody seeth; but the great corruption and decay of faith hereby none see but wise men, who only know that were the Scriptures never so truly translated, yet heretics and ill men that follow their own spirit, and know nothing but their private fantasy, and not the sense of the holy church and doctors, must needs abuse them to their damnation; and that the curious, simple and sensual men which have no taste of the things that be of the Spirit of God, may of infinite places take occasion of pernicious errors. For though the letter or text (in Mark 10:18) have no error, yet (saith St Ambrose) the Arian, or (as we may now speak) the Calvinian, 'interpretation hath errors.'[49] And Tertullian saith: 'The sense adulterated is as perilous as the style corrupted.'[50] St Hilary also speaketh thus: 'Heresy riseth about the understanding, not about the writing; the fault is in the sense, not in the word.'[51] And St Augustine saith that many hold the Scriptures as they do the sacraments: *ad speciem et non ad salutem*; 'to the outward show and not to salvation.'[52]

25. All heretics pretend Scriptures.

Finally, all sect-masters and ravening wolves, yea the devils themselves pretend Scriptures, allege Scriptures, and wholly shroud themselves in Scriptures, as in the wool and fleece of the simple sheep, whereby the vulgar, in these days of general disputes, cannot but be in extreme danger of error, though their books were truly translated, and were truly in themselves God's own Word indeed.

26. The Scriptures have been falsely and heretically translated into the vulgar tongues, and sundry other ways sacrilegiously abused, and so given to the people to read.

But the case now is more lamentable, for the Protestants, such as St Paul calleth: *ambulantes in astutia*; 'walking in deceitfulness,'[53] have so abused the people, and many other in the world, not unwise, that by their false translations they have, instead of God's Law and Testament, and for Christ's written will and word, given them their own wicked writing and fantasies, most shamefully in all their versions, Latin, English and other tongues, corrupting both the letter and sense by false translation, adding, detracting, altering, transposing, pointing, and all other guileful means; specially where it serveth for the advantage of their private opinions, for which they are bold also, partly to disauthorise quiet,

---

[49] Ambrose, *De fide ad Gratianum* II, 1, 16 (PL 16, col. 563).
[50] Tertullian, *De praescriptione haereticorum* 17 (PL 2, coll. 29-30).
[51] Hilary of Poitiers, *De Trinitate* II, 1 (PL 10, col. 51).
[52] Augustine, *De baptismo contra Donatistas* III, 19 (PL 43, coll. 151-4).
[53] 2 Corinthians 4:2.

partly to make doubtful, divers whole books allowed for canonical Scripture by the universal Church of God this thousand years and upward; to alter all the authentical and ecclesiastical words used since our Christianity into new profane novelties of speeches agreeable to their doctrine; to change the titles of works, to put out the names of the authors, to charge the very Evangelist with following untrue translation (Luke 1:78; Beza), to add whole sentences proper to their sect, into their Psalms in metre, even into the very Creed in rhyme. All which the poor deceived people say and sing as though they were God's own Word, being indeed through such sacrilegious treachery made the Devil's word.

27. All this their dealing is noted (as occasion serveth) in the annotations upon this Testament; and more at large in a book lately made purposely of that matter, called 'A Discovery, etc.'

To say nothing of their intolerable liberty and licence to change the accustomed callings of God, angels, men, places and things used by the Apostles and all antiquity, in Greek, Latin and all other languages of Christian nations, into new names, sometimes falsely, and always ridiculously and for ostentation taken from the Hebrews; to frame and fine the phrases of Holy Scriptures after the form of profane writers, sticking not, for the same to supply, add, alter or diminish as freely as if they translated Livy, Vergil or Terence.

28. Calvin complaineth of the new delicate translators, namely, Castalion; himself and Beza being as bad or worse.

Having no religious respect to keep either the majesty or sincere simplicity of that venerable style of Christ's spirit, as St Augustine speaketh, which kind the Holy Ghost did choose of infinite wisdom to have the divine mysteries rather uttered in, than any other more delicate, much less in that meretricious manner of writing that sundry of these new translators do use; of which sort Calvin himself and his pew-fellows, so much complain, that they profess Satan to have gained more by these new interpreters (their number, levity of spirit, and audacity increasing daily) than he did before by keeping the word from the people. And for a pattern of this mischief, they give Castalion, adjuring all their churches and scholars to beware of his translation, as one that hath made a very sport and mockery of God's Holy Word. So they charge him themselves (and the Zwinglians of Zürich, whose translations Luther therefore abhorred)[54] handling the matter with no more fidelity, gravity or sincerity than the others; but rather with much more falsification, or (to use the Apostle's words) *cauponation* and *adulteration* of God's Word,[55] than they, besides many wicked glosses, prayers, confessions of faith, containing both blasphemous errors and plain contradictions to themselves and among themselves, all privileged and authorized to be joined to the Bible, and to be said and sung of the poor people, and to be believed as articles of faith and wholly consonant to God's Word.

29. The purpose and commodity of setting forth this Catholic edition.

We therefore, having compassion to see our beloved countrymen, with extreme danger of their souls, to use only such profane translations and erroneous men's mere fantasies, for the pure and blessed word of truth, much also moved thereunto by the desires of many devout persons; have set forth for you (benign readers) the New Testament to begin withal, trusting that it may give occasion to you, after diligent perusal thereof, to lay away at least such their pure versions as hitherto you have been forced to occupy. How well we have done it, we must not be judges, but refer all to God's church and our superiors in the same. To them we submit ourselves, and this, and all other our labours, to be in part or in the whole, reformed, corrected, altered or quite abolished; most humbly desiring pardon if through our ignorance, temerity or other human infirmity, we have anywhere mistaken the sense of the Holy Ghost. Further promising, that if hereafter we espy any of our own errors, or if any other, either friend of good will or adversary for desire of reprehension, shall open unto us the same; we will not (as Protestants do) for defence of our estimation, or of pride and contention, by wrangling words wilfully persist in them, but be most glad to hear of them, and in the next edition or otherwise to correct them; for it is truth that we seek for, and God's honour, which being had either by good intention or by occasion, all is well.

---

[54] This is probably a reference to the dispute between Luther and Zwingli over the true meaning of Jesus' words at the Last Supper: 'This is my body' etc. Luther took them literally, Zwingli symbolically.

[55] 2 Corinthians 2:17.

30. The religious care and sincerity observed in this translation.

This we profess only, that we have done our endeavour with prayer, much fear and trembling, lest we should dangerously err in so sacred, high and divine a work; that we have done it with all faith, diligence and sincerity; that we have used no partiality for the disadvantage of our adversaries, nor no more licence than is sufferable in translating of Holy Scriptures; continually keeping ourselves as near as is possible to our text and to the very words and phrases which by long use are made venerable, though to some profane or delicate ears they may seem more hard and barbarous, as the whole style of Scripture doth lightly to such at the beginning; acknowledging with St Jerome, that in other writings it is enough to give in translation, sense for sense, but that in Scriptures, lest we miss the sense, we must keep the very words.[56] We must, saith St Augustine, speak according to a set rule, lest licence of words breed some wicked opinion concerning the things contained under the words.[57]

31. The ancient Fathers kept religiously the very barbarisms of the vulgar Latin text.

Whereof our holy Fathers and ancient doctors had such a religious care that they would not change the very barbarisms or incongruities of speech which by long use had prevailed in the old readings or recitings of Scriptures, as *neque nubent, neque nubentur,*[58] in Tertullian;[59] St Hilary[60] and in all the fathers. *Qui me confusus fuerit, confundar et ego sum,* in St Cyprian.[61] *Talis enim nobis decebat sacerdos* (which was an older translation than the vulgar Latin that now is) in St Ambrose,[62] and St Jerome himself, who otherwise corrected the Latin translation that was used before his time, yet keepeth religiously (as himself professeth),[63] these and the like speeches. *Nonne vos magis pluris*

---

[56] Jerome, *Ad Pammachium epistola* CI, 2 (PL 22, col. 829).
[57] Augustine, *De civitate Dei* X, 12 (PL 41, col. 291).
[58] 'They neither marry nor are given in marriage', Matthew 22:30; Luke 10:33.
[59] Tertullian, *Adversus Marcionem* IV, 38 (PL 2, coll. 452-5).
[60] Hilary of Poitiers, *In Matthaeum* XXIII, 4 (PL 9, col. 1045).
[61] Jeremiah 20:7. The ungrammatical Latin reads: 'Who has deceived me, I shall be deceived and I am.' Cyprian of Carthage, *De lapsis* 28 (PL 4, col. 488).
[62] Hebrews 7:26. The Old Latin reads: 'Such a high priest suited us.' Ambrose, *De fuga saeculi* 3, 16 (PL 14, col. 577).
[63] Jerome, *Praefatio in quattuor Evangelia* (PL 29, col. 527).

estis illis?[64] and *Filius hominis non venit ministrari, sed ministrare,*[65] and *neque nubent neque nubentur,*[66] in his commentaries upon these places; and, *Non capit prophetam perire extra Hierusalem,*[67] in his commentaries[68] in Joel 2 (*sub finem*). And St Augustine, who is most religious in all these phrases, counteth it a special pride and infirmity in those that have a little learning in tongues, and none in things, that they easily take offence of the simple speeches or solecisms in the Scriptures.[69] See also the same holy father.[70] But of the manner of our translation, more anon.

Now though the text thus truly translated, might sufficiently in the sight of the learned, and all indifferent men, both control the adversaries' corruptions and prove that the Holy Scripture, whereof they have made so great vaunts, make nothing for their new opinions, but wholly for the Catholic church's belief and doctrine, in all the points of difference betwixt us; yet knowing that the good and simple may easily be seduced by some few obstinate persons of perdition (whom we see given over into a reprobate sense, to whom the Gospel, which in itself is the odour of life to salvation, is made the odour of death to damnation, over whose eyes for sin and disobedience God suffereth a veil or cover to lie, whilst they read the New Testament, even as the Apostle saith the Jews have till this day, in reading of the Old ,[71] that as the one sort cannot find Christ in the Scriptures, read they never so much, so the other cannot find the Catholic church nor her doctrine there neither) and finding by experience this saying of St Augustine to be most true: 'If the prejudice of any erroneous persuasion preoccupate the mind, whatsoever the Scripture hath contrary, men take it for a figurative speech.'[72]

---

[64] Matthew 6:26. The Latin reads: 'Are you not more more than these?'
[65] Matthew 20:28; The Latin reads: 'The Son of Man did not come to be ministered, but to minister.' cf. Mark 10:45.
[66] 'They neither marry nor are given in marriage', Matthew 22:30; Luke 10:33.
[67] Luke 10:33. The Latin reads: 'It does not take a prophet to perish outside Jerusalem.'
[68] Jerome, *Commentary on Joel* 2:32 (PL 25, col. 978).
[69] Augustine, *De doctrina Christiana* II, 13 (PL 34, coll. 44-5).
[70] Augustine, *ibid.* III, 3 (PL 34, coll. 67-8) and *Tractatus in Evangelium Iohannis* 2 (PL 35, coll. 1388-96).
[71] 2 Corinthians 3:13-16.
[72] Augustine, *De doctrina Christiana* III, 10, 15 (PL 34, coll. 42, 46).

32. Of the annotations, why they were made and what matter they contain.

For these causes, and somewhat to help the faithful reader in the difficulties of divers places, we have also set forth reasonable annotations, thereby to show the studious reader in most places pertaining to the controversies of this time, both the heretical corruptions and false deductions, and also the apostolic tradition, the expositions of the holy fathers, the decrees of the Catholic church and most ancient councils; which means, whosoever trusteth not, for the sense of Holy Scriptures, but had rather follow his private judgement or the arrogant spirit of these sectaries, he shall worthily through his own wilfulness be deceived; beseeching all men to look with diligence, sincerity and indifferency, into the case that concerneth no less than everyone's eternal salvation or damnation.

33. Heresies make Catholics more diligent to search and find the senses of Holy Scripture for repelling the same.

Which if he do, we doubt not but he shall to his great contentment, find the Holy Scriptures most clearly and invincibly to prove the articles of Catholic doctrine against our adversaries, which perhaps he had thought before this diligent search, either not to be consonant to God's Word, or at least not contained in the same, and finally he shall prove this saying of St Augustine to be most true. *Multi sensus*, etc.; Many senses of Holy Scriptures lie hidden, and are known to some few of greater understanding; neither are they at any time avouched more commodiously and acceptably than at such times, when the care to answer heretics doth force men thereunto. For then, even they that be negligent in matters of study and learning, shaking off sluggishness, are stirred up to diligent hearing, that the adversaries may be repelled. Again, how many senses of Holy Scriptures, concerning Christ's Godhead, have been avouched against Photinus;[73] how many of his manhood, against Mani;[74] how many of the Trinity,

---

[73] (d. 376). He was accused of believing that Jesus Christ was just a man adopted by God and not the second person of the Trinity.

[74] A Persian prophet who lived in the third century and preached a dualism that said that good and evil were equal, competing forces. The Manichees continued in existence for many centuries, taking different names (Cathars, Albigensians, Bogomils) and did not finally disappear until the fifteenth century.

against Sabellius;[75] how many of the unity in Trinity, against the Arians,[76] Eunomians,[77] Macedonians;[78] how many, of the Catholic church dispersed throughout the whole world, and of the mixture of good and bad in the same until the end of the world, against the Donatists[79] and Luciferians[80] and others of the like error; how many against all other heretics, which it were too long to rehearse? Of which senses and expositions of Holy Scripture the approved authors and avouchers should otherwise not be known at all, or not so well known as the contradictions of proud heretics have made them.'[81]

Thus he saith of such things as not seeming to be in Holy Scriptures to the ignorant or heretics, yet indeed be there. But in other points doubted of, that indeed are not decided by Scripture, he giveth us this goodly rule to be followed in all, as he exemplifieth in one. 'Then do we hold, ' saith he, 'the verity of the Scriptures, when we do that which now hath seemed good to the universal church, which the authority of the Scriptures themselves doth commend; so that, forasmuch as the Holy Scripture cannot deceive, whosoever is afraid to be deceived with the obscurity of questions, let him therein ask counsel of the same church, which the Holy Scripture most certainly and evidently showeth and pointeth unto.'[82]

---

[75] He lived at Rome sometime around 220 and taught that the Father suffered and died on the cross because there was no real difference between him and the Son. This heresy is known as 'Patripassianism.'

[76] The followers of Arius (256-336), the 'arch-heretic' of Alexandria who was condemned at the first council of Nicaea in 325. Many of the Germanic invaders of the Roman Empire were Arians and it was not until 589 that the last of them (the Spanish Visigoths) converted to orthodox Christianity.

[77] Followers of Eunomius (330-92/5) who claimed that the being of the God we know in Christ is not identical with the being of God as he is in eternity.

[78] Followers of Macedonius (d. 364) who denied that the Holy Spirit was fully God.

[79] North African schismatics who broke with the church because of its lenient policy towards penitent apostates. They were named for one of their early leaders, Donatus (early fourth century) and lasted until North Africa was overrun by the Arabs in 698.

[80] Supposed followers of Lucifer of Cagliari who were accused of devil-worship, apparently because of the confusion caused by the name Lucifer.

[81] Augustine, *Enarratio in Psalmum* 67 [68]; 1, 39 (PL 36, coll. 812-13, 836-7).

[82] Augustine, *Contra Cresconium* III, 33 (PL 43, coll. 515-16).

34. Many causes why this New Testament is translated according to the ancient vulgar Latin text.

Now to give thee also intelligence in particular, most gentle reader, of such things as it behoveth thee specially to know concerning our translation – we translate the old vulgar Latin text, not the common Greek text, for these causes:

01. *It is most ancient.* It is so ancient that it was used in the Church of God above 1300 years ago, as appeareth by the Fathers of those times.

02. *Corrected by St Jerome.* It is that (by the common received opinion, and by all probability) which St Jerome afterward corrected according to the Greek, by the appointment of Damasus, then pope, as he maketh mention in his preface before the four evangelists, unto the said Damasus, and in *Catalogo* (*in fine*)[83] and *Epistula* 102.[84]

03. *Commended by St Augustine.* Consequently it is the same which St Augustine so commendeth and alloweth in an epistle to St Jerome.[85]

04. *Used and expounded by the Fathers.* It is that which for the most part ever since hath been used in the church's service, expounded in sermons, alleged and interpreted in the commentaries and writings of the ancient Fathers of the Latin church.

05. *Only authentical, by the holy Council of Trent.* The holy Council of Trent, for these and many other important considerations, hath declared and defined this only of all other Latin translations to be authentical, and so only to be used and taken in public lessons, disputations, preachings, and expositions, and that no man presume upon any pretence to reject or refuse the same.[86]

06. *Most grave, least partial.* It is the gravest, sincerest, of greatest majesty, least partiality, as being without all respect of controversies and contentions, specially these of our

---

[83] Jerome, *De viris illustribus* 35 (PL 23, col. 649).
[84] PL 22, coll. 830-1.
[85] Augustine, *Epistula* LXXI (PL 33, coll. 241-3).
[86] Council of Trent, session 4, 8 April 1546 (second decree).

time, as appeareth by those places which Erasmus and others at this day translate much more to the advantage of the Catholic cause.

07. *Precise in following the Greek.* It is so exact and precise according to the Greek, both the phrase and the word, that delicate heretics therefore reprehend it of rudeness. And that it followeth the Greek far more exactly that the Protestants' translations, beside infinite other places, we appeal to these (Titus 3:14): *Curent bonis operibus praeesse, proistasthai.* English Bible, 1577:[87] 'to maintain good works.' And Hebrews 10:20: *Viam nobis initiavit, enekainisen.* English Bible: 'he prepared.' So in these words, *iustificationes, traditiones, idola,* etc. In all which they come not near the Greek, but avoid it of purpose.

08. *Preferred by Beza himself.* The adversaries themselves, namely Beza, prefer it before all the rest.[88] And again he saith that the old interpreter translated very religiously.[89]

09. *All the rest misliked of the sectaries themselves, each reprehending another.* In the rest, there is such diversity and dissension, and no end of reprehending one another, and translating every man according to his fantasy, that Luther said: 'If the world should stand any long time, we must receive again (which he thought absurd) the decrees of the councils, for preserving the unity of faith, because of so divers interpretations of the Scripture.'[90] And Beza, (in the place above-mentioned) noteth the itching ambition of his fellow translators, that had much rather disagree and dissent from the best, than seem themselves to have said or written nothing. And Beza's translation itself being so esteemed in our country, that the Geneva English Testaments be translated according to the same, yet sometime goeth so wide from the Greek, and from the

---

[87] An edition of the Geneva Bible.
[88] Beza, *Praefatio Novi Testamenti*, 1565. An English translation of this was printed by L. Tomson at the beginning of his revision of the Geneva New Testament, 1576 (see above).
[89] Beza, *Annotationes in Lucam* 1,1 (in his New Testament and translated by Tomson.)
[90] Martin Luther, *On councils and the church* II (1539). See *Luther's works. American edition* XLI, ed. E. W. Gritsch (Philadelphia, PA: Fortress, 1966), p. 138.

meaning of the Holy Ghost, that themselves which protest to translate it, dare not follow it. For example, they have put the words: 'the son of Canaan,'[91] which he wittingly and wilfully left out; and they say: 'with the women,' agreeably to the vulgar Latin, where he saith *cum uxoribus*, with their wives.[92]

10. *It is truer than the vulgar Greek text itself.* It is not only better than all other Latin translations, but than the Greek text itself, in those places where they disagree.

35. The ancient Fathers for proof thereof, and the adversaries themselves.

The proof hereof is evident, because most of the ancient heretics were Grecians, and therefore the Scriptures in Greek were corrupted by them, as the ancient Fathers often complain. Tertullian noteth the Greek text which is at this day to be an old corruption of Marcion the heretic, and the truth to be as in our vulgar Latin: *Secundus homo de coelo coelestis*,[93] the second man from heaven, heavenly.' So read other ancient fathers, and Erasmus thinketh it must needs be so, and Calvin himself followeth it.[94] Again, St Jerome noteth that the Greek text which is at this day, is not the apostolical verity or the true text of the Apostle, but that which is in the vulgar Latin: *Qui cum uxore est, solicitus est quae sunt mundi, quomodo placeat uxori, et divisus est*. 'He that is with a wife is careful of worldly things, how he may please his wife, and is divided or distracted.'[95] The ecclesiastical history called the *Tripartite*, noteth the Greek text that now is to be an old corruption of the ancient Greek copies, by the Nestorian heretics, and the true reading to be as in our vulgar Latin: *omnis spiritus qui solvit IESUM, ex Deo non est*, 'Every spirit that dissolveth JESUS, is not of God'; and Beza confesseth that Socrates in his *Ecclesiastical History* readeth so in the Greek: *pan pneuma ho lyei ton Iesoun Christon*, etc.[96]

---

[91] Luke 3:36.
[92] Acts 1:14.
[93] 1 Corinthians 15:47.
[94] John Calvin, *Institutes of the Christian religion* II,13,2.
[95] 1 Corinthians 7:33.
[96] 1 John 4:3.

36. The Calvinists themselves often forsake the Greek as corrupt, and translate according to the ancient vulgar Latin text.

But the proof is more pregnant out of the adversaries themselves. They forsake the Greek text as corrupted and translate according to the vulgar Latin, namely Beza and his scholars the English translators of the Bible, in these places. Hebrews 9:1, saying: The first covenant, for that which is in the Greek: The first tabernacle. Where they put *covenant*, not as of the text, but in another letter, as to be understood according to the vulgar Latin, which most sincerely leaveth it out altogether, saying: *Habuit quidem et prius iustificationes* etc.; 'The former also indeed had justifications.' Again, Romans 11:21 they translate not according to the Greek text: *Tempori servientes*, 'serving the time', which Beza saith must needs be a corruption; but according to the vulgar Latin: *Domino servientes*, 'serving our Lord'. Again, Revelation 11:2, they translate not the Greek text, *Atrium quod intra templum est*, 'the court which is within the temple'; but clean contrary, according to the vulgar Latin, which Beza saith is the true reading, *Atrium quod est foris templum*, 'the court which is without the temple'. Only in this last place, one English Bible, of the year 1562,[97] followeth the error of the Greek. Again, 2 Timothy 2:14, they add *but* more than is in the Greek, to make the sense more commodious and easy, according as it is in the vulgar Latin. Again, James 5:12, they leave the Greek and follow the vulgar Latin, saying: 'lest you fall into condemnation'. 'I doubt not' saith Beza, 'but this is the true and sincere reading, and I suspect the corruption in the Greek came thus,' etc. It were infinite to set down all such places, where the adversaries, specially Beza, follow the old vulgar Latin and the Greek copy agreeable thereunto, condemning the Greek text that now is, of corruption.

37. Superfluities in the Greek, which Erasmus calleth trifling and rash additions.

Again, Erasmus the best translator of all the later, by Beza's judgement, saith that the Greek sometime hath superfluities corruptly added to the text of Holy Scripture, as Matthew 6 to the end of the *Pater Noster*, these words: 'because thine is the

---

[97] The last edition of the Great Bible of 1538.

kingdom, the power and the glory, for evermore.'[98] Which he calleth *nugas*, trifles rashly added to our Lord's prayer, and reprehendeth Valla for blaming the old vulgar Latin because it hath it not. Likewise Romans 11:6, these words in the Greek, and not in the vulgar Latin: 'But if of works, it is not now grace; otherwise the work is no more a work.' And Mark 10:29, these words, *or wife*, and suchlike. Yea the Greek text in these superfluities condemneth itself, and justifieth the vulgar Latin exceedingly; as being marked throughout in a number of places, that such and such words are superfluous, in all which places our vulgar Latin hath no such thing, but is agreeable to the Greek, which remaineth after the superfluities be taken away. For example, that before mentioned in the end of the *Pater Noster*, hath a mark of superfluity in the Greek text thus, ', and Mark 6:11 these words: '*Amen, I say unto you, it shall be more tolerable for the land of Sodom and Gomorrah in the day of judgement than for that city*'; and Matthew 20:22, these words: '*And be baptized with the baptism that I am baptized with?*' which is also superfluously repeated again,[99] and suchlike places exceeding many; which being noted superfluous in the Greek, and being not in the vulgar Latin, prove the Latin in those places to be better, truer and more sincere than the Greek.

38. The vulgar Latin translation agreeth with the best Greek copies, by Beza's own judgement.

Whereupon we conclude of these premises that it is no derogation to the vulgar Latin text, which we translate, to disagree from the Greek text, whereas it may notwithstanding be not only as good, but also better. And this the adversary himself, their greatest and latest translator of the Greek, doth avouch against Erasmus in behalf of the old vulgar Latin translation, in these notorious words: 'How unworthy and without cause,' saith he, 'doth Erasmus blame the old interpreter as dissenting from the Greek? He dissented, I grant, from those Greek copies which he had gotten, but we have found, not in one place, that same interpretation which he blameth, is grounded upon the authority of other Greek copies, and those most ancient. Yea in some number of places we have observed that the reading of the Latin

---

[98] Matthew 6:13. (Omitted from most modern Bibles.)
[99] Matthew 20:23.

text of the old interpreter, though it agree not sometime with our Greek copies, yet it is much more convenient, for that it seemed he followed some better and truer copy.'[100] Thus for Beza. In which words he unwittingly, but most truly, justifieth and defendeth the old vulgar translation against himself and all other cavillers that accuse the same, because it is not always agreeable to the Greek text.

39. When the Fathers say that the Latin text must yield to the Greek, and be corrected by it, they mean the true and uncorrupted Greek text.

Whereas it was translated out of other Greek copies (partly extant, partly not extant at this day) either as good and as ancient, such as St Augustine speaketh of, calling them: *doctiores et diligentiores*, the more learned and diligent Greek copies,' whereunto the Latin translations that fail in any place, must needs yield.[101] And if it were not too long to exemplify and prove this, which would require a treatise by itself, we could show by many and most close examples throughout the New Testament, these sundry means of justifying the old translation.

40. The vulgar Latin translation is [in] many ways justified by most ancient Greek copies, and the Fathers.

First, if it agree with the Greek text (as commonly it doth, and in the greatest places concerning the controversies of our time, it doth most certainly) so far the adversaries have not to complain; unless they will complain of the Greek also, as they do (James 4:2 and 1 Peter 3:21), where the vulgar Latin followeth exactly the Greek text, saying *occiditis*,[102] and *quod vos similes formae*,[103] etc. But Beza in both places correcteth the Greek text also as false.

If it disagree here and there from the Greek text, it agreeth with another Greek copy set in the margin, whereof see examples in the foresaid Greek Testaments of Robert Stevens[104] and Crispin[105]

---

[100] Beza, *Praefatio in Novum Testamentum*, 1565.
[101] Augustine, *De doctrina Christiana* II, 15 (PL 34, col. 46).
[102] 'You kill'.
[103] 'Because you are like of form'.
[104] Robert l'Estienne (d. 1559) was a prominent French printer. His edition of the *Codex Bezae* in 1550 was the first to use modern verse notations.
[105] Jean Crespin (d. 1572) was a French Biblical scholar.

throughout, namely 2 Peter 1:10: *Satagite ut per bona opera certam vestram vocationem faciatis, dia ton agathon ergon.*[106] And Mark 8:7: *Et ipsos benedixit, eulogesas auta.*[107]

If these marginal Greek copies be thought less authentical than the Greek text, the adversaries themselves tell us the contrary, who in their translations often follow the marginal copies and forsake the Greek text; as in the examples above mentioned (Romans 11; Revelation 11; 2 Timothy 2; James 5, etc.) it is evident.

If all Erasmus' Greek copies have not that which is in the vulgar Latin, Beza had copies which have it, and those most ancient (as he saith) and better. And if all Beza's copies fail in this point and will not help us, Gagney,[108] the French king's preacher, and he that might command in all the king's libraries, he found Greek copies that have just according to the vulgar Latin; and that in such place as would seem otherwise less probable, as James 3:5: *Ecce quantus ignis quam magnam silvam incendit*, 'Behold how much fire, what a great wood it kindleth.' A man would think it must be as in the Greek text: 'A little fire, what a great wood it kindleth!' But an approved ancient Greek copy, alleged by Gagney, hath as it is in the vulgar Latin. And if Gagney's copies also fail sometime, there Beza and Crispin supply Greek copies fully agreeable to the vulgar Latin, as Jude 5: *Scientes semel omnia, quoniam Iesus,*[109] etc. and v.19: *Segregant semetipsos.*[110] Likewise, Ephesians 2:11: *Quod elegerit vos primitias, aparchas*[111] in some Greek copies. Gagney in 2 Corinthians 9:2: *Vestra aemulatio, ho hymon zelos.*[112] So hath one Greek copy (Beza).

---

[106] 'Take care to make your election sure by good works'; the Greek says 'through good works' but this phrase is not in the best Greek manuscripts and is omitted nowadays.

[107] The Latin says: 'and he blessed them', a translation of the Greek 'having blessed them'. Some manuscripts, including the one used by Beza, omit this phrase but it is included in the current Nestlé-Aland Greek New Testament.

[108] Jean Gagney (Gagnaeus) was a prominent French scholar of the first part of the sixteenth century.

[109] 'Knowing once everything, that Jesus, etc.'

[110] 'They separate themselves'.

[111] 'Because he chose you the firstfruits'. Some Greek copies have 'aparchas', which is also 'firstfruits', but the phrase is a mistranslation of the Greek. The Biblical reference is mistaken; it probably should be 2 Thessalonians 2:13 instead.

[112] 'Your zeal' in both Latin and Greek occurs in Beza but not in Gagney.

41. The Greek fathers.

If all their copies be not sufficient, the ancient Greek fathers had copies and expounded them agreeable to our vulgar Latin, as 1 Timothy 6:20: *Profanas vocum novitates*[113] – so readeth St John Chrysostom and expoundeth it against heretical and erroneous novelties. Yet now we know no Greek copy that readeth so. Likewise John 10:29: *Pater meus quod mihi dedit maius omnibus est.*[114] So readeth St Cyril of Alexandria and expoundeth it.[115] Likewise 1 John 4:3: *omnis spiritus qui solvit IESUM, ex Deo non est.*[116] So readeth St Irenaeus,[117] St Augustine,[118] St Leo,[119] besides Socrates in his *Ecclesiastical History*,[120] and the *Tripartite*,[121] who say plainly that this was the old and true reading of this place in Greek. And in what Greek copy extant at this day is there this text: *Est autem Hierosolymis probatica piscina?*[122] And yet St John Chrysostom,[123] St Cyril[124] and Theophylact[125] read so in the Greek, and Beza saith it is the better reading. And so is the Latin text of the Roman Mass Book justified, and eight other Latin copies that read so. For our vulgar Latin here is according to the Greek text, *super probatica*, and Romans 5:17: *Donationis et iustitiae.*[126] So readeth Theodoret in Greek.[127] And Luke 2:14 Origen[128] and St John Chrysostom[129] read: *Hominibus bonae voluntatis*,[130] and Beza liketh it better than the Greek text that now is.

---

[113] 'Ungodly novelties of voices.' Not in any Greek manuscript.
[114] 'My Father that gave to me is greater than all.' This is now the preferred variant reading.
[115] Cyril of Alexandria, *In Iohannem* VII (PG 74, coll. 20-1).
[116] 'Every spirit that denies Jesus is not of God.' The preferred modern reading is: 'Every spirit that does not confess Jesus is not of God.'
[117] Irenaeus, *Adversus omnes haereses* III, 16, 8 (PG 7, col. 927).
[118] Augustine, *Tractatus in Iohannem* VI, 14 (PL 35, col. 1432).
[119] Leo I of Rome, *Epistula* XXVIII, 5 (PL 54, coll. 773-5).
[120] Socrates, *Historia ecclesiastica* VII, 22 (PG 67, col. 785).
[121] Theodorus Lector, *Historia tripartita* XII, 4.
[122] John 5:2: 'There is at Jerusalem a sheep pool.' The Latin Vulgate reads, according to the Greek, 'by the Sheep Gate'.
[123] John Chrysostom, *Homiliae in Iohannem* 36 (PG 59, coll. 203-4).
[124] Cyril of Alexandria, *In Iohannem* II (PG 73, col. 536).
[125] Theophylact of Ochrid, *In Iohannem* 5:2 (PG 123, col. 1257).
[126] 'Of free gift and righteousness.'
[127] Theodoret of Cyrus, *In Iohannem* 5:2 (PG 82, col. 101).
[128] Origen, *Homiliae in Lucam* 13 (PG 13, col. 1830).
[129] John Chrysostom, *Homiliae in Matthaeum* 68, 3 (PG 58, col. 644).
[130] 'To men of good will'.

Where there is no such sign of any ancient Greek copy in the fathers, yet these later interpreters tell us that the old interpreter did follow some other Greek copy, as Mark 7:3: *Nisi crebro laverint*. Erasmus thinketh that he did read in the Greek *pyknei*, 'often'; and Beza and others commend his conjecture, yea and the English Bibles are so translated. Whereas now it is *pygmei*, which signifieth the length of the arm up to the elbow. And who would not think that the Evangelist should say: 'The Pharisees wash often, because otherwise they eat not' rather than thus: 'Unless they wash up to the elbow, they eat not'?

42. The Latin fathers.

If all such conjectures, and all the Greek fathers help us not, yet the Latin Fathers with great consent will easily justify the old vulgar translation, which for the most part they follow and expound, as John 7:39: *Nondum erat Spiritus datus*.[131] So readeth St Augustine;[132] Leo.[133] Whose authority were sufficient, but indeed Didymus, also a Greek doctor, readeth so,[134] translated by St Jerome, and a Greek copy in the Vatican, and the Syriac New Testament. Likewise John 21:22: *Sic eum volo manere*,[135] so readeth St Ambrose;[136] St Augustine[137] and the Venerable Bede upon St John's Gospel.[138]

And lastly, if some other Latin Fathers of ancient time read otherwise, either here or in other places, not all agreeing with the text of our vulgar Latin, the cause is the great diversity and multitude that was then of Latin copies (whereof St Jerome complaineth), till this one vulgar Latin grew only into use. Neither doth their divers reading make more for the Greek than for the vulgar Latin, differing oftentimes from both, as when St Jerome in this last place readeth: *Si sic eum volo manere*,[139] it is according

---

[131] 'The Spirit was not yet given.'
[132] Augustine, *De Trinitate* IV,20 (PL 42, coll. 906-9); *Quaestiones* LXXXIII (PL 35, coll. 2276-8); *Tractatus in Iohannem* LII, 8 (PL 35, col. 1772).
[133] Leo I of Rome, *Sermo* LXXVI, 8 (PL 54, col. 411).
[134] Didymus the Blind of Alexandria, *De Spiritu Sancto* II, 33 (PG 39, col. 1063).
[135] 'So I want him to remain.'
[136] Ambrose, *Expositio in Psalmum 45* 11 (PL 14, col. 1138) and *Expositio in Psalmum 118 Resh* XX, 12 (PL 15, col. 1487).
[137] Augustine, *Tractatus in Iohannem* CXXIV, 1 (PL 35, coll. 1969-70).
[138] Bede, *In Iohannem* 21 (PL 92, col. 931).
[139] 'If I want him to remain so.' Jerome, *Adversus Iovinianum* I, 26 (PL 23, coll. 322-3).

to no Greek copy now extant. And if yet there be some doubt that the readings of some Greek or Latin fathers, differing from the vulgar Latin, be a check or condemnation to the same; let Beza, that is, let the adversary himself, tell us his opinion in this case also. 'Whosoever,' saith he, 'shall take upon him to correct these things' (speaking of the vulgar Latin translation) 'out of the ancient fathers' writings, either Greek or Latin, unless he do it very circumspectly and advisedly, he shall surely corrupt all rather than amend it, because it is not to be thought that as often as they cited any place, they did always look into the book or number every word.' As if he should say: 'We may not by and by think that the vulgar Latin is faulty and to be corrected, when we read otherwise in the Fathers either Greek or Latin, because they did not always exactly cite the words, but followed some commodious and godly sense thereof.

43. The few and small faults negligently crept into the vulgar Latin translation.

Thus then we see that by all means the old vulgar Latin translation is approved good, and better than the Greek text itself, and that there is no cause why it should give place to any other text, copies or readings. Marry, if there be any faults evidently crept in by those that heretofore wrote or copied out the Scriptures (as there be some) them we grant no less, than we would grant faults nowadays committed by the printer, and they are exactly noted of Catholic writers, namely in all Plantin's Bibles set forth by the divines of Louvain;[140] and the holy Council of Trent willeth that the vulgar Latin text be in such points throughly mended, and so to be most authentical.[141] Such faults as these, *in fide* for *in fine*, *praescientiam* for *praesentiam*, *suscipiens* for *suspiciens*; and such like very rare, which are evident corruptions made by the copyists, or grown by the similitude of words. These being taken away, which are no part of those corruptions and differences before talked of, we translate that text which is most sincere, and in our opinion, and as we have proved, incorrupt. The adversaries contrary, translate that text, which themselves confess both by their writings and doings, to be corrupt in a

---

[140] Christophe Plantin (1520-89) was a Belgian printer who produced an important edition of the Bible in the original languages in 1569.

[141] Council of Trent, session 4, 8 April 1546 (second decree).

number of places and more corrupt than our vulgar Latin, as is before declared.

44. Calvinists confessing the Greek to be most corrupt, yet translate that only, and hold that only for authentical Scripture.

And if we would here stand to recite the places in the Greek which Beza pronounceth to be corrupted, we should make the reader to wonder how they can either so plead otherwise for the Greek text, as though there were no other truth of the New Testament but that; or how they translate only that (to deface, as they think, the old vulgar Latin) which themselves so shamefully disgrace, more than the vulgar Latin, inventing corruptions where none are, nor can be, in such universal consent of all both Greek and Latin copies. For example, Matthew 10:2: 'The first Simon, who is called Peter.' I think, saith Beza, this word *protos*, 'first,' hath been added to the text of some that would establish Peter's primacy. Again, Luke 22:20: 'The chalice, *that is shed for you.*' It is most likely (saith he) that these words, being sometime but a marginal note, came by corruption out of the margin into the text. Again, Acts 7:43: 'Figures which they made, *to adore them.*' It may be suspected (saith he) that these words, as many other, have crept by corruption into the text out of the margin. And 1 Corinthians 15:57: He thinketh the Apostle said not *nikos* (victory), as it is in all Greek copies, but *neikos* (contention). And Acts 13:20 – he calleth it a manifest error, that in the Greek it is 400 years for 300. And Ac 7:16, he reckoneth up a whole catalogue of corruptions, namely Mark 12:42: *ho esti kodrantes*, 'which is a farthing'; and Acts 8:26: *haute estin eremos*, 'this is a desert'. And Acts 7:16, the name of Abraham, and such like. All which he thinketh to have been added or altered into the Greek text by corruption.

45. They standing precisely upon the Hebrew of the Old, and Greek text of the New Testament, must of force deny the one of them.

But among other places he laboureth exceedingly to prove a great corruption[142] where it is said (according to the Septuagint, that is, the Greek text of the Old Testament) that Jacob went down into Egypt with 75 souls. And Luke 3:36, he thinketh these words *tou Kainan*, 'which was of Canaan', to be so false that he leaveth them

---

[142] Acts 7:14.

clean out in both his editions of the New Testament;[143] saying that he is bold so to do by the authority of Moses. Whereby he will signify that it is not in the Hebrew text of Moses or of the Old Testament, and therefore it is false in the Greek of the New Testament. Which consequence of theirs (for it is common among them and concerneth all Scriptures), if it were true, all places of the Greek text of the New Testament, cited out of the Old according to the Septuagint, and not according to the Hebrew (which they know are very many) should be false; and so by tying themselves only to the Hebrew in the Old Testament, they are forced to forsake the Greek of the New; or if they will maintain the Greek of the New, they must forsake sometime the Hebrew in the Old; but this argument shall be forced against them elsewhere.

46. They say the Greek is more corrupt than we will grant them.

By this little, the reader may see what gay patrons they are of the Greek text, and how little cause they have in their own judgements to translate it, or vaunt of it as in derogation of the vulgar Latin translation, and how easily we might answer them in a word why we translate not the Greek; forsooth because it is so infinitely corrupted. But the truth is, we do by no means grant it so corrupted as they say, though in comparison we know it less sincere and incorrupt than the vulgar Latin, and for that cause and others before alleged, we prefer the said Latin and have translated it.

47. We prefer not the vulgar Latin text as making more for us.

The Greek text maketh for us more than the vulgar Latin. If there yet remain one thing which perhaps they will say, when they cannot answer our reasons aforesaid; to wit, that we prefer the vulgar Latin before the Greek text, because the Greek maketh more against us; we protest that, as for other causes we prefer the Latin, so in this respect of making for us or against us, we allow the Greek as much as the Latin, yea in sundry places more than the Latin, being assured that they have not one, and that we have many advantages in the Greek more than in the Latin, as by the annotations of this New Testament shall evidently appear; namely in all such places where they dare not translate the Greek, because

---

[143] Those of 1556 and 1565.

it is for us and against them, as when they translate *dikaiomata* 'ordinances' and not 'justifications,' and that of purpose as Beza confesseth; Luke 1:6, *paradoseis*, 'ordinances' or 'instructions' and not 'traditions,' in the better part. 2 Thessalonians 2:15, *presbyterous*, 'elders' and not 'priests'; *eidola*, 'images' rather than 'idols.'

For the real presence. And especially when St Luke in the Greek so maketh for us (the vulgar Latin being indifferent for them and us) that Beza saith it is a corruption crept out of the margin into the text. What need these absurd devices and false dealings with the Greek text, if it made for them more than for us, yea if it made not for us against them?

For fasting. But that the Greek maketh more for us, see 1 Corinthians 7:5. In the Latin, *Defraud not one another, but for a time, that you give yourselves to prayer,* in the Greek, *to fasting and prayer.* Acts 10:30, in the Latin Cornelius saith: *From the fourth day past until this hour I was praying in my house, and behold a man,* etc.; in the Greek, *I was fasting and praying.*

For free will. 1 John 5:18 in the Latin: *We know that everyone which is born of God sinneth not, but the generation of God preserveth him, etc.*; in the Greek: *but he that is born of God preserveth himself.*

Against only faith. Revelation 22:14, in the Latin: *Blessed are they that wash their garments in the blood of the Lamb, etc.*; in the Greek: *Blessed are they that do his commandments.*

Against special assurance of salvation. Romans 8:38. *Certus sum,* etc. *I am sure that neither death nor life, nor other creature is able to separate us from the charity of God.* As though he were assured, or we might and should assure ourselves of our predestination; in the Greek *pepeismai, I am probably persuaded that neither death nor life*, etc.

For the sacrifice of Christ's body and blood. In the Evangelists about the sacrifice and blessed sacrament, in the Latin thus: *This is my blood that shall be shed for you,*[144] and in St Paul, *This is my body which shall be betrayed* or *delivered for you,*[145] both being

---

[144] Luke 22:20.
[145] 1 Corinthians 11:24.

referred to the time to come and to the sacrifice on the cross; in the Greek, *This is my blood which is shed for you*, and *my body which is broken for you*, both being referred to that present time when Christ gave his body and blood at his supper, then shedding the one and breaking the other, that is sacrificing it sacramentally and mystically. Lo these and the like our advantages in the Greek, more than in the Latin.

48. The Protestants condemning the old vulgar translation as making for us, condemn themselves.

But is the vulgar translation for all this papistical and therefore do we follow it? (For so some of them call it, and say it is the worst of all other.) If it be, the Greek (as you see) is more, and so both Greek and Latin and consequently the Holy Scripture of the New Testament is papistical. Again, if the vulgar Latin be papistical, papistry is very ancient and the Church of God for so many hundred years wherein it hath used and allowed this translation, hath been papistical. But wherein is it papistical? Forsooth in these phrases and speeches: *Paenitentiam agite*,[146] *Sacramentum hoc magnum est*,[147] *Ave, gratia plena*,[148] *Talibus hostiis promeretur Deus*,[149] and such like. First, doth not the Greek say the same? See the annotations upon these places. Secondly, could he translate these things papistically or partially, or rather prophetically so long before they were in controversy? Thirdly, doth he not say for *paenitentiam agite*, in another place, *paenitemini*,[150] and doth he not translate other mysteries, by the word *sacramentum*, as Revelation 17:5: *sacramentum mulieris*,[151] and as he translateth one word *gratia plena*, so doth he not translate the very like word *plenus ulceribus*,[152] which themselves do follow also? Is this also papistry?

49. It is void of all partiality.

When he said: *Quanto deteriora merebitur supplicia*, etc.,[153] and

---

[146] 'Do penance', Matthew 3:2, etc.
[147] 'This is a great sacrament', Ephesians 5:32.
[148] 'Hail, full of grace', Luke 1:28.
[149] 'God is placated by such sacrifices', Hebrews 13:16.
[150] 'Repent'.
[151] 'Sacrament (mystery) of the woman'.
[152] 'Full of ulcers', Luke 16:20.
[153] 'How much worse punishments will he merit', Hebrews 10:29.

they like it well enough, might he not have said according to the same Greek word: *Vigilate ut mereamini fugere ista omnia et stare ante filium hominis*[154] and *Qui merebuntur saeculum illud et resurrectionem ex mortuis*, etc.,[155] and *Tribulationes quas sustinetis ut mereamini regnum Dei, pro quo et patimini.*[156] Might he not (we say) if he had partially affectated the word 'merit,' have used it in all these places, according to his and your own translation of the same Greek word?[157] Which he doth not, but in all these places saith simply: *Ut digni habeamini,*[158] and *Qui digni habebuntur.*[159] And how can it be judged papistical or partial, when he saith *Talibus hostiis promeretur Deus*?[160] Was Primasius, also St Augustine's scholar, a papist for using this text, and all the rest that have done the like? Was St Cyprian a papist, for using so often this speech: *promereri Dominum iustis operibus, paenitentia,* etc.?[161] Or is there any difference, but that St Cyprian useth it as a deponent, more Latinly; the other as a passive, less finely? Was it papistry, to say *senior*[162] for *presbyter, ministrantibus* for *sacrificantibus,* or *liturgiam celebrantibus,*[163] *simulacris* for *idolis,*[164] *fides tua te salvum fecit* sometime for *sanum fecit*?[165] Or shall we think he was a Calvinist for translating thus, as they think he was a papist, when any word soundeth for us?

50. The papistry thereof (as they term it) is in the very sentences of the Holy Ghost, more than in the translation.

Again, was he a papist in these kinds of words only, and was he

---

[154] 'Stay awake, so that you may merit to flee all these things and stand befor the Son of Man', Luke 21:36.
[155] 'Those who will merit that age and the resurrection from the dead, etc.', Luke 20:35.
[156] 'The tribulations which you are enduring in order to merit the kingdom of God, for which you are also suffering', 2 Thessalonians 1:5.
[157] Hebrews 10:29.
[158] 'That you may be accounted worthy'.
[159] 'Who will be accounted worthy'.
[160] 'God is placated by such sacrifices', Hebrews 13:16.
[161] 'The Lord is placated by righteous works, penance, etc.', Cyprian of Carthage, *Epistula* XVII (PL 4, col. 269).
[162] 'Elder'.
[163] 'Ministers' for 'sacrificers' or 'celebrants of the liturgy', Acts 13:2.
[164] 'Images' for 'idols', 1 Thessalonians 1:9; 1 John 5:21.
[165] 'Your faith has made you saved' for 'made you whole', Matthew 9:22, etc.

not in whole sentences? As *Tibi dabo claves*, etc.[166] *Quidquid solveris in terra, erit solutum et in coelis*;[167] and *Quorum remiseritis peccata, remittuntur eis*;[168] and, *Tunc reddet unicuique secundum opera sua*;[169] and *Nunquid poterit fides salvare eum? Ex operibus iustificatur homo et non ex fide tantum*;[170] and *Nubere volunt, damnationem habentes quia primam fidem irritam fecerunt*;[171] and, *Mandata eius gravia non sunt*;[172] and *Aspexerit in remunerationem*.[173] Are all these and such like papistical translations because they are most plain for the Catholic faith which they call papistry? Are they not word for word as in the Greek, and the very words of the Holy Ghost? And if in these there be no accusation of papistical partiality, why in the other? Lastly, are the ancient fathers, General Councils, the churches of all the west part, that use all these speeches and phrases now so many hundred years, are they all papistical? Be it so, and let us in the name of God follow them, speak as they speak, translate as they translated, interpret as they interpreted, because we believe as they believed. And thus far for defence of the old vulgar Latin translation, and why we translated it before all others.

51. The manner of this translation and what hath been observed therein.

In this our translation, because we wish it to be most sincere, as becometh a Catholic translation, and have endeavoured so to make it; we are very precise and religious in following our copy, the old vulgar approved Latin; not only in sense, which we hope we always do, but sometime in the very words and phrases, which may seem to the vulgar reader and to common English ears not yet acquainted therewith, rudeness or ignorance; but to the discreet reader that deeply weigheth and considereth the importance of sacred words and speeches, and how easily the

---

[166] 'I shall give you the keys', Matthew 16:19.
[167] 'Whatever you loose on earth shall be loosed in heaven also', Matthew 16:19.
[168] 'Whose sins you remit, they shall be remitted', Matthew 16:19.
[169] 'Then he shall render to each one according to his works', Romans 2:6.
[170] 'Will faith be able to save him? A man is justified by works and not by faith alone', James 2:24.
[171] 'They want to marry, having damnation because they have made their first faith invalid', 1 Timothy 5:11-12.
[172] 'His commandments are not hard', 1 John 5:3.
[173] 'He was looking for a reward', Hebrews 11:26.

voluntary translator may miss the true sense of the Holy Ghost, we doubt not but our consideration and doing therein shall seem reasonable and necessary; yea and that all sorts of Catholic readers will in short time think that familiar, which at the first may seem strange, and will esteem it more when they shall otherwise be taught to understand it, than if it were the common known English.

52. Certain words not English nor as yet familiar in the English tongue.

Amen. For example, we translate often thus, *Amen, amen, I say unto you.* Which as yet seemeth strange, but after a while it will be as familiar as *Amen* in the end of all prayers and psalms, and even as when we end with *Amen*, it soundeth far better than *so be it*, so in the beginning, *Amen, amen* must needs by use and custom sound far better than *verily, verily*. Which indeed, doth not express the asseveration and assurance signified in this Hebrew word; besides that is the solemn and usual word of our Saviour to express a vehement asseveration, and therefore is not changed, neither in the Syriac nor Greek nor vulgar Latin Testament, but is preserved and used of the Evangelists and Apostles themselves, even as Christ spake it, *propter sanctiorem auctoritatem*, as St Augustine saith of this and of *Alleluia*, 'for the more holy and sacred authority thereof.'[174]

Alleluia. And therefore do we keep the word *alleluia* as it is both in Greek and Latin, yea and in all the English translations,[175] though in their Books of Common Prayer they translate it, *Praise ye the Lord.*

Paraskeve. Again, if *hosanna, raca, Belial* and such like be untranslated in the English Bibles, why may we not say *Corbanna* and *Paraskeve*, specially when they, Englishing this latter thus, '*the preparation of the Sabbath*', put three words more into the text than the Greek word doth signify.[176] And others saying thus, after the day of '*preparing*', make a cold translation and short of the sense; as if they should translate the Sabbath, '*the resting*', for *Paraskeve* is as solemn a word for the Sabbath eve as *Sabbath* is

---

[174] Augustine, *De doctrina Christiana* II, 11 (PL 34, coll. 44-5).
[175] Revelation 19:4.
[176] Matthew 27:62.

for the Jews' seventh day; and now among Christians much more solemner, taken for Good Friday only. These words then we thought it far better to keep in the text and to tell their signification in the margin or in a table for that purpose, than to disgrace both the text and them with translating them.

Pasche. Azymes. Such are also these words, the *Pasche*, the feast of *azymes*, the bread of *proposition*. Which they translate the *Passover*, the feast of *sweet bread*,[177] the *shewbread*. But if *Pentecost*[178] be yet untranslated in their Bibles and seemeth not strange, why should not *Pasche* and *azymes* so remain also, being solemn feasts, as Pentecost was? Or why should they English one rather than the other? Specially whereas *Passover* at the first was as strange as *Pasche* may seem now, and perhaps as many now understand *Pasche* as *Passover*. And as for *azymes*, when they English it as the feast of *sweet bread*, it is a false interpretation of the word and nothing expresseth that which belongeth to the feast, concerning unleavened bread. And as for their term of *shewbread*, it is very strange and ridiculous.

Neophyte. Again, if *proselyte* be a received word in the English Bibles,[179] why may we not be bold to say *neophyte*?[180] Specially when they, translating it into English, do falsely express the signification of the word thus, '*a young scholar*'. Whereas it is a peculiar word to signify them that were lately baptized, as *cathechumenus* signifieth the newly instructed in faith not yet baptized, who is also a young scholar rather than the other; and many that have been old scholars may be *neophytes*, by deferring baptism. And if *phylacteries* be allowed for English,[181] we hope that *didrachms* also, *prepuce*, *Paraclete* and such like will easily grow to be current and familiar. And in good sooth there is in all these such necessity, that they cannot be conveniently translated, as when St Paul saith, *concisio, non circumcisio*,[182] how can we but follow his very words and allusion? And how is it possible to express *evangelizo*, but as we do, *evangelize*? For *evangelium* being the Gospel, what is *evangelizo*, or '*to evangelize*', but to

---

[177] More familiarly, 'unleavened bread.'
[178] Acts 2:1.
[179] Matthew 23:15; Acts 2:11.
[180] 1 Timothy 3:6.
[181] Matthew 23:5.
[182] 'Concision, not circumcision', Philippians 3:2.

show the glad tidings of the Gospel, of the time of grace of all Christ's benefits? All which signification is lost by translating as the English Bibles do, '*I bring you good tidings*'.[183] Therefore we say *depositum*,[184] and he *exinanited* himself,[185] and, You have *reflourished*,[186] and to *exhaust*,[187] because we cannot possibly attain to express these words fully in English and we think much better, that the reader, staying at the difficulty of them, should take an occasion to look in the table following, or otherwise to ask the full meaning of them, than by putting some usual English words that express them not, so to deceive the reader.

53. Catholic terms proceeding from the very text of Scripture.

Sometime also we do it for another cause, as when we say, *the advent of our Lord*, and, *imposing of hands*, because one is a solemn time, the other a solemn action in the Catholic church; to signify to the people that these and suchlike names come out of the very Latin text of the Scripture. So did *penance, doing penance, chalice, priest, deacon, traditions, altar, host* and the like (which we exactly keep as Catholic terms) proceed even from the very words of Scripture.

54. Certain hard speeches and phrases.

Moreover, we presume not in hard places to mollify the speeches or phrases, but religiously keep them word for word, and point for point, for fear of missing or restraining the sense of the Holy Ghost to our fantasy, as Ephesians 6:12: '*Against the spiritual of wickedness in the celestials.*' And, '*What to me and thee, woman?*'[188] whereof, see the annotation upon this place. And 1 Peter 2:2: '*As infants even now born, reasonable, milk without guile desire ye.*' We do so place '*reasonable*' of purpose, that it may be indifferent both to infants going before, as in our Latin text; or to milk that followeth after, as in other Latin copies and in the Greek.

---

[183] Luke 2:10.
[184] 1 Timothy 6:20.
[185] Philippians 2:7.
[186] Philippians 4:10.
[187] Hebrews 9:28.
[188] John 2:4.

55. The Protestants' presumptuous boldness and liberty in translating.

John 3:8 we translate: *'The spirit breatheth where he will,'* etc., leaving it indifferent to signify either the Holy Ghost, or wind, which, the Protestants translating 'wind,' take away the other sense more common and usual in the ancient fathers. We translate Luke 8:23: *'They were filled,'* not adding of our own, *'with water'*, to mollify the sentence, as the Protestants do, and [Luke] 22:20: *'This is the chalice, the New Testament,'* etc., not *'This chalice is the New Testament'*. Likewise Mark 13:19: *'Those days shall be such tribulation,'* etc. not as the adversaries: *'In those days'*, both our text and theirs being otherwise. Likewise James 4:6: *'And giveth greater grace,'* leaving it indifferent to the *'Scripture,'* or to the *'Holy Ghost,'* both going before. Whereas the adversaries do too boldly and presumptuously add, saying: *'The Scripture* giveth', taking away the other sense, which is far more probable. Likewise Hebrews 12:21 we translate: *'So terrible was it which was seen,* Moses said,' etc. Neither doth Greek or Latin permit us to add *'that'* Moses said, as the Protestants presume to do. So we say: *'Men brethren,'*[189] *'a widow woman,'*[190] *'a woman a sinner,'*[191] *'James of Alphaeus,'* and the like. Sometime also we follow of purpose the Scripture's phrase, as: *'the hell of fire,'* according to Greek and Latin, which we might say perhaps, *'the fiery hell,'* by the Hebrew phrase in such speeches, but not *'hellfire'*, as commonly it is translated. Likewise Luke 4:36: 'What *word* is this, that in power and authority he commandeth the unclean spirits?' As also Luke 2:15: 'Let us pass over, and see the *word* that is done,' where we might say *thing*, by the Hebrew phrase, but there is a certain majesty and more signification in these speeches, and therefore both Greek and Latin keep them, although it is no more the Greek or Latin phrase than it is the English. And why should we be squeamish at new words or phrases in the Scripture, which are necessary, when we do easily admit and follow new words coined in court and in courtly or other secular writings?

---

[189] Acts 1:16; 2:29.
[190] Luke 4:26.
[191] Luke 7:37.

56.   The Greek added often in the margin for many causes.

We add the Greek in the margin for divers causes. Sometime when the sense is hard, then the learned reader may consider of it and see if he can help himself better than by our translation, as Luke 11: *Nolite extolli; me meteorizesthe*,[192] and again: *Quod superest date; eleemosynam, ta enonta*.[193] Sometime to take away the ambiguity of the Latin or English, as Luke 11:17: *Et domum supra domum cadet*, which we must needs [render in] English, '*and house upon house shall fall*'. By the Greek the sense is not, one house shall fall upon another, but if one house rise upon itself, that is, against itself, it shall perish, according as he speaketh of a kingdom divided against itself, in the words before. And Acts 14:12: *Sacerdos Iovis qui erat*,[194] in the Greek, *qui* is referred to Jupiter. Sometime to satisfy the reader that might otherwise conceive the translation to be false, as Philippians 4:6: '*But in everything by prayer*,' etc., *en panti proseuchei*, not '*in all prayer*,' as in the Latin it may seem. Sometime when the Latin neither doth, nor can reach to the signification of the Greek word, we add the Greek also as more significant. *Illi soli servies*, 'him only shalt thou serve', *latreuseis*. And Acts 6:5: Nicholas, a *stranger* of Antioch, *proselytos*. And Romans 9:4, 'the service,' *he latreia*. And Ephesians 1:10: 'to perfect,' *instaurare omnia in Christo; anakephalaiosasthai*.[195] And: 'Wherein he hath gratified us,' *echaritosen*[196] and Ephesians 6:11: 'Put on the armour,' *panoplian*, and a number the like. Sometime, when the Greek hath two senses and the Latin but one, we add the Greek. 2 Corinthians 1:4: 'By the exhortation wherewith we also are exhorted,' the Greek signifieth also *consolation*, etc.; and 2 Corinthians 10:15: 'But having hope of your faith increasing, to be' etc., where the Greek may also signify, *as* or *when* your faith increaseth. Sometime for advantage of the Catholic cause, when the Greek maketh for us more than the Latin, as: *seniores, presbyterous*,[197] *Ut digni habeamini, hina axiothete*,[198] *Qui*

---

[192] 'Do not be exalted'. The Greek says: 'Do no t be worried'. Actually Luke 12:29.
[193] 'Give as alms what is left over'. The Greek says: 'what is within'. Luke 11:41.
[194] 'A priest of Jupiter who was'.
[195] 'To restore all things in Christ'. The Greek says: 'to recapitulate'.
[196] Ephesians 1:6.
[197] 'Elders, presbyters'.

effundetur, to ekchynomenon;[199] *praecepta, paradoseis*;[200] and John 21:15: *poimaine; pasce et rege.*[201] And sometime to show the false translation of the heretic, as when Beza saith: *Hoc poculum in meo sanguine qui; to poterion en toi emoi haimati to ekchynomenon*[202] and *Quem oportet coelo contineri; hon dei ouranon dechesthai.*[203] Thus we use the Greek divers ways, and esteem of it as it is worthy, and take all commodities thereof for the better understanding of the Latin, which being a translation, cannot always attain to the full sense of the principal tongue, as we see in all translations.

57. The Latin text sometime noted in the margin.

Item, we add the Latin word sometime in the margin, when either we cannot fully express it, as Acts 8:2: 'They took order for Stephen's funeral, *curaverunt Stephanum*'[204] and: 'All take not this word, *non omnes capiunt*',[205] or when the reader might think, it cannot be as we translate, as Luke 8:23: 'A storm of wind descended into the lake and *they were filled*, and *complebantur*';[206] and John 5:6, 'when Jesus knew that he had now a long time, *quia iam multum tempus haberet*',[207] meaning, in his infirmity.

58. In the beginning of books, Matthew, Paul etc., not St Matthew, St Paul, etc.

This precise following of our Latin text, in neither adding nor diminishing, is the cause why we say not in the title of books, in the first page, St Matthew, St Paul; because it is so neither in Greek nor Latin, though in the tops of the leaves following, where we may be bolder, we add St Matthew, etc. to satisfy the reader.

---

[198] 'That you may ve accounted worthy'. The Greek says: 'that you may be considered worthy', 2 Thessalonians 1:5.
[199] 'Which will be poured out'. The Greek says: 'poured out', Luke 22:20.
[200] 2 Thessalonians 2:14.
[201] In Greek, 'Shepherd'. The Latin says: 'Shepherd and rule'.
[202] 'This cup in my blood which...' The Greek says: 'the cup in my blood that is poured out', Luke 22:20.
[203] 'Who must be kept in heaven'. The Greek says: 'whom heaven must receive', Acts 3:21.
[204] 'They took care of Stephen'.
[205] 'Not all take', Matthew 19:11.
[206] 'They were being filled'.
[207] 'For he already had much time'.

Much unlike to the Protestants our adversaries, which make no scruple to leave out the name of Paul in the title of the Epistle to the Hebrews, though it be in every Greek book which they translate.[208] And their most authorized English Bibles leave out *Catholic* in the title of St James' Epistle and the rest, which were famously known in the primitive church by the name of *Catholicae Epistulae*.[209]

59. Another reading in the margin.

Item, we give the reader in places of some importance, another reading in the margin, specially when the Greek is agreeable to the same, as John 4: '*transiet de morte ad vitam.*'[210] Other Latin copies have, *transiit*,[211] and so it is in the Greek.

60. The pointing something altered.

We bind not ourselves to the points of any one copy, print or edition of the vulgar Latin, in places of no controversy, but follow the pointing most agreeable to the Greek and to the Fathers' commentaries. As Colossians 1:10: *Ambulantes digni Deo, per omnia placentes.* 'Walking worthy of God, in all things pleasing.' *Axios tou Kyriou eis pasan areskeian* we point thus: *Deus Domini nostri Iesu Christi, pater gloriae*,[212] as in the Greek and St John Chrysostom,[213] and St Jerome both in text and commentaries.[214] Which the Catholic reader specially must mark, lest he find fault, when he seeth our translation disagree in such places from the pointing of his Latin Testament.

61. The margin reading sometime preferred before the text.

We translate sometime the word that is in the Latin margin, and not that in the text, when by the Greek or the fathers we see it is a manifest fault of the writers heretofore, that mistook one word for

---

[208] The epistle to the Hebrews was not generally regarded as Pauline in the early church, and modern scholarship has confirmed this opinion. The name of the apostle was attached to it at a late stage and with no textual authority.
[209] Eusebius of Caesarea, *Historia ecclesiastica* III, 25 (PG 20, coll. 268-9). Eusebius gives the books but does not call them 'catholic epistles.'
[210] 'He will go over from death to life', Actually John 5:24.
[211] 'He is going over'.
[212] 'The God of our Lord Jesus Christ, the Father of glory', Ephesians 1:17.
[213] Jerome, *In Ephesios* I (PL 26, col. 458). The translation of the text is in PL 29, col. 779.
[214] John Chrysostom, *In Ephesios* I, PG 62, col. 23.

another. As *in fine*, not *in fide*,[215] *praesentiam*, not *praescientiam*,[216] *latuerunt*, not *placuerunt*.[217]

Thus we have endeavoured by all means to satisfy the indifferent[218] reader and to help his understanding every way, both in the text and by Annotations; and withal to deal most sincerely before God and man, in translating and expounding the most sacred text of the holy Testament. Farewell good reader, and if we profit the any whit by our poor pains, let us for God's sake be partakers of thy devout prayers, and together with humble and contrite heart call upon our Saviour Christ to cease these troubles and storms of his dearest spouse; in the meantime comforting ourselves with this saying of St Augustine: *That heretics, when they receive power corporally to afflict the Church, do exercise her patience; but when they oppugn her only by their evil doctrine or opinion, then they exercise her wisdom.*[219]

---

[215] 1 Peter 3:8.
[216] 2 Peter 1:16.
[217] Hebrews 13:2.
[218] 'Non-specialist'.
[219] Augustine, *De civitate Dei* XVIII, 51 (PL 41, coll. 612-14).

11. Preface to the Douai Old Testament, 1609

To the right well-beloved English reader, grace and glory in Jesus Christ everlasting.

01. The cause of delay in setting forth this English Bible.

    At last through God's goodness (most dearly beloved) we send you here the greater part of the Old Testament, as long since you received the New, faithfully translated into English. The residue is in hand to be finished, and your desire thereof shall not now (God prospering our intention) be long frustrate. As for the impediments which hitherto have hindered this work, they all proceeded (as many do know) of one general cause, our poor estate in banishment. Wherein expecting better means, greater difficulties rather ensued. Nevertheless you will hereby the more perceive our fervent good will, ever to serve you, in that we have brought forth this Tome, in these hardest times, of above forty years, since this college was most happily begun. Wherefore we nothing doubt, but you our dearest, for whom we have dedicated our lives, will both pardon the long delay which we could not well prevent, and accept now this fruit of our labours, with like good affection, as we acknowledge them due, and offer the same unto you.

02. Why and how it is allowed to have Holy Scriptures in vulgar tongues.

    If any demand why it is now allowed to have the Holy Scriptures in vulgar tongues, which generally is not permitted, but in the three sacred only; for further declaration of this and other like points, we remit you to the Preface before the New Testament. Only here, as by an epitome, we shall repeat the sum of all that is there more largely discussed.

03. Scriptures being hard are not to be read of all.

    To this first question therefore we answer that both just reason and highest authority of the Church judge it not absolutely necessary, nor always convenient that Holy Scriptures should be in vulgar tongues. For being as they are, hard to be understood, even by the learned, reason doth dictate to reasonable men, that they were not written, nor ordained to be read indifferently of all men.

04. Many take harm by reading Holy Scriptures.

Experience also teacheth that through ignorance, joined often with pride and presumption, many reading Scriptures have erred grossly, by misunderstanding God's Word. Which, though it be most pure in itself, yet the sense being adulterated is as perilous (saith Tertullian) as the style corrupted.[1] St Ambrose observeth that where the text is true, the Arians' interpretation hath errors.[2] St Augustine also teacheth that heresies and perverse doctrines, entangling souls, and throwing them down headlong into the depth, do not otherwise spring up, but when good (or true) Scriptures are not well (and truly) understood, and when that which in them is not well understood, is also rashly and boldly avouched.[3] For in the same cause St Jerome utterly disallowed that all sorts of men and women, old and young, presumed to read and talk of the Scriptures, whereas no artisan nor tradesman dare presume to teach any faculty which he hath not first learned.[4]

05. Reading of Scriptures moderated.

Seeing therefore that dangers and hurts happen in many, the careful chief pastors in God's church have always moderated the reading of Holy Scriptures, according to persons, times and other circumstances; prohibiting some and permitting some, to have and read them in their mother tongue.

06. Scriptures translated into divers tongues.

So St John Chrysostom translated the Psalms and some other parts of Holy Scriptures for the Armenians when he was there in banishment.[5] The Slavonians and Goths say they have the Bible in their languages.[6] It was translated into Italian by an Archbishop of Genoa.[7] Into French in the time of King Charles V, especially

---

[1] Tertullian, *De praescriptione haereticorum* 17 (PL 2, coll. 29-30).
[2] Ambrose, *De fide ad Gratianum* II, 1 16 (PL 16, col. 563).
[3] Augustine, *Tractatus in Iohannem* XVIII, 1 (PL 35, coll. 1535-6).
[4] Augustine, *Epistulae* LIII, 7 (PL 33, col. 199).
[5] This is purely legendary.
[6] The Slavonic Bible was translated by Methodius (d. 885) and his assistants. The Gothic Bible was translated by Ulfilas (Wulfila) in the fourth century.
[7] Jacopo de Voragine was archbishop of Genoa (1292-8) but although he was reputed to have translated the Bible into Italian, there has never been any sign of it.

because the Waldensian heretics had corruptly translated it, to maintain their errors.[8] We had some parts in English translated by Venerable Bede, as Malmesbury witnesseth.[9] And Thomas Arundel, Archbishop of Canterbury, in a council holden at Oxford, straightly ordained that no heretical translation set forth by Wycliffe and his accomplices, nor any other vulgar edition should be suffered till it were approved by the ordinary of the diocese, alleging St Jerome's judgement of the difficulty and danger in translating Holy Scriptures out of one tongue into another.[10] And therefore it must needs be much more dangerous, when ignorant people read also corrupted translations.

07. A calumnious suggestion of Lutherans.

Now since Luther and his followers have pretended that the Catholic Roman faith and doctrine should be contrary to God's written Word and that the Scriptures were not suffered in vulgar languages, lest the people could see the truth, and withal these new masters corruptly turning the Scriptures into divers tongues, as might best serve their own opinions; against this false suggestion and practice, Catholic pastors have, for one special remedy, set forth true and sincere translations in most languages of the Latin Church. But so, that people must read them with licence of their spiritual superior, as in former times they were in like sort limited. Such also of the laity, yea and of the meaner learned clergy, as were permitted to read Holy Scriptures, did not presume to interpret hard places, nor high mysteries, much less to dispute and contend; but leaving the discussion thereof to the more learned, searched rather, and noted the godly and imitable examples of good life, and so learned more humility, obedience, hatred of sin, fear of God, zeal of religion and other virtues. And thus Holy Scriptures may be rightly used in any tongue, 'to teach, to argue, to correct, to instruct in justice, that the man of God may be perfect, and (as St Paul addeth) instructed to every good work,'[11] when men labour rather to be 'doers of God's will and word, than

---

[8] The translation by Raoul de Presles done in 1377 and dedicated to King Charles V (1364-80).
[9] William of Malmesbury, *Gesta regum Anglorum* I, 60 (PL 179, col. 1017).
[10] In 1407. See the introduction.
[11] 2 Timothy 3:16-17.

readers or hearers only, deceiving themselves."[12]

08. Why we translate the old Latin text.

But here another question may be proposed: Why we translate the Latin text, rather than the Hebrew or Greek, which Protestants prefer, as the fountain tongues wherein Holy Scriptures were first written?

09. More pure than the Hebrew or Greek now extant.

To this we answer, that if indeed those first pure editions were now extant, or if such as be extant were more pure than the Latin, we would also prefer such fountains before the rivers, in whatsoever they should be found to disagree. But the ancient best learned fathers and doctors of the church do much complain and testify to us that both the Hebrew and the Greek editions are foully corrupted by Jews and heretics, since the Latin was truly translated out of them whilst they were more pure. And that the same Latin hath been far better conserved from corruptions. So that the old Vulgate Latin edition hath been preferred and used for the most authentical above a thousand and three hundred years. For by this very term St Jerome calleth that version the Vulgate, or common, which he conferred with the Hebrew of the Old Testament and with the Greek of the New; which he also purged from faults committed by writers, rather amending than translating it. Though in regard of this amending, St Gregory calleth it the new version of St Jerome;[13] who nevertheless in another place calleth the selfsame the old Latin edition, judging it most worthy to be followed. St Augustine calleth it the Italian. St Isidore witnesseth that St Jerome's version was received and approved by all Christian churches.[14] Sophronius, also a most learned man, seeing St Jerome's edition so much esteemed, not only of the Latins but also of the Grecians, turned the Psalter and Prophets out of the same Latin into Greek.[15] Of latter times what

---

[12] James 1:22.
[13] Gregory the Great, *Moralia in Hiob* XX, 24.
[14] Isidore of Seville, *De officiis* I, 12.
[15] Jerome, *Praefatio in librum Psalmorum iuxta Hebraicam veritatem* (PL 28, coll. 1124-5).

shall we need to recite other most learned men? St Bede,[16] St Anselm,[17] St Bernard,[18] St Thomas Aquinas,[19] St Bonaventure[20] and the rest? Who all uniformly allege this only text as authentical. In so much that all other Latin editions, which St Jerome saith were in his time almost innumerable, are as it were fallen out of all divines' hands, and grown out of credit and use. If moreover, we consider St Jerome's learning, piety, diligence and sincerity, together with the commodities he had of best copies, in all languages then extant, and of other learned men with whom he conferred; and if we so compare the same with the best means that hath been since, surely no man of indifferent judgement will match any other edition with St Jerome's, but easily acknowledge with the whole Church, God's particular providence in this great doctor, as well for expounding as most especially for the true text and edition of Holy Scriptures.

10. His edition free from partiality.

Neither do we flee unto this old Latin text for more advantage. For besides that it is free from partiality, as being most ancient of all Latin copies, and long before the particular controversies of those days began; the Hebrew also and the Greek when they are truly translated, yea and Erasmus his Latin, in sundry places, prove more plainly the Catholic Roman doctrine than this which we rely upon. So that Beza and his followers take also exception against the Greek, when Catholics allege it against them.

---

[16] (673-735). Easily the greatest Anglo-Saxon writer and theologian, but also a figure of major European importance. His commentaries on Scripture were standard fare until the Reformation.

[17] (1033-1109). Archbishop of Canterbury from 1093 until his death, he was the leading theologian of his time and remains a significant figure today.

[18] Bernard of Clairvaux (1090-1153). Abbot of Clairvaux and a leading figure of monastic reform. He was also an acclaimed writer whose devotional works, mostly based on Scripture, were very popular with the Reformers.

[19] (1226-74). The greatest scholastic theologian and author of the famous *Summa theologiae*. He was somewhat out of fashion in the sixteenth century, but his reputation was revived by Pope Leo XIII (1878-93) and became the basis of a neo-Thomist movement in the Roman Catholic church which was influential until the mid-twentieth century.

[20] (1218-74). Another leading theologian of the thirteenth century who became minister-general of the Franciscan order of friars in 1257. His writings have always been prized for their deep piety and learning.

11. Preferred before all other editions by Beza.

Yea the same Beza preferreth the old Latin version before all others and freely testifieth that the old interpreter translated religiously.

12. None yet in England allowed for sufficient.

What then do our countrymen that refuse this Latin, but deprive themselves of the best, and yet all this while have set forth none that is allowed by all Protestants, for good or sufficient.

13. What is done in this edition.

How well this is done the learned may judge, when by mature conference they shall have made trial thereof. And if anything be mistaken, we will (as still we promise) gladly correct it. Those that translated it about thirty years since were well known to the world to have been excellent in the tongues, sincere men, and great divines.

14. Divers readings resolved upon, and none left in the margin.

Only one thing we have done touching the text, whereof we are especially to give notice. That whereas heretofore in the best Latin editions there remained many places differing in words, some also in sense, as in long process of time, the writers erred in their copies; now lately, and by the care and diligence of the church, those divers readings were maturely and judiciously examined and conferred with sundry the best written and printed books, and so resolved upon, that all which before were left in the margin are either restored into the text or else omitted, so that now none such remain in the margin. For which cause we have again conferred this English translation, and conformed it to the most perfect Latin edition.

15. They touched not present controversies.

Where yet by the way we must give the vulgar reader to understand, that very few or none of the former varieties touched controversies of this time; so that this recognition is no way suspicious of partiality, but is merely done for the more secure conservation of the true text; and more ease and satisfaction of such as otherwise should have remained more doubtful.

16. Why some words are not translated into vulgar English.

Now for the strictness observed in translating some words, or rather the not translating of some, which is in more danger to be disliked, we doubt not but the discreet learned reader, deeply weighing and considering the importance of sacred words, and how easily the translator may miss the sense of the Holy Ghost, will hold that which is here done for reasonable and necessary.

17. Some Hebrew words not translated into Latin nor Greek.

We have also the example of the Latin and Greek, where some words are not translated, but left in Hebrew, as they were first spoken and written; which seeing they could not or were not convenient to be translated into Latin or Greek, how much less could they, or was it reason to turn them into English?

18. More authority in sacred tongues.

St Augustine also yieldeth a reason, exemplifying in the words *amen* and *alleluia*, for the more sacred authority thereof; which doubtless is the cause why some names of solemn feasts, sacrifices and other holy things are reserved in sacred tongues, Hebrew, Greek or Latin.

19. Some words cannot be turned into English.

Again for necessity, English not having a name, or sufficient term, we either keep the word as we find it, or only turn it to our English termination, because it would otherwise require many words in English, to signify one word of another tongue. In which cases, we commonly put the explication in the margin.

20. Protestants leave some words untranslated.

Briefly, our apology is easy against English Protestants, because they also reserve some words in the original tongues, not translated into English, as *Sabbath, ephod, Pentecost, proselyte*, and some others. The sense whereof is indeed as soon learned as if they were turned so near as is possible into English. And why then may we not say *prepuce, phase* or *Pasch, azymes, breads of proposition, holocaust* and the like? Rather than as Protestants translate them: *foreskin, Passover, the feast of sweet breads, shewbreads, burnt offerings*, etc. By which terms, whether they be truly translated into English or no, we will pass over. Sure it is, an Englishman is still to seek what they mean, as if they remained in Hebrew or Greek.

21. Corruptions in Protestants' translations of Holy Scriptures.

It more importeth that nothing be wittingly and falsely translated for advantage of doctrine in matter of faith. Wherein as we dare boldly avouch the sincerity of this translation, and that nothing is here either untruly or obscurely done of purpose, in favour of Catholic Roman religion, so we cannot but complain and challenge English Protestants, for corrupting the text contrary to the Hebrew and Greek, which they profess to translate for the more show and maintaining of their peculiar opinions against Catholics, as is proved in the discovery of manifold corruptions.

22. Of purpose against Catholic doctrine.

For example, we shall put the reader in memory of one or two. Genesis 4:7, whereas (God speaking to Cain) the Hebrew words in grammatical construction may be translated either thus: *Unto thee also pertaineth the lust THEREOF and thou shalt have dominion over IT*, or thus: *Also unto thee HIS desire shall be subject, and thou shalt rule over HIM*; though the coherence of the text require the former and in the Bibles printed (1552 and 1577) Protestants did so translate it, yet in the year 1579 and 1603[21] they translate it the other way, rather saying that Abel was subject to Cain, and that Cain by God's ordinance had dominion over his brother Abel, than that concupiscence or lust of sin is subject to man's will, or that man hath power of free will, to resist (by God's grace) temptation of sin. But as we hear in a new edition (which we have not yet seen) they translate it almost as the first.

23. Against Melchizedek's sacrifice.

In like sort Genesis 14:18. The Hebrew particle *waw*, which St Jerome and all antiquity translated *enim* (for), Protestants will by no means admit it, because (besides other arguments) we prove thereby Melchizedek's sacrifice. And yet themselves translate the same, as St Jerome doth saying: *for she is a man's wife*, etc.[22]

24. And against holy images.

Again, Genesis 31:19. The English Bibles (1552 and 1577) translate

---

[21] The 1552 Bible was a reprint of the Great Bible of 1538; the 1577 edition is the Bishops' Bible and the other two are editions of the Geneva Bible. Hence the differences.

[22] Genesis 20:3.

theraphim 'images.' Which the edition of 1603 correcting, translateth 'idols.' And the marginal annotation well proveth that it ought to be so translated.[23]

25. This edition dedicated to all that understand English.

With this then we will conclude, most dear (we speak to you all that understand our tongue, whether you be of contrary opinions in faith, or of mundane fear participate with another congregation, or profess with us the same Catholic religion) to you all we present this work, daily beseeching God Almighty, the divine wisdom, eternal goodness, to create, illuminate and replenish your spirits with his grace, that you may attain eternal glory, every one in his measure, in those many mansions prepared and promised by our Saviour in his Father's house. Not only to those which first received and followed his divine doctrine, but to all that should afterwards believe in him and keep the same precepts.

26. Christ redeemed all but all are not saved.

For there is one God, one also Mediator of God and men, [the] Man Christ Jesus, who gave himself a redemption for all. Whereby appeareth his will that all should be saved. Why then are all not saved? The Apostle addeth that they must first come to the knowledge of the truth, because without faith it is impossible to please God.

27. True faith first necessary.

This groundwork therefore of our creation in Christ by true faith, St Paul laboured most seriously by word and writing, to establish in the hearts of all men. In this he confirmed the Romans by his Epistle, commending their faith as already received, and renowned in the whole world. He preached the same faith to many nations, amongst others, to the learned Athenians. Where it seemed to some as absurd as strange, in so much that they scornfully called him a *word-sower*, and a preacher of new gods.[24]

---

[23] The 1552 Bible was a reprint of the Great Bible of 1538. The 1577 Bible is an edition of the Bishops' Bible of 1568. The 1603 Bible is an edition of the Geneva Bible of 1560.
[24] Acts 17:18.

28. The twelve apostles were first reapers before they were sowers.

   St Paul [was] at first a sower, or seminary apostle. But St Augustine alloweth the term for good, which was reproachfully spoken of the ignorant. And so distinguishing between reapers and sowers in God's church, he teacheth that whereas the other apostles reaped in the Jews that which the patriarchs and prophets had sown, St Paul sowed the seed of Christian religion in the Gentiles. And so in respect of the Israelites to whom they were first sent, calleth the other Apostles *messores*, reapers, and St Paul being specially sent to the Gentiles, *seminatorem*, a sower, or seminary apostle[25].

29. Pastoral cures and apostolical missions.

   Which two sorts of God's workmen are still in the church, with distinct offices of pastoral cures and apostolical missions; the one for the perpetual government of Catholic countries; the other for conversion of such as either have not received Christian religion, or are relapsed. As at this time in our country, for the divers sorts of pretended religions, these divers spiritual works are necessary to teach and feed all Britain's people.

30. New doctrine is falsely called the Gospel.

   Because some in error of opinions preach another Gospel, whereas in verity there is no other Gospel. They preach indeed new doctrines which cannot save.[26]

31. The seduced and externally conformable are punished with the authors of iniquity.

   Others follow them, believing falsehood. But when the blind lead the blind not the one only, but both fall into the ditch.[27] Others conform themselves in external show, fearing them that can punish and kill the body.[28] But our Lord will bring such as decline unto (unjust) obligations, and them that work iniquity.[29] The relics and final flock of Catholics in our country have great sadness and sorrow of heart, not so much for our own affliction,

---

[25] *Tractatus in Iohannem XV*, 4, 32 (PL 35, col. 1521).
[26] Cf. Galatians 1:6-9; Jeremiah 7:8.
[27] Matthew 15:14.
[28] Matthew 10:28.
[29] Psalm 125:5.

for that is comfortable, but for you our brethren and kinsmen in flesh and blood. Wishing, with our own temporal damage whatsoever, your salvation.

32. Grace in the New Testament more abundant than in the Old.

Now is the acceptable time, now are the days of salvation,[30] the time of grace by Christ, whose days many kings and prophets desired to see;[31] they saw them (in spirit) and rejoiced. But we are made partakers of Christ and his mysteries, so that ourselves neglect not his heavenly riches; if we receive and keep the beginning of his substance firm unto the end;[32] that is, the true Catholic faith; building thereon good works by his grace,[33] without which we cannot think a good thought, by which we can do all things necessary to salvation.[34] But if we hold not fast this ground, all the building faileth.

33. Both wicked works and omission of good works are damnable.

Or if, confessing to know God in words, we deny him in deeds; committing works of darkness,[35] or omitting works of mercy, when we may do them to our distressed neighbours;[36] briefly, if we have not charity, the form and perfection of all virtues, all is lost and nothing worth.[37] But if we build upon firm ground, gold, silver and precious stones, such building shall abide and make our vocation sure by good works, as St Peter speaketh.[38] These (saith St Paul) are the heirs of God, coheirs of Christ.[39]

34. Innumerable saved by Christ.

Neither is the number of Christ's blessed children counted, as of the Jews, an hundred forty-four thousand, of every tribe of Israel twelve thousand signed;[40] but a most great multitude of Catholic Christians which no man can number, of all nations and tribes

---

[30] 2 Corinthians 6:2.
[31] Luke 10:24.
[32] Hebrews 3:6.
[33] Revelation 2:10, 19.
[34] Hebrews 6:9-12.
[35] Titus 1:16.
[36] Matthew 25:31-2.
[37] 1 Corinthians 13:2.
[38] 2 Peter 1:10.
[39] Romans 8:17.
[40] Revelation 7:4.

and peoples and tongues, standing before the throne of the Lamb, clothed in white robes and palms (of triumph) in their hands, having overcome temptations in the virtuous race of good life.

35. They are more happy that suffer persecution for the truth.

Much more those which also endure persecution for the truth's sake shall receive most copious great rewards in heaven. For albeit the passions of time (in themselves) are not condign[41] to the glory to come that shall be revealed in us; yet our tribulation, which presently is momentary and light, worketh (through grace) above measure exceedingly an eternal weight of glory.[42]

36. English Catholics most happy in this age.

What shall we therefore meditate of the especial prerogative of English Catholics at this time? For to you it is given for Christ, not only that you believe in him, but also that you suffer for him. A little now, if you must be made pensive in divers temptations, that the probation of your faith, much more precious than gold which is proved by the fire,[43] may be found unto praise and glory and honour in the revelation of Jesus Christ. Many of you have sustained the spoil of your goods with joy, knowing that you have a better and permanent substance. Others have been deprived of your children, fathers, mothers, brothers, sisters and nearest friends, in ready resolution also, some with sentence of death, to lose your own lives.[44] Others have had trials of reproaches, mockeries and stripes. Others of bands, prisons and banishments.

37. The due praise of martyrs and other glorious saints exceedeth mortal tongues.

The innumerable renowned late English martyrs and confessors, whose happy souls for confessing true faith before men, are now most glorious in heaven, we pass here with silence; because their due praise, requiring longer discourse, yea rather angels', than English tongues, far surpasseth the reach of our conceits. And so we leave it to your devout meditation. They now secure for

---

[41] 'Worthy'.
[42] Romans 8:18; cf. 2 Corinthians 4:8f.
[43] 1 Peter 1:6-7.
[44] Hebrews 11:35-8.

themselves, and solicitous for us their dearest clients, incessantly (we are well assured) intercede before Christ's divine Majesty for our happy consummation, with the conversion of our whole country.

38. Patience necessary to the end of man's life.

To you therefore (dearest friends mortal) we direct this speech, admonishing ourselves and you, in the apostles' words, that for so much as we have not yet resisted temptations to (last) blood (and death itself) patience is still necessary for us, that doing the will of God, we may receive the promise.[45] So we repine not in tribulation but ever love them that hate us, pitying their case and rejoicing in our own.

39. Persecution profitable.

For neither can we see during this life how much good they do us, nor know how many of them shall be (as we heartily desire they all may be) saved; our Lord and Saviour having paid the same price by his death, for them and for us. Love all therefore, pray for all.[46] Do not lose your confidence, which hath a great remuneration. For yet a little and very little while, he that is to come will come, and he will not slack.[47]

40. Confession of faith before men necessary to salvation.

Now the just liveth by faith,[48] believing with heart to justice, and confessing with mouth to salvation.[49] But he that withdraweth himself shall not please Christ's soul. Attend to your salvation, dearest countrymen. You that are far off, draw near,[50] put on Christ. And you that are within Christ's fold, keep your standing, persevere in him to the end. His grace dwell and remain in you, that glorious crowns may be given you. Amen.

From the English College at Douai, the Octave of All Saints [08 November] 1609.

The God of patience and comfort give you to be of one mind, one

---

[45] Hebrews 12:1-4.
[46] John 17:20.
[47] 2 Peter 3:9-10.
[48] Romans 1:17.
[49] Romans 10:9.
[50] Isaiah 33:13.

towards one another in Jesus Christ; that of one mind, with one mouth you may glorify God.[51]

---

[51] See 2 Corinthians 13:11.

12. Preface to the Authorised (King James) Version, 1611

Epistle Dedicatory

To the most high and mighty prince James by the grace of God, king of Great Britain, France, and Ireland, defender of the faith, etc. the translators of the Bible wish grace, mercy and peace, through Jesus Christ our Lord.

Great and manifold were the blessings, most dread Sovereign, which Almighty God, the Father of all mercies, bestowed upon us the people of England, when first he sent your Majesty's royal person to rule and reign over us. For whereas it was the expectation of many, who wished not well unto our Zion, that upon the setting of that bright occidental star, Queen Elizabeth of most happy memory, some thick and palpable clouds of darkness would so have overshadowed this land that men should have been in doubt which way they were to walk, and that it should hardly be known who was to direct the unsettled state; the appearance of your Majesty, as of the sun in his strength, instantly dispelled those supposed and surmised mists and gave unto all that were well affected exceeding cause of comfort; especially when we beheld the government established in your Highness, and your hopeful seed, by an undoubted title, and this also accompanied with peace and tranquillity at home and abroad.[1]

But among all our joys, there was no one that more filled our hearts, than the blessed continuance of the preaching of God's sacred Word among us; which is that inestimable treasure, which excelleth all the riches of the earth; because the fruit thereof extendeth itself, not only to the time spent in this transitory world, but directeth and disposeth men unto that eternal happiness which is above in heaven.

Then not to suffer this to fall to the ground, but rather to take it

---

[1] Queen Elizabeth I died on 24 March 1603 and was succeeded by James VI of Scotland, her distant cousin and the son of her erstwhile rival, Mary Queen of Scots. The paragraph alludes to Catholic plots to kill James, of which the most famous was the 'Gunpowder Plot' in which Guy Fawkes tried to blow up the houses of parliament on 5 November 1605.

up, and to continue it in that state, wherein the famous predecessor of Your Highness did leave it: nay, to go forward with the confidence and resolution of a Man in maintaining the truth of Christ, and propagating it far and near, is that which hath so bound and firmly knit the hearts of all your Majesty's loyal and religious people unto you, that your very name is precious among them: their eye doth behold you with comfort, and they bless You in their hearts, as that sanctified person, who, under God, is the immediate author of their true happiness. And thus their contentment doth not diminish or decay, but every day increaseth and taketh strength when they observe, that the zeal of your Majesty toward the house of God doth not slack or go backward, but is more and more kindled, manifesting itself abroad in the farthest parts of Christendom, by writing in defence of the truth, (which hath given such a blow unto that man of sin, as will not be healed,) and every day at home, by religious and learned discourse, by frequenting the house of God, by hearing the Word preached, by cherishing the teachers thereof, by caring for the Church, as a most tender and loving nursing Father.[2]

There are infinite arguments of this right Christian and religious affection in Your Majesty; but none is more forcible to declare it to others than the vehement and perpetual desire of accomplishing and publishing of this work, which now with all humility we present unto your Majesty. For when your Highness had once out of deep judgment apprehended how convenient it was, that out of the Original Sacred Tongues, together with comparing of the labours, both in our own, and other foreign languages, of many worthy men who went before us, there should be one more exact translation of the Holy Scriptures into the English tongue; your Majesty did never desist to urge and to excite those to whom it was commended, that the work might be hastened, and that the business might be expedited in so decent a manner, as a matter of such importance might justly require.

And now at last, by the mercy of God, and the continuance of our labours, it being brought unto such a conclusion, as that we have great hopes that the Church of England shall reap good fruit thereby; we hold it our duty to offer it to your Majesty, not only as to our King and Sovereign, but as to the principal mover and author of the work, humbly craving of your most sacred Majesty, that since things of this quality have ever been subject to the censures of ill-meaning and discontented

---

[2] James had received an excellent theological education in his youth and was noted as an accomplished writer and defender of the divine right of kings.

persons, it may receive approbation and patronage from so learned and judicious a prince as your Highness is, whose allowance and acceptance of our labours shall more honour and encourage us, than all the calumniations and hard interpretations of other men shall dismay us. So that if, on the one side, we shall be traduced[3] by popish persons at home or abroad, who therefore will malign us, because we are poor instruments to make God's holy truth to be yet more and more known unto the people, whom they desire still to keep in ignorance and darkness; or if, on the other side, we shall be maligned by self-conceited brethren, who run their own ways, and give liking unto nothing, but what is framed by themselves, and hammered on their anvil we may rest secure, supported within by the truth and innocency of a good conscience, having walked the ways of simplicity and integrity, as before the Lord; and sustained without by the powerful protection of your Majesty's grace and favour, which will ever give countenance to honest and Christian endeavours against bitter censures and uncharitable imputations.

The Lord of heaven and earth bless your Majesty with many and happy days, that, as his heavenly hand hath enriched your Highness with many singular and extraordinary graces, so you may be the wonder of the world in this latter age for happiness and true felicity, to the honour of that great GOD, and the good of his Church, through Jesus Christ our Lord and only Saviour.

The translators to the reader

01. The best things have been calumniated[4].

Zeal to promote the common good, whether it be by devising anything ourselves, or revising that which hath been laboured by others, deserveth certainly much respect and esteem, but yet findeth but cold entertainment in the world. It is welcomed with suspicion instead of love, and with emulation instead of thanks: and if there be any hole left for cavil[5] to enter, (and cavil, if it do not find a hole, will make one) it is sure to be misconstrued, and in danger to be condemned. This will easily be granted by as many as know history, or have any experience. For, was there ever

---

[3] 'Attacked'.
[4] 'Scorned'.
[5] 'Objections'.

anything projected, that savoured any way of newness or renewing, but the same endured many a storm of gain-saying, or opposition? A man would think that civility, wholesome laws, learning and eloquence, synods, and church maintenance, (that we speak of no more things of this kind) should be as safe as a sanctuary, and out of the danger of the dart, as they say, that no man would lift up the heel, no, nor dog move his tongue against the motioners of them. For by the first, we are distinguished from brute beasts led with sensuality: By the second, we are bridled and restrained from outrageous behaviour, and from doing of injuries, whether by fraud or by violence: by the third, we are enabled to inform and reform others, by the light and feeling that we have attained unto ourselves: Briefly, by the fourth being brought together to a parley face to face, we sooner compose our differences than by writings, which are endless: And lastly, that the church be sufficiently provided for, is so agreeable to good reason and conscience, that those mothers are holden to be less cruel, that kill their children as soon as they are born, than those nursing fathers and mothers (wheresoever they be) that withdraw from them who hang upon their breasts (and upon whose breasts again themselves do hang to receive the spiritual and sincere milk of the word) livelihood and support fit for their estates. Thus it is apparent, that these things which we speak of, are of most necessary use, and therefore, that none, either without absurdity can speak against them, or without note of wickedness, can spurn against them.

Yet for all that, the learned know that certain worthy men have been brought to untimely death for none other fault, but for seeking to reduce their countrymen to good order and discipline:[6] and that in some commonwealths it was made a capital crime, once to motion the making of a new law for the abrogating of an old, though the same were most pernicious:[7] And that certain, which would be counted pillars of the state,[8] and patterns of virtue and prudence, could not be brought for a long time to give way to good letters and refined speech, but bare themselves as averse from them, as from rocks, or boxes of poison: And fourthly, that

---

[6] This was traditionally ascribed to Anacharsis, a Scythian who lived in the sixth century BC.
[7] This was the case in the ancient Greek city of Locri, for example.
[8] Cato the Elder (234-149 BC) who was famous for his rough speech and manners.

he was no babe, but a great clerk[9], that gave forth (and in writing to remain to posterity) in passion peradventure, but yet he gave forth, that he had not seen any profit to come by any synod, or meeting of the clergy, but rather the contrary: And lastly, against church maintenance and allowance, in such sort, as the ambassadors and messengers of the great King of kings should be furnished, it is not unknown what a fiction or fable (so it is esteemed, and for no better by the reporter himself, though superstitious) was devised: Namely, that at such time as the professors and teachers of Christianity in the Church of Rome, then a true church, were liberally endowed, a voice forsooth was heard from heaven, saying; 'Now is poison poured down into the church, etc.'[10] Thus not only as oft as we speak, as one saith, but also as oft as we do anything of note or consequence, we subject ourselves to everyone's censure, and happy is he that is least tossed upon tongues: for utterly to escape the snatch of them it is impossible. If any man conceit, that this is the lot and portion of the meaner sort only, and that princes are privileged by their high estate, he is deceived. As the sword devoureth as well one as the other, as it is in Samuel,[11] nay as the great commander charged his soldiers in a certain battle, to strike at no part of the enemy, but at the face;[12] And as the king of Syria commanded his chief captains to fight neither with small nor great, save only against the king of Israel:[13] so it is too true, that envy striketh most spitefully at the fairest, and at the chiefest. David was a worthy prince, and no man to be compared to him for his first deeds, and yet for as worthy an act as ever he did, (even for bringing back the ark of God in solemnity) he was scorned and scoffed at by his own wife.[14] Solomon was greater than David though not in virtue, yet in power: and by his power and wisdom he built a Temple to the LORD, such a one as was the glory of the land of Israel, and the

---

[9] Gregory of Nazianzus, *Orationes* XLII, 21-2 (PG 36, coll. 481-5).
[10] William Langland, *Piers Plowman*, C Text, Passus XVIII, 220. The legend was a commonplace in the middle ages and claimed that when the Emperor Constantine endowed the church, an angel from heaven cried: '*Hodie venenum effusum est in ecclesia Dei*,' the words translated here.
[11] 2 Samuel 11:25.
[12] Scipio Africanus (235-183 BC)
[13] 1 Kings 22:31.
[14] 2 Samuel 6:16.

wonder of the whole world.[15] But was that his magnificence liked of by all? We doubt of it. Otherwise, why do they lay it in his son's dish, and call unto him for easing of the burden. Make, say they, the grievous servitude of thy Father, and his sore yoke, lighter.[16] Belike he had charged them with some levies, and troubled them with some carriages; Hereupon they raise up a tragedy, and wish in their heart the temple had never been built. So hard a thing it is to please all, even when we please God best, and do seek to approve ourselves to everyone's conscience.

02. The highest personages have been calumniated.

If we all descend to later times, we shall find many the like examples of such kind, or rather unkind acceptance. The first Roman emperor did never do a more pleasing deed to the learned, nor more profitable to posterity, for conserving the record of times in true supputation,[17] than when he corrected the calendar, and ordered the year according to the course of the Sun: and yet this was imputed to him for novelty, and arrogancy, and procured to him great obloquy.[18] So the first christened emperor (at the leastwise that openly professed the faith himself, and allowed others to do the like) for strengthening the empire at his great charges, and providing for the church, as he did, got for his labour the name Pupillus, as one who would say, a wasteful prince, that had need of a guardian, or overseer.[19] So the best christened emperor,[20] for the love that he bare unto peace, thereby to enrich both himself and his subjects, and because he did not seek war but find it, was judged to be no man at arms (though indeed he excelled in feats of chivalry, and showed so much when he was provoked) and condemned for giving himself to his ease, and to his pleasure. To be short, the most learned emperor of former times, (at the least, the greatest politician) what thanks had he for cutting off the superfluities of the laws, and digesting

---

[15] An allusion to 2 Chronicles 9:1.
[16] 1 Kings 12:4.
[17] 'Accuracy'.
[18] This was Julius Caesar, who reformed the Roman calendar in 46 BC. The opposition to him was recorded by Plutarch in his life of Caesar.
[19] This was Constantine the Great (306-37), who legalised Christianity in 313.
[20] Theodosius I (378-95), so called because he made Christianity the official religion of the Roman Empire. His debauchery is recorded by the contemporary pagan historian Zosimus, *Historia nova*, IV.

them into some order and method?[21] This, that he hath been blotted by some to be an epitomist, that is, one that extinguished worthy whole volumes, to bring his abridgements into request. This is the measure that hath been rendered to excellent princes in former times, even *Cum bene facerent, male audire.* (For their good deeds to be evil spoken of.) Neither is there any likelihood, that envy and malignity died, and were buried with the ancient. No, no, the reproof of Moses taketh hold of most ages: '*You are risen up in your fathers' stead, an increase of sinful men.*'[22] '*What is that that hath been done? That which shall be done, and there is no new thing under the sun, saith the wise man.*'[23] and St Stephen, '*As your fathers did, so do you.*'[24]

03. His Majesty's constancy notwithstanding calumniation, for the survey of the English translations.

This, and more to this purpose, his Majesty that now reigneth (and long, and long may he reign, and his offspring for ever, himself and children, and children's children always) knew full well, according to the singular wisdom given unto him by God, and the rare learning and experience that he hath attained unto; namely, that whosoever attempteth any thing for the public (specially if it pertain to religion, and to the opening and clearing of the Word of God) the same setteth himself upon a stage to be gloated upon by every evil eye, yea, he casteth himself headlong upon pikes, to be gored by every sharp tongue. For he that meddleth with men's religion in any part, meddleth with their custom, nay, with their freehold; and though they find no content in that which they have, yet they cannot abide to hear of altering. Notwithstanding his royal heart was not daunted or discouraged for this or that colour, but stood resolute, as a statue immoveable, and an anvil not easy to be beaten into plates, as one saith; he knew who had chosen him to be a soldier, or rather a captain, and being assured that the course which he intended, made much for the glory of God, and the building up of his church, he would not suffer it to be broken off for whatsoever speeches or practices. It

---

[21] Justinian I (527-65), whose famous *Digest* is the basis of modern civil law in most European countries.
[22] Numbers 32:14.
[23] Ecclesiastes 1:9.
[24] Acts 7:51.

doth certainly belong unto Kings, yea, it doth specially belong unto them, to have care of religion, yea, to know it aright, yea, to profess it zealously, yea, to promote it to the uttermost of their power. This is their glory before all nations which mean well, and this will bring unto them a far most excellent weight of glory in the day of the Lord Jesus. For the Scripture saith not in vain, '*Them that honour me, I will honour,*'[25] neither was it a vain word that Eusebius delivered long ago, that piety towards God was the weapon, and the only weapon that both preserved Constantine's person, and avenged him of his enemies.[26]

04. The praise of the Holy Scriptures.

But now what piety without truth? What truth (what saving truth) without the Word of God? What Word of God (whereof we may be sure) without the Scripture? The Scriptures we are commanded to search.[27] They are commended that searched and studied them.[28] They are reproved that were unskillful in them, or slow to believe them.[29] They can make us wise unto salvation.[30] If we be ignorant, they will instruct us; if out of the way, they will bring us home; if out of order, they will reform us; if in heaviness, comfort us; if dull, quicken us; if cold, inflame us. *Tolle, lege; tolle, lege,* 'take up and read, take up and read' the Scriptures, (for unto them was the direction) it was said unto St Augustine by a supernatural voice.[31] 'Whatsoever is in the Scriptures, believe me,' saith the same St Augustine, 'is high and divine; there is verily truth and a doctrine most fit for the refreshing and renewing of men's minds, and truly so tempered that everyone may draw from thence that which is sufficient for him, if he come to draw with a devout and pious mind, as true religion requireth.'[32] Thus St Augustine. And St Jerome: *Ama Scripturas et amabit te sapientia,* etc. ('Love the Scriptures, and wisdom will love thee.')[33] And St Cyril against Julian: 'Even boys that are bred up in the Scriptures become most

---

[25] 1 Samuel 2:30.
[26] Eusebius of Caesarea, *Historia ecclesiastica* X, 8 (PG 20, col. 893).
[27] John 5:39; Isaiah 8:20.
[28] Acts 17:11; 8:28-9.
[29] Matthew 22:29; Luke 24:25.
[30] 2 Timothy 3:15.
[31] Augustine, *Confessiones* VIII, 12 (PL 32, coll. 761-4).
[32] Augustine, *De utilitate credendi,* 6 (PL 42, coll. 74-5).
[33] Jerome, *Epistula* CXXX, 20 (PL 22, col. 1124).

religious,' etc.³⁴ But what mention we three or four uses of the Scripture, whereas whatsoever is to be believed or practised, or hoped for, is contained in them? Or three or four sentences of the fathers, since whosoever is worthy the name of a father, from Christ's time downward, hath likewise written not only of the riches, but also of the perfection of the Scripture? 'I adore the fullness of the Scripture,' saith Tertullian against Hermogenes.³⁵ And again, to Apelles, a heretic of the like stamp, he saith: 'I do not admit that which thou bringest in (or concludest) of thine own (head or store, *de tuo*) without Scripture.'³⁶ So Saint Justin Martyr before him: 'We must know by all means, saith he, that it is not lawful (or possible) to learn (anything) of God or of right piety, save only out of the prophets, who teach us by divine inspiration.'³⁷ So Saint Basil after Tertullian: 'It is a manifest falling away from the faith and a fault of presumption, either to reject any of those things that are written, or to bring in (upon the head of them, *epeisagein*) any of those things that are not written.'³⁸ We omit to cite to the same effect, St Cyril, Bishop of Jerusalem in his fourth *Cathechesis*,³⁹ St Jerome against Helvidius,⁴⁰ Saint Augustine, in his third book against the letters of Petilian,⁴¹ and in very many other places of his works. Also we forbear to descend to later fathers, because we will not weary the reader. The Scripture then being acknowledged to be so full and so perfect, how can we excuse ourselves of negligence, if we do not study them, of curiosity, it we be not content with them? Men talk much of *eiresione*,⁴² how many sweet and goodly things it had hanging on it; of the philosophers' stone, that it turneth copper into gold: of cornucopia, that it had all things necessary for food in it, of *panaces* the herb, that it was good for all diseases: of *catholicon* the drug, that it is instead of all purges; of Vulcan's armour, that it was an armour of proof against all thrusts, and all

---

³⁴ Cyril of Alexandria, *Contra Iulianum* 7 (PG 76, coll. 833-7).
³⁵ Tertullian, *Adversus Hermogenem* 24 (PL 2, col. 219).
³⁶ Tertullian, *De carne Christi* 7 (PL 2, coll. 766-9).
³⁷ Justin Martyr, *Cohortatio ad Graecos* 8 (PG 6, coll. 256-7).
³⁸ Basil of Caesarea, *De sancta et orthodoxa fide* (PG 30, coll. 831-6).
³⁹ Cyril of Jerusalem, *Cathecheses*, IV, 33-7 (PG 33, coll. 493-504).
⁴⁰ Jerome, *De perpetua virginitate Beatae Mariae adversus Helvidium* (PL 23, coll. 183-206).
⁴¹ Augustine, *Contra litteras Petiliani* III, (PL 43, coll. 345-88).
⁴² An olive or laurel branch dedicated to Apollo.

blows, etc. Well, that which they falsely or vainly attributed to these things for bodily good, we may justly and with full measure ascribe unto the Scripture, for spiritual. It is not only an armour, but also a whole armour of weapons, both offensive, and defensive; whereby we may save ourselves, and put the enemy to flight.[43] It is not an herb, but a tree, or rather a whole paradise of trees of life, which bring forth fruit every month, and the fruit thereof is for meat, and the leaves for medicine.[44] It is not a pot of manna,[45] or a cruse of oil,[46] which were for memory only, or for a meal's meat or two, but as it were a shower of heavenly bread, sufficient for a whole host,[47] be it never so great; and as it were a whole cellar full of oil vessels, whereby all our necessities may be provided for, and our debts discharged. In a word, it is a panary of wholesome food against fenowed[48] traditions; a physician's shop (Saint Basil called it) of preservatives against poisoned heresies;[49] a pandect[50] of profitable laws against rebellious spirits; a treasure of most costly jewels,[51] against beggarly rudiments; finally, a fountain of most pure water springing up unto everlasting life.[52] And what marvel? The original thereof being from heaven, not from earth; the author being God, not man; the indicter, the Holy Spirit, not the wit of the apostles or prophets; the penmen such as were sanctified from the womb, and endued with a principal portion of God's Spirit; the matter, verity, piety, purity, uprightness; the form, God's Word, God's testimony, God's oracles, the Word of truth,[53] the Word of salvation,[54] etc., the effects, light of understanding,[55] stableness of persuasion,[56] repentance from dead works,[57] newness of life,[58] holiness, peace,

---

[43] Ephesians 6:10-17.
[44] Revelation 22:2.
[45] Hebrews 9:4.
[46] 1 Kings 17:12-16.
[47] Exodus 16:15-35; Numbers 11:6-9.
[48] 'Mouldy, musty.'
[49] Basil of Caesarea, *In psalmos* I, 1 (PG 29, coll. 209-12).
[50] 'Digest'.
[51] An allusion to Malachi 3:17.
[52] An allusion to Jeremiah 2:13
[53] John 17:17.
[54] Ephesians 6:17; 2 Timothy 3:15.
[55] Psalm 119:130.
[56] Hebrews 11:13.
[57] Hebrews 6:1.

joy in the Holy Ghost;[59] lastly, the end and reward of the study thereof, fellowship with the saints,[60] participation of the heavenly nature,[61] fruition of an inheritance immortal, undefiled, and that never shall fade away:[62] Happy is the man that delighteth in the Scripture, and thrice happy that meditateth in it day and night.[63]

05. Translation necessary.

But how shall men meditate in that, which they cannot understand? How shall they understand that, which is kept close in an unknown tongue? As it is written: 'Except I know the power of the voice, I shall be to him that speaketh a barbarian, and he that speaketh shall be a barbarian to me.'[64] The Apostle excepteth no tongue; not Hebrew the ancientest, not Greek the most copious, not Latin the finest. Nature taught a natural man to confess, that all of us in those tongues which we do not understand, are plainly deaf; we may turn the deaf ear unto them. The Scythian counted the Athenian, whom he did not understand, barbarous:[65] so the Roman did the Syrian, and the Jew, (even Saint Jerome himself calleth the Hebrew tongue barbarous, belike because it was strange to so many)[66] so the emperor of Constantinople called the Latin tongue barbarous, though Pope Nicholas do storm at it:[67] so the Jews long before Christ, called all other nations *lognazim*, which is little better than barbarous. Therefore as one complaineth, that always in the Senate of Rome there was one or other that called for an interpreter,[68] so lest the Church be driven to the like exigent, it is necessary to have translations in a readiness. Translation it is that openeth the window, to let in the light; that breaketh the shell, that we may eat the kernel; that putteth aside the curtain, that we

---

[58] Romans 6:4.
[59] Romans 14:17.
[60] 2 Corinthians 8:4.
[61] 2 Peter 1:4.
[62] 1 Peter 1:4.
[63] Psalm 1:1-6.
[64] 1 Corinthians 14:11.
[65] Clement of Alexandria, *Stromateis* I, 16, 133. 2 (PG 8, col. 792).
[66] Jerome, *Epistula* XVIII, 6 (PL 22, col. 365) appears to be the place referred to, but it does not support this statement.
[67] *Concilia omnia*, ed. P. Crabbe (Cologne, 1538), II, fo. 130v.
[68] Cicero, *De finibus* 5.

may look into the most holy place⁶⁹; that removeth the cover of the well, that we may come by the water, even as Jacob rolled away the stone from the mouth of the well, by which means the flocks of Laban were watered.⁷⁰ Indeed without translation into the vulgar tongue, the unlearned are but like children at Jacob's well (which was deep) without a bucket, or something to draw with:⁷¹ or as that person mentioned by Isaiah, to whom when a sealed book was delivered, with this motion, 'Read this, I pray thee', he was fain to make this answer, 'I cannot, for it is sealed'.⁷²

06. The translation out of the Hebrew into Greek.⁷³

While God would be known only in Jacob, and have his name great in Israel, and in none other place⁷⁴, while the dew lay on Gideon's fleece only, and all the earth besides was dry⁷⁵; then for one and the same people, which spake all of them the language of Canaan, that is, Hebrew, one and the same original in Hebrew was sufficient. But when the fulness of time drew near that the Sun of Righteousness,⁷⁶ the Son of God should come into the world, whom God ordained to be a reconciliation through faith in his blood,⁷⁷ not of the Jews only, but also of the Greek,⁷⁸ yea, of all them that were scattered abroad; then lo, it pleased the Lord to stir up the spirit of a Greek prince, (Greek for descent and language) even of Ptolemy Philadelphus king of Egypt, to procure the translating of the Book of God out of Hebrew into Greek.⁷⁹ This is the translation of the seventy interpreters, commonly so called (i.e. the Septuagint), which prepared the way for our Saviour among the Gentiles by written preaching, as Saint John Baptist

---

⁶⁹ Matthew 27:51; See also 2 Corinthians 3:13-16.
⁷⁰ Genesis 29:10.
⁷¹ John 4:11.
⁷² Isaiah 29:11.
⁷³ The translators copied the story from Augustine, *Contra Faustum* XII, 32 (PL 42, col. 271).
⁷⁴ Deuteronomy 7:1-16.
⁷⁵ Judges 6:39-40.
⁷⁶ Malachi 4:2.
⁷⁷ 2 Corinthians 5:18-20.
⁷⁸ Romans 10:12-13.
⁷⁹ Ptolemy II Philadelphus (285-246 BC) created the great library at Alexandria. Judaea was part of his realm and many Jews settled in the city in the late fourth and early third centuries BC.

did among the Jews by vocal.[80] For the Grecians being desirous of learning, were not wont to suffer books of worth to lie moulding in kings' libraries, but had many of their servants, ready scribes, to copy them out, and so they were dispersed and made common. Again, the Greek tongue was well known, and made familiar to most inhabitants in Asia, by reason of the conquests that there the Grecians had made, as also by the colonies, which thither they had sent. For the same causes also it was well understood in many places of Europe, yea, and of Africa too. Therefore the Word of God being set forth in Greek, becometh hereby like a candle set upon a candlestick, which giveth light to all that are in the house,[81] or like a proclamation sounded forth in the market place, which most men presently take knowledge of; and therefore the language was fittest to contain the Scriptures, both for the first preachers of the Gospel to appeal unto for witness, and for the learners also of those times to make search and trial by. It is certain, that that translation was not so sound and so perfect, but that it needed in many places correction; and who had been so sufficient for this work as the apostles or apostolic men? Yet it seemed good to the Holy Ghost and to them, to take that which they found, (the same being for the greatest part true and sufficient) rather then by making a new, in that new world and green age of the Church, to expose themselves to many exceptions and cavillations, as though they made a translation to serve their own turn, and therefore bearing witness to themselves, their witness not to be regarded.[82] This may be supposed to be some cause, why the translation of the Seventy was allowed to pass for current. Notwithstanding though it was commended generally, yet it did not fully content the learned, no not of the Jews. For not long after Christ, Aquila fell in hand with a new translation, and after him Theodotion, and after him Symmachus: yea, there was a fifth and a sixth edition, the authors whereof were not known. These with the Seventy made up the Hexapla, and were worthily and to great purpose compiled together by Origen. Howbeit the edition of the Seventy went away with the credit, and therefore not only was placed in the midst by Origen (for the worth and

---

[80] Mark 1:2-8.
[81] Matthew 5:15.
[82] Cf. John 8:17.

excellency thereof above the rest, as Epiphanius gathereth)[83] but also was used by the Greek fathers for the ground and foundation of their commentaries.[84] Yea, Epiphanius above named doth attribute so much unto it, that he holdeth the authors thereof not only for interpreters, but also for prophets in some respect: and Justinian the emperor enjoining the Jews his subjects to use specially the translation of the Seventy, rendereth this reason thereof, because they were as it were enlightened with prophetical grace.[85] Yet for all that, as the Egyptians are said of the prophet to be men and not God, and their bones flesh and not spirit:[86] so it is evident (and Saint Jerome affirmeth as much) that the Seventy were interpreters, they were not prophets; they did many things well, as learned men; but yet as men they stumbled and fell, one while through oversight, another while through ignorance, yea, sometimes they may be noted to add to the original, and sometimes to take from it; which made the apostles to leave them many times, when they left the Hebrew, and to deliver the sense thereof according to the truth of the word, as the Spirit gave them utterance.[87] This may suffice touching the Greek translations of the Old Testament.

07. The translating of the Scripture into the vulgar tongues.

There were also within a few hundred years after Christ, translations many into the Latin tongue: for this tongue also was very fit to convey the Law and the Gospel by, because in those times very many countries of the West, yea, of the South, East, and North, spake or understood Latin, being made provinces to the Romans. But now the Latin translations were too many to be all good, for they were infinite (*Latini interpres nullo modo numerari possunt*, saith Saint Augustine.)[88] Again, they were not out of the Hebrew fountain (we speak of the Latin translations of the Old Testament) but out of the Greek stream, therefore the Greek being not altogether clear, the Latin derived from it, must needs be muddy. This moved St Jerome a most learned father, and the best linguist, without controversy, of his age, or of any

---

[83] Epiphanius, *De mensuribus et ponderibus* 2 (PG 43, col. 240).
[84] Augustine, *De doctrina Christiana* II, 15 (PL 34, col. 46).
[85] *Novellae*, diatax. 146.
[86] Isaiah 31:3.
[87] Jerome, *Epistula* XVIII, 17 (PL 22, col. 372).
[88] Augustine, *De doctrina Christiana* II, 11 (PL 34, coll. 44-5).

that went before him, to undertake the translating of the Old Testament, out of the very fountains themselves, which he performed with that evidence of great learning, judgement, industry and faithfulness, that he hath for ever bound the church unto him, in a debt of special remembrance and thankfulness.

08. Translation out of Hebrew and Greek into Latin.

Now though the church were thus furnished with Greek and Latin translations, even before the faith of Christ was generally embraced in the empire: (for the learned know that even in St Jerome's time, the consul of Rome and his wife were both ethnics,[89] and about the same time the greatest part of the Senate also) yet for all that the godly-learned were not content to have the Scriptures in the language which themselves understood, Greek and Latin, (as the good lepers were not content to fare well themselves, but acquainted their neighbours with the store that God had sent, that they also might provide for themselves)[90] but also for the behoof and edifying of the unlearned, which hungered and thirsted after righteousness, and had souls to be saved as well as they, they provided translations into the vulgar for their countrymen, insomuch that most nations under heaven did shortly after their conversion, hear Christ speaking unto them in their mother tongue, not by the voice of their minister only, but also by the written word translated. If any doubt hereof, he may be satisfied by examples enough, if enough will serve the turn. First Saint Jerome saith, *Multarum gentium linguis Scriptura ante translata, docet falsa esse qua addita sunt*, etc., i.e. 'The Scripture being translated before in the languages of many nations, doth show that those things that were added [by Lucian or Hesychius] are false.'[91] So St Jerome in that place. The same St Jerome elsewhere affirmeth, that he, the time was, had set forth the translation of the Seventy, *sua lingua hominibus*, i.e. for his countrymen of Dalmatia.[92] Which words not only Erasmus doth understand to purport, that Saint Jerome translated the Scripture

---

[89] 'Gentiles.'
[90] 2 Kings 7:9.
[91] Jerome, *Praefatio in quattuor evangelia* (PL 29, col. 527).
[92] Jerome, *Praefatio in librum Psalmorum iuxta Hebraicam veritatem* (PL 28, coll. 1124-5).

into the Dalmatian tongue, but also Sixtus Senensis,[93] and Alphonsus a Castro[94] (that we speak of no more), men not to be excepted against by them of Rome, do ingenuously confess as much. So St John Chrysostom that lived in St Jerome's time giveth evidence with him: 'The doctrine of St John (saith he) did not in such sort (as the philosophers did) vanish away: but the Syrians, Egyptians, Indians, Persians, Ethiopians and infinite other nations, being barbarous people, translated it into their own (mother) tongue and have learned to be (true) philosophers,'[95] he meaneth Christians. To this may be added Theodoret, as next unto him, both for antiquity, and for learning. His words be these: 'Every country that is under the sun is full of these words, [of the Apostles and Prophets] and the Hebrew tongue (he meaneth the Scriptures in the Hebrew tongue) is turned not only into the language of the Grecians, but also of the Romans and Egyptians, and Persians and Indians, and Armenians and Scythians, and Sarmatians[96], and briefly into all the languages that any nation useth.'[97] So he. In like manner, Ulfilas [Wulfila] is reported by Paulus Diaconus and Isidore (and before them by Sozomen) to have translated the Scriptures into the Gothic tongue;[98] John, Bishop of Seville by Vasseus, to have turned them into Arabic, about the year of our Lord 717;[99] Bede by Cisterciensis to have turned a great part of them into Saxon;[100] Einhard by Trithemius, to have abridged the French Psalter, as Bede had done the Hebrew, about the year 800;[101] King Alfred by the same Cisterciensis, to have turned the Psalter into Saxon;[102] Methodius by Aventinus (printed at Ingolstadt) to have turned the Scriptures

---

[93] Sixtus Senensis, *Bibliotheca sancta ex praecipuis Catholicae Ecclesiae auctoribus collecta*, (Venice, 1566), 4, p. 243.
[94] Alphonsus a Castro, *Adversus omnes haereses* I, 23 (Paris, 1534).
[95] John Chrysostom, *Homiliae in Iohannem* II (I), 2 (PG 59, col. 32).
[96] The Scythians and the Sarmatians were nomadic tribes living in what is now Ukraine.
[97] Theodoret, *Therapeutica* V (81). (PG 83, col. 948).
[98] Paul the Deacon, *Historia Gottorum, Vandalorum et Langobardum* 12; Isidore of Seville, *Chronicon* 103 (PL 83, col. 1050); Sozomen, *Historia ecclesiastica* VI, 37 (PG 67, col. 1404).
[99] Johannes Vasaeus, *Rerum Hispaniae memorabilium annales* (Cologne, 1577), p. 461.
[100] Willaim of Malmesbury, *Gesta regum Anglorum* I, 60 (PL 179, col. 1017).
[101] Johannes Trithemius, *Opera historica* (Frankfurt, 1601), p. 252.
[102] William of Malmesbury, *Gesta regum Anglorum* II, 123 (PL 179, col. 1085); see also Polydore Vergil, *Historia Anglorum* (Basel, 1534) V, p. 262.

into Slavonian;[103] Waldo, Bishop of Friesing, by Beatus Rhenanus, to have caused about that time, the Gospels to be translated into Dutch[104] rhyme, yet extant in the library of Corbinian;[105] Valdus, by divers to have turned them himself, or to have gotten them turned into French, about the year 1160;[106] Charles, the fifth of that name, surnamed 'the Wise,' to have caused them to be turned into French, about 200 years after Valdus his time, of which translation there may be many copies yet extant, as witnesseth Beroaldus.[107] Much about that time, even in our King Richard the Second's days, John Trevisa translated them into English, and many English Bibles in written hand are yet to be seen with divers, translated, as it is very probable, in that age.[108] So the Syrian translation of the New Testament is in most learned men's libraries, of Widminstodius his setting forth;[109] and the Psalter in Arabic is with many, of Augustinus Nebiensis setting forth.[110] So Postel affirmeth, that in his travail he saw the Gospels in the Ethiopian tongue.[111] And Ambrose Thesius allegeth the Psalter of the Indians, which he testifieth to have been set forth by Potken in Syrian characters.[112] So that to have the Scriptures in the mother tongue, is not a quaint conceit lately taken up, either by

---

[103] Johannes Aventinus, *Annales Boiorum* (Ingolstadt, 1534), IV, 16, 17, p. 401.

[104] 'German.'

[105] Beatus Rhenanus, *Res Germanicae* (Basel, 1531), II, p. 201.

[106] Peter Waldo, the founder of the Waldensians, either translated or commissioned a friar of Lyon to translate, the New Testament into Franco-Provençal sometime between 1175-85.

[107] Matthaeus Beroaldus, *Chronicum Scripturae sacrae authoritate constitutum* (Frankfurt, 1606), p. 337. The translation was done in 1377 by Raoul de Presles and dedicated to King Charles V (1364-80).

[108] John (of) Trevisa (1342-1402) was a Cornishman who became vicar of Berkeley, Gloucestershire and a follower of John Wycliffe. He made several translations from Latin into English and may have helped produce the first of the two Wycliffite versions of the Bible.

[109] Johann Albrecht von Widmanstetter (1506-57) published a Syriac New Testament at Vienna in 1555.

[110] Agostino Guistiniani (1470-1536) was bishop of Nebbio (Corsica) and published a polyglot psalter at Genoa in 1515, which included an Arabic version. He visited England shortly afterwards.

[111] Guillaume Postel (1510-81) was a French scholar who made this claim in his introduction to twelve languages and their scripts, published in 1538.

[112] Johannes Potken (1470-1525) was papal secretary. In 1513 he printed a Ge'ez psalter at Rome, which he misleadingly called 'Chaldaean.' Ambrosius Theseus was a sixteenth-century orientalist who published an introduction to ten eastern languages, including 'Chaldaean,' at Pavia in 1539.

the Lord Cromwell in England,[113] or by the Lord Radziwill in Poland,[114] or by the Lord Ungnadius in the Emperor's dominion,[115] but hath been thought upon, and put in practice of old, even from the first times of the conversion or reformation of any nation; no doubt, because it was esteemed most profitable to cause faith to grow in men's hearts the sooner, and to make them to be able to say with the words of the Psalm: *As we have heard, so we have seen.*[116]

09. The unwillingness of our chief adversaries, that the Scriptures should be divulged in the mother tongue, etc.

Now the Church of Rome would seem at the length to bear a motherly affection towards her children, and to allow them the Scriptures in their mother tongue: but indeed it is a gift, not deserving to be called a gift, an unprofitable gift: they must first get a licence in writing before they may use them, and to get that, they must approve themselves to their confessor, that is, to be such as are, if not frozen in the dregs, yet soured with the leaven of their superstition. Howbeit, it seemed too much to Clement VIII that there should be any licence granted to have them in the vulgar tongue, and therefore he overruleth and frustrateth the grant of Pius IV.[117] So much are they afraid of the light of the Scripture, (*lucifugae Scripturarum*, fleers of the light of Scripture, as Tertullian speaketh)[118] that they will not trust the people with it, no not as it is set forth by their own sworn men, no not with the licence of their own bishops and inquisitors. Yea, so unwilling they are to communicate the Scriptures to the people's understanding in any sort, that they are not ashamed to confess, that we forced them to translate it into English against their wills. This seemeth to argue a bad cause, or a bad conscience, or both.

---

[113] Thomas Cromwell (1485-1540) was Henry VIII's chief minister from 1532 and instrumental in the publication of the first officially sanctioned, complete English Bible in 1538.

[114] Mikolaj Krysztof Radziwill (1515-65), known as the 'Black,' was a high-ranking Polish-Lithuanian nobleman who sponsored the publication of the first Polish-language Bible at Brest in 1564.

[115] Krsto Ungnad (1540-?) was ban (governor) of Croatia (1578-83) during which time he sponsored the publication of a Croatian Bible.

[116] Psalm 48:8.

[117] *Index librorum prohibitorum*, p. 15, v. 5.

[118] Tertullian, *De resurrectione carnis* 47 (PL 2, col. 863).

Sure we are, that it is not he that hath good gold, that is afraid to bring it to the touchstone, but he that hath the counterfeit; neither is it the true man that shunneth the light, but the malefactor, lest his deeds should be reproved:[119] neither is it the plain-dealing merchant that is unwilling to have the weights, or the meteyard brought in place, but he that useth deceit. But we will let him alone for this fault, and return to translation.

10. The speeches and reasons, both of our brethren and of our adversaries, against this work.

Many men's mouths have been open a good while, (and yet are not stopped) with speeches about the translation so long in hand, or rather perusals of translations made before: and ask what may be the reason, what the necessity of the employment: Hath the church been deceived, say they, all this while? Hath her sweet bread been mingled with leaven, her silver with dross, her wine with water, her milk with lime? (*Lacte gypsum male miscetur*, saith St Irenaeus).[120] We hoped that we had been in the right way, that we had had the oracles of God delivered unto us, and that though all the world had cause to be offended and to complain, yet that we had none. Hath the nurse holden out the breast, and nothing but wind in it? Hath the bread been delivered by the fathers of the church, and the same proved to be *lapidosus*, as Seneca speaketh?[121] What is it to handle the word of God deceitfully, if this be not? Thus certain brethren. Also the adversaries of Judah and Jerusalem, like Sanballat in Nehemiah, mock, as we hear, both at the work and workmen, saying: '*What do these weak Jews, etc.; will they make the stones whole again out of the heaps of dust which are burnt? Although they build, yet if a fox go up, he shall even break down their stony wall.*'[122] Was their translation good before? Why do they now mend it? Was it not good? Why then was it obtruded to the people? Yea, why did the Catholics (meaning popish Romanists), always go in jeopardy, for refusing to go to hear it? Nay, if it must be translated into English, Catholics are fittest to do it. They have learning, and they

---

[119] John 3:20.
[120] Irenaeus, *Adversus omnes haereses* III, 17, 4 (PG 7, col. 932).
[121] Lucius Annaeus Seneca (4 BC – AD 65) was a Stoic philosopher and Nero's tutor. Some of his ideas appealed to the early Christians, who had a high opinion of him.
[122] Nehemiah 4:2-3.

know when a thing is well, they can *manum de tabula*.[123] We will answer them both briefly: and the former, being brethren, thus, with St Jerome: *Damnamus veteres? minime, sed post priorum studio in domo Domini, quod possumus laboramus.* That is: 'Do we condemn the ancient? In no case, but after the endeavours of them that were before us, we take the best pains we can in the house of God.'[124] As if he said: 'Being provoked by the example of the learned that lived before my time, I have thought it my duty, to essay whether my talent in the knowledge of the tongues, may be profitable in any measure to God's church, lest I should seem to have laboured in them in vain, and lest I should be thought to glory in men, (although ancient,) above that which was in them.' Thus St Jerome may be thought to speak.

11. A satisfaction to our brethren.

And to the same effect say we, that we are so far off from condemning any of their labours that travailed before us in this kind, either in this land or beyond sea, either in King Henry's time, or King Edward's (if there were any translation, or correction of a translation in his time) or Queen Elizabeth's of ever renowned memory, that we acknowledge them to have been raised up of God, for the building and furnishing of his church, and that they deserve to be had of us and of posterity in everlasting remembrance. The judgement of Aristotle is worthy and well known: 'If Timotheus had not been, we had not had much sweet music, but if Phrynis (Timotheus his master) had not been, we had not had Timotheus.'[125] Therefore blessed be they, and most honoured be their name, that break the ice, and give the onset upon that which helpeth forward to the saving of souls. Now what can be more available thereto, than to deliver God's book unto God's people in a tongue which they understand? Since of an hidden treasure, and of a fountain that is sealed, there is no profit, as Ptolemy Philadelphus wrote to the rabbis or masters of the Jews, as witnesseth Epiphanius;[126] and as St Augustine saith: 'A man had rather be with his dog than with a stranger (whose

---

[123] 'Size a thing up.'
[124] Jerome, *Apologia adversus libros Rufini* II, 25 (PL 23, col. 449).
[125] Aristotle, *Metaphysica* I.
[126] Epiphanius of Salamis, *De mensuribus et ponderibus* 10-11 (PG 43, coll. 252-6).

tongue is strange unto him.)'¹²⁷ Yet for all that, as nothing is begun and perfected at the same time, and the later thoughts are thought to be the wiser; so if we building upon their foundation that went before us, and being holpen by their labours, do endeavour to make that better which they left so good; no man, we are sure, hath cause to mislike us; they, we persuade ourselves, if they were alive, would thank us. The vintage of Abiezer that struck the stroke; yet the gleaning of grapes of Ephraim was not to be despised.¹²⁸ Joash the king of Israel did not satisfy himself, till he had smitten the ground three times; and yet he offended the prophet for giving over then.¹²⁹ Aquila, of whom we spake before, translated the Bible as carefully, and as skilfully as he could; and yet he thought good to go over it again, and then it got the credit with the Jews, to be called *kat'akribeian*, that is, accurately done, as Saint Jerome witnesseth.¹³⁰ How many books of profane learning have been gone over again and again, by the same translators, by others? Of one and the same book of Aristotle's *Ethics*, there are extant not so few as six or seven several translations. Now if this cost may be bestowed upon the gourd, which affordeth us a little shade, and which today nourisheth, but tomorrow is cut down¹³¹; what may we bestow, nay, what ought we not to bestow upon the vine, the fruit whereof maketh glad the conscience of man, and the stem whereof abideth for ever?¹³² And this is the Word of God, which we translate: 'What is the chaff to the wheat, saith the Lord?'¹³³ *Tanti vitreum, quanti verum margaritum?* (saith Tertullian) 'if a toy of glass be of that reckoning with us, how ought we to value the true pearl?'¹³⁴ Therefore let no man's eye be evil, because his Majesty's is good; neither let any be grieved, that we have a prince that seeketh the increase of the spiritual wealth of Israel (let Sanballats and Tobiahs do so, which therefore do bear their just reproof)¹³⁵ but let us rather bless God from the ground of our heart, for

---

[127] Augustine, *De civitate Dei* XIX, 7 (PL 41, coll. 633-4).
[128] See Judges 8:2.
[129] 2 Kings 13:18-19.
[130] Jerome, *In Ezechiel* 3 (PL 25, col. 75).
[131] Jonah 4:6-7.
[132] Psalm 104:15.
[133] Jeremiah 23:28.
[134] Tertullian, *Ad martyras* 4 (PL 1, col. 626).
[135] Nehemiah 4:7.

working this religious care in him, to have the translations of the Bible maturely considered and examined. For by this means it cometh to pass, that whatsoever is sound already (and all is sound for substance, in one or other of our editions, and the worst of ours far better than their authentic vulgar) the same will shine as gold more brightly, being rubbed and polished; also, if anything be halting, or superfluous, or not so agreeable to the original, the same may be corrected, and the truth set in place. And what can the King command to be done, that will bring him more true honour than this? And wherein could they that have been set a work, approve their duty to the King, yea their obedience to God, and love to his saints more, than by yielding their service, and all that is within them, for the furnishing of the work? But besides all this, they were the principal motives of it, and therefore ought least to quarrel it: for the very historical truth is, that upon the importunate petitions of the Puritans, at his Majesty's coming to this crown, the conference at Hampton Court having been appointed for hearing their complaints; when by force of reason they were put from all other grounds, they had recourse at the last, to this shift, that they could not with good conscience subscribe to the communion book, since it maintained the Bible as it was there translated, which was, as they said, a most corrupted translation. And although this was judged to be but a very poor and empty shift; yet even hereupon did his Majesty begin to bethink himself of the good that might ensue by a new translation, and presently after gave order for this translation which is now presented unto thee. Thus much to satisfy our scrupulous brethren.

12. An answer to the imputations of our adversaries.

Now to the latter we answer; that we do not deny, nay we affirm and avow, that the very meanest translation of the Bible in English, set forth by men of our profession (for we have seen none of theirs of the whole Bible as yet) containeth the Word of God, nay, is the Word of God. As the king's speech which he uttered in parliament, being translated into French, Dutch,[136] Italian, and Latin, is still the king's speech, though it be not interpreted by every translator with the like grace, nor peradventure so fitly for phrase, nor so expressly for sense,

---

[136] 'German.'

everywhere. For it is confessed, that things are to take their denomination of the greater part; and a natural man could say, *Verbum ubi multa nitent in carmine, non ego paucis offendor maculis*, etc.[137] A man may be counted a virtuous man, though he have made many slips in his life, (else, there were none virtuous, for in many things we offend all)[138] also a comely man and lovely, though he have some warts upon his hand, yea, not only freckles upon his face, but also scars. No cause therefore why the word translated should be denied to be the word, or forbidden to be current, notwithstanding that some imperfections and blemishes may be noted in the setting forth of it. For what ever was perfect under the sun, where apostles or apostolic men, that is, men indued with an extraordinary measure of God's Spirit, and privileged with the privilege of infallibility, had not their hand? The Romanists therefore in refusing to hear, and daring to burn the Word translated, did no less than despite the Spirit of grace, from whom originally it proceeded, and whose sense and meaning, as well as man's weakness would enable, it did express. Judge by an example or two. Plutarch writeth, that after that Rome had been burnt by the Gauls, they fell soon to build it again: but doing it in haste, they did not cast the streets, nor proportion the houses in such comely fashion, as had been most sightly and convenient.[139] Was Catiline therefore an honest man, or a good patriot, that sought to bring it to a combustion?[140] Or Nero a good prince, that did indeed set it on fire?[141] So, by the story of Ezra, and the prophecy of Haggai it may be gathered, that the temple built by Zerubbabel after the return from Babylon, was by no means to be compared to the former built by Solomon (for they that remembered the former, wept when they considered the latter)[142]

---

[137] 'When a word radiates with many splendours in song, I am not offended by a few blemishes.' Horace, *Ars poetica* 351.
[138] James 3:2.
[139] In Plutarch's life of (Marcus Furius) Camillus (446-365 BC).
[140] Catiline (108-62 BC) was a notorious subverter of the Roman republic who was famously opposed by Cicero. Catiline was accused of planning to burn Rome in 63 BC, in the course of what is known as his second conspiracy against the state (though modern scholars doubt whether there was ever a 'first' one, as Cicero alleged).
[141] Nero (AD 54-68) was alleged to have set the city of Rome on fire in AD 64. Seeking a scapegoat, he blamed the Christians for it, and thus began the first official persecution of the church, in the course of which Peter and Paul were both probably martyred.
[142] Ezra 3:12.

notwithstanding, might this latter either have been abhorred and forsaken by the Jews, or profaned by the Greeks? The like we are to think of translations. The translation of the Seventy dissenteth from the original in many places, neither doth it come near it for perspicuity, gravity, majesty; yet which of the apostles did condemn it? Condemn it? Nay, they used it, (as it is apparent, and as St Jerome and most learned men do confess) which they would not have done, nor by their example of using it, so grace and commend it to the church, if it had been unworthy the appellation and name of the Word of God. And whereas they urge for their second defence of their vilifying and abusing of the English Bibles, or some pieces thereof, which they meet with, for that heretics (forsooth) were the authors of the translations, (heretics they call us by the same right that they call themselves catholics, both being wrong) we marvel what divinity taught them so. We are sure Tertullian was of another mind: *Ex personis probamus fidem, an ex fide personas?* 'So we try men's faith by their person? We should try their persons by their faith.'[143] Also St Augustine was of another mind: for he lighting upon certain rules made by Tyconius a Donatist, for the better understanding of the word, was not ashamed to make use of them, yea to insert them into his own book, with giving commendation to them so far forth as they were worthy to be commended, as is to be seen in St Augustine's third book *De doctrina Christiana*.[144] To be short, Origen, and the whole church of God for certain years, were of another mind: for they were so far from treading under foot, (much more from burning) the translation of Aquila a proselyte, that is, one that had turned Jew; of Symmachus, and Theodotion, both Ebionites, that is, most vile heretics, that they joined them together with the Hebrew original, and the translation of the Seventy, (as hath been before signified out of Epiphanius) and set them forth openly to be considered of and perused by all. But we weary the unlearned, who need not know so much, and trouble the learned, who know it already.

Yet before we end we must answer a third cavil and objection of theirs against us, for altering and amending our translation so oft; wherein truly they deal hardly, and strangely with us. For to

---

[143] Tertullian, *De praescriptione haereticorum* 3 (PL 2, col. 15).
[144] Augustine, *De doctrina Christiana* III, 30 (PL 34, coll. 81-2).

whom ever was it imputed for a fault (by such as were wise) to go over that which he had done, and to amend it where he saw cause? St Augustine was not afraid to exhort St Jerome to a *palinodia* or recantation;[145] the same St Augustine was not ashamed to retractate, we might say, revoke, many things that had passed him, and doth even glory that he seeth his infirmities.[146] If we will be sons of the truth, we must consider what it speaketh, and trample upon our own credit, yea, and upon other men's too, if either be any way an hindrance to it. This to the cause: then to the persons we say, that of all men they ought to be most silent in this case. For what varieties have they, and what alterations have they made, not only of their service books, portesses and breviaries, but also of their Latin translation? The service book supposed to be made by St Ambrose (*Officium Ambrosianum*) was a great while in special use and request: but Pope Hadrian calling a council with the aid of Charles the emperor, abolished it, yea, burnt it, and commanded the service book of St Gregory universally to be used.[147] Well, *Officium Gregorianum* gets by this means to be in credit, but doth it continue without change or altering? No, the very Roman service was of two fashions, the new fashion, and the old, (the one used in one church, the other in another) as is to be seen in Pamelius a Romanist, his preface, before *Micrologus*.[148] The same Pamelius reporteth out of Radulphus de Rivo, that about the year of our Lord 1277, Pope Nicholas III removed out of the churches of Rome, the more ancient books (of service) and brought into use the missals of the Friars Minorites, and commanded them to be observed there; insomuch that about an hundred years after, when the above-named Radulphus happened to be at Rome, he found all the books to be new, (of the new stamp.)[149] Neither was there this chopping and changing in the more ancient times only, but also of late: Pius V himself confesseth, that every bishopric almost had a peculiar kind of service, most unlike to that which others had: which moved him to abolish all other breviaries, though never so

---

[145] Augustine, *Epistula* IX (PL 33, coll. 72-3).
[146] Augustine, *Retractationes* (PL 32, coll. 583-656); *Epistula* XXVIII, 4: *Video interdum vitia mea* (PL 33, col. 114).
[147] Guillaume Durand, *Speculum iudiciale* V, 2.
[148] Jacob Pamelius (1536-87), a Flemish theologian. His *Micrologus de ecclesiasticis observationibus* was published at Antwerp in 1565.
[149] Ralph de Rivo (d. 403) wrote an important history of the Roman Breviary.

ancient, and privileged, and published by bishops in their dioceses, and to establish and ratify that only which was of his own setting forth, in the year 1568.[150] Now, when the father of their Church, who gladly would heal the sore of the daughter of his people softly and sleightly, and make the best of it, findeth so great fault with them for their odds and jarring; we hope the children have no great cause to vaunt of their uniformity. But the difference that appeareth between our translations, and our often correcting of them, is the thing we are specially charged with; let us see therefore whether they themselves be without fault this way, (if it be to be counted a fault, to correct) and whether they be fit men to throw stones at us: *O tandem maior pareas insani minori*: they that are less sound themselves, ought not to object infirmities to others. If we should tell them that Valla,[151] Stapulensis,[152] Erasmus,[153] and Vives[154] found fault with their vulgar translation, and consequently wished the same to be mended, or a new one to be made, they would answer peradventure, that we produced their enemies for witnesses against them; albeit, they were in no other sort enemies, than as St Paul was to the Galatians, for telling them the truth: and it were to be wished, that they had dared to tell it them plainlier and oftener.[155] But what will they say to this, that Pope Leo X allowed Erasmus' translation of the New Testament, so much different from the vulgar, by his apostolic letter and bull; That the same Leo exhorted Pagninus to translate the whole Bible, and bare whatsoever charges were

---

[150] Pius V (1566-72) was one of the major implementers of the centralising decisions taken at the Council of Trent. His Breviary was the forerunner of the Missal of 1570, known to us as the Tridentine Mass.

[151] Lorenzo Valla (1406-57) was one of the earliest and most important renaissance humanists. It was he who exposed the papal claim to rule Rome as a gift of the Emperor Constantine as a forgery.

[152] Jacques Lefèvre d'Etaples (1455-1536) was a prominent French humanist scholar who was very close to the early Reformers but never left the Roman church.

[153] Desiderius Erasmus (1466-1536) was the most famous scholar of his time. He edited the Greek New Testament in 1516 and provided a Latin translation of it that differed significantly from the standard Vulgate.

[154] Juan Luis Vives (1493-1540) was a prominent Spanish humanist who came to England as tutor for the young Princess Mary in 1523 but left a few years later because he opposed Henry VIII's plans to have his marriage annulled.

[155] Galatians 4:16.

necessary for the work?[156] Surely, as the Apostle reasoneth to the Hebrews, that if the former law had been sufficient, there had been no need of the latter:[157] so we may say, that if the old vulgar had been at all points allowable, to small purpose had labour and charges been undergone, about framing of a new. If they say, it was one pope's private opinion, and that he consulted only himself; then we are able to go further with them, and to aver that more of their chief men of all sorts, even their own Trent-champions Paiva[158] and Vega,[159] and their own inquisitor Hieronymus ab Oleastro,[160] and their own Bishop Isidorus Clarius,[161] and their own Cardinal Thomas a Vio Cajetan,[162] do either make new translations themselves, or follow new ones of other men's making, or note the vulgar interpreter for halting; none of them fear to dissent from him, nor yet to except against him. And call they this an uniform tenor of text and judgement about the text, so many of their worthies disclaiming the now received conceit? Nay, we will yet come nearer the quick: doth not their Paris edition differ from the Louvain, and Hentenius,[163] his from them both, and yet all of them allowed by authority? Nay, doth not Sixtus V confess that certain Catholics (he meaneth certain of his own side) were in such an humour of translating the Scriptures into Latin that Satan, taking occasion by them, though they thought of no such matter, did strive what he could, out of so uncertain and manifold a variety of translations, so to mingle all things, that nothing might seem to be left certain and

---

[156] Sixtus Senensis, *Bibliotheca sancta ex praecipuis Catholicae Ecclesiae auctoribus collecta* (Venice, 1566).
[157] Hebrews 7:11; 8:7.
[158] Diogo de Paiva de Andrada (1528-75) was a Portuguese theologian whose *Defensio Tridentinae fidei* was published in 1578.
[159] Andreas de Vega (d. 1560) wrote a defence of the Tridentine doctrine of justification in answer to John Calvin's attack on it. It was published in 1548.
[160] Hieronymus ab Oleastro (d. 1563) translated the Pentateuch, though it was not published until 1588.
[161] Isidoro Chiari (1495-1555) was a father of the Council of Trent (1545-63) and produced a Latin Bible in 1542. In 1547 he became bishop of Foligno, on the recommendation of Reginald Cardinal Pole.
[162] Tomasso de Vio Cajetan (1469-1534) was one of Luther's chief opponents. He translated most of the Bible towards the end of his life.
[163] Johannes Hentenius (1499-1566) was a Flemish Biblical scholar who produced a critical edition of the Latin Vulgate in 1547.

firm in them, etc.?[164] Nay further, did not the same Sixtus ordain by an inviolable decree, and that with the counsel and consent of his cardinals, that the Latin edition of the Old and New Testament which the Council of Trent would have to be authentic, is the same without controversy which he then set forth, being diligently corrected and printed in the printing house of the Vatican? Thus Sixtus in his preface before his Bible. And yet Clement VIII his immediate successor, to account of, publisheth another edition of the Bible, containing in it infinite differences from that of Sixtus, (and many of them weighty and material) and yet this must be authentic by all means.[165] What is to have the faith of our glorious Lord Jesus Christ with Yea and Nay, if this be not? Again, what is sweet harmony and consent, if this be? Therefore as Demaratus of Corinth[166] advised a great king, before he talked of the dissensions among the Grecians, to compose his domestic broils: (for at that time his queen and his son and heir were at deadly feud with him) so all the while that our adversaries do make so many and so various editions themselves, and do jar so much about the worth and authority of them, they can with no show of equity challenge us for changing and correcting.

13. The purpose of the translators, with their number, furniture, care, etc.

But it is high time to leave them, and to show in brief what we proposed to ourselves, and what course we held in this our perusal and survey of the Bible. Truly (good Christian reader) we never thought from the beginning, that we should need to make a new translation, nor yet to make of a bad one a good one, (for then the imputation of Sixtus had been true in some sort, that our people had been fed with gall of dragons instead of wine, with whey instead of milk;) but to make a good one better, or out of many good ones, one principal good one, not justly to be excepted

---

[164] Pope Sixtus V (1585-90) commissioned an official edition of the Latin Vulgate which appeared in 1590 but was so defective that it had to be withdrawn almost immediately.

[165] Pope Clement VIII (1592-1605) issued a revised version of Sixtus V's Bible, which remained authoritative in the Roman Catholic church until the twentieth century. He was not Sixtus' immediate successor as is stated here. Between 1590 and 1592 there were three popes, Urban VII (1590), Gregory XIV (1590-1) and Innocent IX (1591).

[166] He migrated from Corinth to Italy in 655 BC and his son Lucius Tarquinius Priscus (616-579 BC) was the fifth of the seven kings of ancient Rome.

against; that hath been our endeavour, that our mark. To that purpose there were many chosen, that were greater in other men's eyes than in their own, and that sought the truth rather than their own praise. Again, they came or were thought to come to the work, not *exercendi causa* (as one saith) but *exercitati*, that is, learned, not to learn: For the chief overseer and *ergodioktes*[167] under his Majesty, to whom not only we, but also our whole church was much bound, knew by his own wisdom, which thing also Nazianzene taught so long ago, that it is a preposterous order to teach first and to learn after, yea that *to en pithoi keramian manthanein*, 'to learn and practise together, is neither commendable for the workman nor safe for the work.'[168] Therefore such were thought upon, as could say modestly with St Jerome: *Et Hebraeum sermonem ex parte didicimus, et in Latino paene ab ipsis incunabulis etc. detriti sumus.* ('Both we have learned the Hebrew tongue in part, and in the Latin we have been exercised almost from our very cradle.')[169] Saint Jerome maketh no mention of the Greek tongue, wherein yet he did excel, because he translated not the Old Testament out of Greek, but out of Hebrew. And in what sort did these assemble? In the trust of their own knowledge, or of their sharpness of wit, or deepness of judgement, as it were in an arm of flesh? At no hand. They trusted in him that hath the key of David, opening and no man shutting;[170] they prayed to the Lord the Father of our Lord, to the effect that St Augustine did: 'O let thy Scriptures be my pure delight, let me not be deceived in them, neither let me deceive by them.'[171] In this confidence, and with this devotion did they assemble together; not too many, lest one should trouble another; and yet many, lest many things haply might escape them. If you ask what they had before them, truly it was the Hebrew text of the Old Testament, the Greek of the New. These are the two golden pipes, or rather conduits, wherethrough the olive branches empty themselves into the gold. St Augustine calleth them precedent, or original tongues;[172] St Jerome, fountains.[173] The same St Jerome

---

[167] Foreman or supervisor.
[168] Gregory of Nazianzus, *Oratio* II, 47 (PG 35, col. 456).
[169] Jerome, *apologia adversus libros Rufini* II, 29 (PL 23, col. 453).
[170] Revelation 3:7.
[171] Augustine, *Confessiones* XI, 2 (PL 32, coll. 809-11).
[172] Augustine, *De doctrina Christiana* III, 3 (PL 34, coll. 67-8).
[173] Jerome, *Epistula* CVI, 45 (PL 22, col. 852).

affirmeth, and Gratian hath not spared to put into his *Decree*, 'That as the credit of the old books (he meaneth of the Old Testament) is to be tried by the Hebrew volumes, so of the New by the Greek tongue,'[174] he meaneth by the original Greek. If truth be to be tried by these tongues, then whence should a translation be made, but out of them? These tongues therefore, the Scriptures we say in those tongues, we set before us to translate, being the tongues wherein God was pleased to speak to his church by his prophets and apostles. Neither did we run over the work with that posting haste that the Septuagint did, if that be true which is reported of them, that they finished it in seventy-two days;[175] neither were we barred or hindered from going over it again, having once done it, like Saint Jerome, if that be true which himself reporteth, that he could no sooner write anything, but presently it was caught from him, and published, and he could not have leave to mend it:[176] neither, to be short, were we the first that fell in hand with translating the Scripture into English, and consequently destitute of former helps, as it is written of Origen, that he was the first in a manner, that put his hand to write commentaries upon the Scriptures, and therefore no marvel, if he overshot himself many times. None of these things: the work hath not been huddled up in seventy-two days, but hath cost the workmen, as light as it seemeth, the pains of twice seven times seventy-two days and more: matters of such weight and consequently destitute of former helps are to be speeded with maturity, as it is written: 'Of business of moment, a man feareth not the blame of convenient slackness.'[177] Neither did we think [it too] much to consult the translators or commentators, Chaldee, Hebrew, Syrian, Greek or Latin, no nor the Spanish, French, Italian, or Dutch;[178] neither did we disdain to revise that which we had done, and to bring back to the anvil that which we had hammered: but having and using as great helps as were needful, and fearing no reproach for slowness, nor coveting praise for expedition, we have at the length, through the good hand of the

---

[174] Jerome, *Epistula* LXXI, 5 (PL 22, col. 671); *Corpus iuris canonici* I, *distinctio* 9, 6.
[175] Josephus, *Antiquitates*, 12.
[176] Jerome, *Epistula* XLVIII (PL 22, coll. 493-511). It was the book against Jovinian that he was talking about.
[177] Sophocles, *Electra*, 990.
[178] 'German.'

Lord upon us, brought the work to that pass that you see.

14. Reasons moving us to set diversity of senses in the margin, where there is great probability for each.

Some peradventure would have no variety of senses to be set in the margin, lest the authority of the Scriptures for deciding of controversies by that show of uncertainty, should somewhat be shaken. But we hold their judgement not to be so sound in this point. For though, 'Whatsoever things are necessary are manifest,' as St John Chrysostom saith,[179] and as St Augustine: 'In those things that are plainly set down in the Scriptures all such matters are found that concern faith, hope and charity.'[180] Yet for all that it cannot be dissembled, that partly to exercise and whet our wits, partly to wean the curious from loathing of them for their everywhere-plainness, partly also to stir up our devotion to crave the assistance of God's Spirit by prayer, and lastly, that we might be forward to seek aid of our brethren by conference, and never scorn those that be not in all respects so complete as they should be, being to seek in many things ourselves, it hath pleased God in his divine providence, here and there to scatter words and sentences of that difficulty and doubtfulness, not in doctrinal points that concern salvation (for in such it hath been vouched that the Scriptures are plain) but in matters of less moment, that fearfulness would better beseem us than confidence, and if we will resolve, to resolve upon modesty with St Augustine, (though not in this same case altogether, yet upon the same ground) *Melius est dubitare de occultis, quam litigare de incertis*, ('it is better to make doubt of those things which are secret, than to strive about those things that are uncertain.')[181] There be many words in the Scriptures, which be never found there but once, (having neither brother nor neighbour, as the Hebrews speak) so that we cannot be holpen by conference of places. Again, there be many rare names of certain birds, beasts and precious stones, etc. concerning which the Hebrews themselves are so divided among themselves for judgement, that they may seem to have defined this or that, rather because they would say something, than because they were sure of that which they said, as Saint Jerome

---

[179] John Chrysostom, *Homiliae in 2 Thessalonicenses* II (PG 62, coll. 471-2).
[180] Augustine, *De doctrina Christiana* II, 9 (PL 34, col. 42).
[181] Augustine, *De Genesi ad litteram* III, 5 (PL 34, col. 282).

somewhere saith of the Septuagint.[182] Now in such a case, doth not a margin do well to admonish the reader to seek further, and not to conclude or dogmatize upon this or that peremptorily? For as it is a fault of incredulity, to doubt of those things that are evident: so to determine of such things as the Spirit of God hath left (even in the judgement of the judicious) questionable, can be no less then presumption. Therefore as Saint Augustine saith, that variety of translations is profitable for the finding out of the sense of the Scriptures:[183] so diversity of signification and sense in the margin, when the text is not so clear, must needs do good, yea, is necessary as we are persuaded. We know that Sixtus V expressly forbiddeth, that any variety of readings of their vulgar edition, should be put in the margin (which though it be not altogether the same thing to that we have in hand, yet it looketh that way) but we think he hath not all of his own side his favourers, for this conceit. They that are wise, had rather have their judgements at liberty in differences of readings, than to be captivated to one, when it may be the other. If they were sure that their high priest had all laws shut up in his breast, as Paul II bragged,[184] and that he were as free from error by special privilege, as the dictators of Rome were made by law inviolable, it were another matter; then his word were an oracle, his opinion a decision. But the eyes of the world are now open, God be thanked, and have been a great while, they find that he is subject to the same affections and infirmities that others be, that his body is subject to wounds, and therefore so much as he proveth, not as much as he claimeth, they grant and embrace.

15. Reasons inducing us not to stand curiously upon an identity of phrasing.

Another thing we think good to admonish thee of (gentle reader) that we have not tied ourselves to an uniformity of phrasing, or to an identity of words, as some peradventure would wish that we had done, because they observe, that some learned men somewhere, have been as exact as they could that way. Truly, that we might not vary from the sense of that which we had translated

---

[182] Jerome, *In Ezechiel*, 3 (PL 25, col. 75).
[183] Augustine, *De doctrina Christiana* II, 1 (PL 34, coll. 35-7).
[184] Pope Paul II (1464-71) was a strong but controversial occupant of the Roman see whose posthumous reputation is amply attested by this anecdote.

before, if the word signified the same thing in both places (for, there be some words that be not of the same sense everywhere) we were especially careful, and made a conscience, according to our duty. But, that we should express the same notion in the same particular word; as for example, if we translate the Hebrew or Greek word once by *purpose*, never to call it *intent*; if one where *journeying*, never *travelling*; if one where *think*, never *suppose*; if one where *pain*, never *ache*; if one where *joy*, never *gladness*, etc. Thus to mince the matter, we thought to favour more of curiosity than wisdom, and that rather it would breed scorn in the atheist, than bring profit to the godly reader. For is the kingdom of God become words or syllables? Why should we be in bondage to them if we may be free, use one precisely when we may use another no less fit, as commodiously? A godly Father in the primitive time showed himself greatly moved, that one of newfangledness called *krabbaton skimpous*, the difference be little or none;[185] and another reporteth, that he was much abused for turning *cucurbita* (to which reading the people had been used) into *hedera*.[186] Now if this happen in better times, and upon so small occasions, we might justly fear hard censure, if generally we should make verbal and unnecessary changings. We might also be charged (by scoffers) with some unequal dealing toward a great number of good English words. For as it is written of a certain great philosopher, that he should say, that those logs were happy that were made images to be worshipped; for their fellows, as good as they, lay for blocks behind the fire; so if we should say, as it were, unto certain words, Stand up higher, have a place in the Bible always, and to others of like quality, Get ye hence, be banished for ever, we might be taxed peradventure with St James his words, namely, *To be partial in ourselves, and judges of evil thoughts.*[187] Add hereunto, that niceness in words was always counted the next step to trifling, and so was to be curious about names too: also that we cannot follow a better pattern for elocution than God himself; therefore he using divers words, in his Holy Writ, and indifferently for one thing in nature: we, if we will not be

---

[185] Two different Greek words for 'bed'. Nicephorus Callistus Xanthopulus, *Historia ecclesiastica* VIII, 42 (PG 146, coll. 165-8).

[186] Two different Latin words for 'vines'. Jerome, *In Ionam* 4:6 (PL 25, col.1148). See Augustine, *Epistulae* X (PL 33, coll. 73-4).

[187] James 2:4.

superstitious, may use the same liberty in our English versions out of Hebrew and Greek, for that copy or store that he hath given us. Lastly, we have on the one side avoided the scrupulosity of the puritans, who leave the old ecclesiastical words, and betake them to other, as when they put *washing* for *baptism*, and *congregation* instead of *church*: as also on the other side, we have shunned the obscurity of the papists, in their *azymes, tunic, rational, holocausts, prepuce, Pasche*, and a number of such like, whereof their late translation is full, and that of purpose to darken the sense, that since they must needs translate the Bible, yet by the language thereof, it may be kept from being understood. But we desire that the Scripture may speak like itself, as in the language of Canaan,[188] that it may be understood even of the very vulgar.

Many other things we might give thee warning of (gentle reader) if we had not exceeded the measure of a preface already. It remaineth, that we commend thee to God, and to the Spirit of his grace, which is able to build further than we can ask or think. He removeth the scales from our eyes,[189] the veil from our hearts,[190] opening our wits, that we may understand his Word, enabling our hearts, yea correcting our affections, that we may love it above gold and silver,[191] yea that we may love it to the end. Ye are brought unto fountains of living water which ye digged not;[192] do not cast earth into them with the Philistines,[193] neither prefer broken pits before them with the wicked Jews.[194] Others have laboured, and you may enter into their labours; O receive not so great things in vain![195] O despise not so great salvation![196] Be not like swine to tread under foot so precious things, neither yet like dogs to tear and abuse holy things.[197] Say not to our Saviour with the Gergasites: *Depart out of our coasts*,[198] neither yet with Esau:

---

[188] Hebrew. The expression 'language of Canaan' was popularly (and pejoratively) used to refer to pious talk in pseudo-Biblical phrases.
[189] Acts 9:18.
[190] 2 Corinthians 3:16.
[191] Deuteronomy 7:25; Psalm 119:72; Proverbs 8:10; 1 Peter 1:18.
[192] Genesis 26:15; Jeremiah 2:13.
[193] Genesis 26:15-18.
[194] Jeremiah 2:13.
[195] John 4:38.
[196] Hebrews 2:3.
[197] Matthew 7:6.
[198] Matthew 8:34.

Sell your birthright for a mess of pottage.[199] If light be come into the world, love not darkness more than light:[200] if food, if clothing be offered, go not naked, starve not yourselves.[201] Remember the advice of Nazianzene: 'It is a grievous thing (or dangerous) to neglect a great fair, and to seek to make markets afterwards.'[202] Also the encouragement of St John Chrysostom: 'It is altogether impossible, that he that is sober and watchful should at any time be neglected.'[203] Lastly, the admonition and menacing of St Augustine: 'They that despise God's will inviting them shall feel God's will taking vengeance of them.'[204] It is a fearful thing to fall into the hands of the living God:[205] but a blessed thing it is, and will bring us to everlasting blessedness in the end, when God speaketh unto us, to hearken; when he setteth his Word before us, to read it; when he stretcheth out his hand and calleth, to answer: 'Here am I; here we are to do thy will, O God.'[206] The Lord work a care and conscience in us to know him and serve him, that we may be acknowledged of him at the appearing of our Lord Jesus Christ,[207] to whom with the Holy Ghost, be all praise and thanksgiving. Amen.

---

[199] Hebrews 12:16.
[200] John 3:19.
[201] Matthew 25:36-44; James 2:15.
[202] Gregory of Nazianzus, *Oratio* XL, 24 (PG 36, col. 392).
[203] John Chrysostom, *Homiliae in Romanos* XXVI, 3 (PG 60, col. 341).
[204] A note in the margin of the text attributes this to Augustine, *Ad articulum sibi false obiectum*, but it is not found in his works. A similar statement appears in Augustine, *Sermones de symbolo* I, 1 (PL 40, col. 659).
[205] Hebrews 10:31.
[206] Hebrews 10:7; Psalm 40:7-8.
[207] 1 Peter 1:7.

For further reading:

The Bible in English by David Daniell (New Haven: Yale University Press, 2003) is by far the most comprehensive study of the English Bible in its many translations, from Anglo-Saxon times to the present. As a specialist in the writings of William Tyndale, Professor Daniell is especially well-placed to assess the importance and impact of sixteenth-century translations on the English language. His approach leans more to the literary than to the theological, though of course it is impossible to ignore the latter, especially in the Reformation period.

The battle for the Bible in England, 1557–1582 by Cameron A. MacKenzie (New York: Peter Lang, 2002). This book is the published version of a thesis defended at the University of Notre Dame and covers the key period during which different approaches towards translating the Bible into English were crystallised. Despite the dates in the title, Dr MacKenzie does in fact go back to William Tyndale and looks forward to the 1611 translation, so that his book may fairly be said to cover the entire period. He pays particular attention to the political and theological implications of the various editions, considering *inter alia* the way they were illustrated and the degree of deference they showed to royal and ecclesiastical authority. At the same time, he pays close attention to theological questions and brings out the importance that Roman Catholic translation attempts had for the development of the Protestant English Bible.

The textual history of the King James Bible by David Norton (Cambridge: Cambridge University Press, 2005) is the definitive study of the alterations made to the King James Version in the years after 1611, leading up to the final stabilisation of the text in 1761. It gives a complete account of when and why the changes were made, allowing readers to pinpoint the date of particular modifications of special interest to them.

Latimer Publications

LS 01	The Evangelical Anglican Identity Problem – Jim Packer	LS 20/21	The Thirty-Nine Articles: Their Place and Use Today – Jim Packer, Roger Beckwith
LS 02	The ASB Rite A Communion: A Way Forward – Roger Beckwith	LS 22	How We Got Our Prayer Book – T. W. Drury, Roger Beckwith
LS 03	The Doctrine of Justification in the Church of England – Robin Leaver	LS 23/24	Creation or Evolution: a False Antithesis? – Mike Poole, Gordon Wenham
LS 04	Justification Today: The Roman Catholic and Anglican Debate – R. G. England	LS 25	Christianity and the Craft – Gerard Moate
LS 05/06	Homosexuals in the Christian Fellowship – David Atkinson	LS 26	ARCIC II and Justification – Alister McGrath
LS 07	Nationhood: A Christian Perspective – O. R. Johnston	LS 27	The Challenge of the Housechurches – Tony Higton, Gilbert Kirby
LS 08	Evangelical Anglican Identity: Problems and Prospects – Tom Wright	LS 28	Communion for Children? The Current Debate – A. A. Langdon
LS 09	Confessing the Faith in the Church of England Today – Roger Beckwith	LS 29/30	Theological Politics – Nigel Biggar
LS 10	A Kind of Noah's Ark? The Anglican Commitment to Comprehensiveness – Jim Packer	LS 31	Eucharistic Consecration in the First Four Centuries and its Implications for Liturgical Reform – Nigel Scotland
LS 11	Sickness and Healing in the Church – Donald Allister	LS 32	A Christian Theological Language – Gerald Bray
LS 12	Rome and Reformation Today: How Luther Speaks to the New Situation – James Atkinson	LS 33	Mission in Unity: The Bible and Missionary Structures – Duncan McMann
LS 13	Music as Preaching: Bach, Passions and Music in Worship – Robin Leaver	LS 34	Stewards of Creation: Environmentalism in the Light of Biblical Teaching – Lawrence Osborn
LS 14	Jesus Through Other Eyes: Christology in a Multi-faith Context – Christopher Lamb	LS 35/36	Mission and Evangelism in Recent Thinking: 1974–1986 – Robert Bashford
LS 15	Church and State Under God – James Atkinson	LS 37	Future Patterns of Episcopacy: Reflections in Retirement – Stuart Blanch
LS 16	Language and Liturgy – Gerald Bray, Steve Wilcockson, Robin Leaver	LS 38	Christian Character: Jeremy Taylor and Christian Ethics Today – David Scott
LS 17	Christianity and Judaism: New Understanding, New Relationship – James Atkinson	LS 39	Islam: Towards a Christian Assessment – Hugh Goddard
LS 18	Sacraments and Ministry in Ecumenical Perspective – Gerald Bray	LS 40	Liberal Catholicism: Charles Gore and the Question of Authority – G. F. Grimes
LS 19	The Functions of a National Church – Max Warren	LS 41/42	The Christian Message in a Multi-faith Society – Colin Chapman
		LS 43	The Way of Holiness 1: Principles – D. A. Ousley

Latimer Publications

LS 44/45	The Lambeth Articles – V. C. Miller	LS 67	Heresy, Schism & Apostasy – Gerald Bray
LS 46	The Way of Holiness 2: Issues – D. A. Ousley	LS 68	Paul in 3D: Preaching Paul as Pastor, Story-teller and Sage – Ben Cooper
LS 47	Building Multi-Racial Churches – John Root	LS69	Christianity and the Tolerance of Liberalism: J.Gresham Machen and the Presbyterian Controversy of 1922 – 1937 – Lee Gatiss
LS 48	Episcopal Oversight: A Case for Reform – David Holloway		
LS 49	Euthanasia: A Christian Evaluation – Henk Jochemsen	LS70	An Anglican Evangelical Identity Crisis: The Churchman – Anvil Affair of 1981–1984 – Andrew Atherstone
LS 50/51	The Rough Places Plain: AEA 1995		
LS 52	A Critique of Spirituality – John Pearce	LS71	Empty and Evil: The worship of other faiths in 1 Corinthians 8-10 and today – Rohintan Mody
LS 53/54	The Toronto Blessing – Martyn Percy	LS72	To Plough or to Preach: Mission Strategies in New Zealand during the 1820s – Malcolm Falloon
LS 55	The Theology of Rowan Williams – Garry Williams		
LS 56/57	Reforming Forwards? The Process of Reception and the Consecration of Women as Bishops – Peter Toon	LS73	Plastic People: How Queer Theory is Changing Us – Peter Sanlon
		LB01	The Church of England: What it is, and what it stands for – R. T. Beckwith
LS 58	The Oath of Canonical Obedience – Gerald Bray		
LS 59	The Parish System: The Same Yesterday, Today And For Ever? – Mark Burkill	LB02	Praying with Understanding: Explanations of Words and Passages in the Book of Common Prayer – R. T. Beckwith
LS 60	'I Absolve You': Private Confession and the Church of England – Andrew Atherstone	LB03	The Failure of the Church of England? The Church, the Nation and the Anglican Communion – A. Pollard
LS 61	The Water and the Wine: A Contribution to the Debate on Children and Holy Communion – Roger Beckwith, Andrew Daunton-Fear	LB04	Towards a Heritage Renewed – H.R.M. Craig
		LB05	Christ's Gospel to the Nations: The Heart & Mind of Evangelicalism Past, Present & Future – Peter Jensen
LS 62	Must God Punish Sin? – Ben Cooper		
LS 63	Too Big For Words?: The Transcendence of God and Finite Human Speech – Mark D. Thompson	LB06	Passion for the Gospel: Hugh Latimer (1485–1555) Then and Now. A commemorative lecture to mark the 450th anniversary of his martyrdom in Oxford – A. McGrath
LS 64	A Step Too Far: An Evangelical Critique of Christian Mysticism – Marian Raikes	LB07	Truth and Unity in Christian Fellowship – Michael Nazir-Ali
LS 65	The New Testament and Slavery: Approaches and Implications – Mark Meynell	LB08	Unworthy Ministers: Donatism and Discipline Today – Mark Burkill
LS 66	The Tragedy of 1662: The Ejection and Persecution of the Puritans – Lee Gatiss		

Latimer Publications

GGC	*God, Gays and the Church: Human Sexuality and Experience in Christian Thinking* – eds. Lisa Nolland, Chris Sugden, Sarah Finch
WTL	*The Way, the Truth and the Life: Theological Resources for a Pilgrimage to a Global Anglican Future* – eds. Vinay Samuel, Chris Sugden, Sarah Finch
AEID	*Anglican Evangelical Identity – Yesterday and Today* – J.I.Packer and N.T.Wright
IB	*The Anglican Evangelical Doctrine of Infant Baptism* – John Stott and J.Alec Motyer
BF	*Being Faithful: The Shape of Historic Anglicanism Today* – Theological Resource Group of GAFCON
FWC	*The Faith we confess: An exposition of the 39 Articles* – Gerald Bray
TPG	*The True Profession of the Gospel: Augustus Toplady and Reclaiming our Reformed Foundations* – Lee Gatiss

www.ingramcontent.com/pod-product-compliance
Lightning Source LLC
LaVergne TN
LVHW091250080426
835510LV00007B/196